D0142760

Labyrinth

AN ESSAY ON THE POLITICAL PSYCHOLOGY OF CHANGE

Richard Wilson

M. E. Sharpe, Inc.
ARMONK, NEW YORK
LONDON, ENGLAND

80 Business Park Drive, Armonk, New York 10504.

Available in the United Kingdom and Europe from M. E. Sharpe, Publishers, 3 Henrietta Street, London WC2E 8LU.

Library of Congress Cataloging-in-Publication Data

Wilson, Richard W., 1933–
Labyrinth : an essay on the political psychology of change.

Bibliography: p.
Includes index.
1. Political psychology. 2. Moral development. 3. Motivation (Psychology). 4. Change (Psychology). I. Title.

JA745.W55 1988 320′.01′9 88–4525
ISBN 0-87332-485-4

Printed in the United States of America.

Contents

List of Figures

Preface

This book is about the political aspirations of modern men and women and the psychological motivations that underlie them. Many writers in the field of political science have enriched their analyses with assumptions about motivations. What those in the growing field of political psychology seek is to make these assumptions explicit, to explain political behavior by reference to clearly articulated psychological motivations.

In their study of mankind the various disciplines of the social sciences traditionally concentrated on different areas. Economists studied exchange, sociologists organization, anthropologists culture, psychologists motivation, and political scientists power. As social analysis has become more sophisticated, these divisions have become increasingly inappropriate. A focus on power and motivation, for instance, is incomplete without reference to social institutions. Having power, after all, is only a point on a continuum. At the other end lies subjugation. Most people at all times live somewhere in between, their chances hedged constantly by the constraints of the institutions within which they live. A better world therefore means not just better people, however these elusive concepts may be defined. It also means better institutions, ones that can provide scope for expanding aspirations. This book, therefore, is also about the complex, bureaucratic organizations that are now dominant in all modern political systems and the way that these organizations influence people's perceptions of their world.

While all contemporary political systems have instituted policies that partially fulfill people's aspirations, they also embody forms of power that impede progress. These are perversions that are inherent in the bureaucratic mode of organization itself; they take on particular forms depending on the kinds of rewards that elites obtain in their pursuit and manipulation of power. Yet if modern organizations are flawed, they are also perfectable. In the effort to fulfill that hope all modern people restlessly seek change. This book, then, is also about social change and the creative and destructive forces that surround us in the modern world. Needless to say, no thinking person needs to be told of the extraordinary perils that confront us. Increased technological capability alone has brought us face to face with the possibility of worldwide destruction. At the same time the death camps, slave labor systems, and other forms of brutal oppression and exploitation serve as reminders that barbarism is by no means a thing of the past. Those who seek to advance human dignity, in fact, feel beleaguered in a world where compromise and good will are often submerged by the rhetoric of hate. The need to understand the reasons for this have never been more imperative.

I wish to dedicate this essay to those who have given their lives, often unwillingly, to end oppression and exploitation. In our century alone, surely the bloodiest on record, over one hundred million people have been cruelly destroyed by others, clubbed, shot, burned, bombed, gassed, speared, and tortured in countless ways. These people had no special color or religion and they came from no special place. They were everywhere. And every one of them deserves our remembrance.

My appreciation for guidance is owed to many. Some, like Sidney L. Greenblatt, Jack L. Nelson, Gordon J. Schochet, and David C. Harrop, are close colleagues whose advice and criticism have been indispensable. Others, too numerous to name but who I hope will recognize in these words my indebtedness, have given suggestions about my work over the years. The Faculty Academic Study Program of Rutgers University provided me with the time for research. Catherine Tranfo at the Rutgers International Center and Phyllis Moditz of the Rutgers political science department provided indispensable assistance in typing. Finally, I owe a lasting debt to Linda C. Frenkel, who over the years provided support and assistance in pushing me to complete this book.

Labyrinth

AN ESSAY ON THE POLITICAL PSYCHOLOGY OF CHANGE

Introduction

In analyzing change, no problem has been as vexatious as understanding the motives of those who are involved. One of the major differences between the natural and social sciences is the crucial necessity of dealing with motivation in the latter. Herein lies much of the reason for the "soft" nature of scientific inquiry in the social area. Freudian theories of motivation are difficult to apply even at the individual level and have not proven to be useful for large-scale aggregate analysis. Social learning theories, which are less subjective, have been widely used in behavior modification and socialization studies. The latter, especially, have been severely criticized on the grounds that attitudes and beliefs lack stability over time.[1] Psychohistorical studies remain popular but, like psychological analyses of great men generally, are largely single case studies.[2] National character studies, once highly popular, have fallen from grace.[3] Marx and others focused on alienation as the prime cause of change; during the 1960s studies of alienation were much in vogue in attempts to understand youth unrest.[4] Unfortunately, alienation loses much of its explanatory power for instances of peaceful, affirmative change. David McClelland suggested that need achievement is a major factor underlying development in the modern world.[5] This informative lead, however, was never followed up extensively by political scientists. More popular three decades ago, but now out of fashion, were studies of the authoritarian personality made widely known by Adorno and his associates.[6] Criticisms, especially of a methodological nature, brought some of the findings about authoritarianism into question although intuitively the studies as a whole struck responsive chords.

Motivation, in short, has proven to be a difficult subject. As a consequence, at the group or system level problems of motivation are often dealt with by the use of sociological approaches that treat groups as having properties that cannot be deduced from individual choices. In most cases, in fact, the question of motivation is simply shunted aside or allowed to be implicit, with the reader free to supply whatever motivations seem appropriate for the circumstance under consideration.[7]

When motivation is made explicit the current most widely used theory assumes individual rational calculation of the costs and benefits of alternative actions. Borrowed from the discipline of economics, this theory is used in political science in the subfield of political economy to explain questions about distributive politics; it is also widely used in international relations in the study of interactions among systems, which are conceived of as individual actors.

Rational actor theory is based on the assumption that people have calculated preferences and behave instrumentally in order to get what they want. In situations of uncertainty, people choose actions that will maximize the possibility of achieving their goals. Put another way, people attempt to minimize regret (i.e., a motivating anxiety) by acting in such a way as to bring about a desired result. For such aspects of politics as voting behavior or budget setting, rational choice models are consistent with observations of individual and aggregate behavior. Even in cases where a person does something that he clearly thinks is wrong, the action can be consistent with a rational choice perspective if it leads to the avoidance of punishment.

Unfortunately, nonmarket effects, what economists refer to as externalities, are often the central problems of politics. Why, for instance, will some people act in a manner that clearly can lead to punishment? Surely political prisoners, who sometimes experience severe torture, must in many cases know that this undesirable outcome is a highly possible consequence of their actions. Some individuals will apparently deliberately sacrifice their well-being, not on the basis of any objective calculus of self-interest but because of some contrary psychic income that provides satisfaction from doing—and persuading others to do—what they consider to be right. In politics not to account for altruism (defined as behavior where "the actor could have done better for himself had he chosen to ignore the effect of his choice on others"[8]) is to suggest that self-sacrifice has no importance, a conclusion that would leave out those who are willing to die for a cause—people like Martin Luther, Gandhi, and a host of others. Equally important is the problem that what is rational at the group level may not be so at the individual level and vice versa. For instance, in the tragedy of the commons problem, rational individual behavior (adding one more cow to the common grazing land in order to secure maximum advantage for oneself) can lead to disaster at the group level with serious consequences for every member of the group.

Rational choice models of motivation seem clearly to have difficulties. They cannot account for important aspects of behavior such as altruism, and they lack consistency between the individual and the group level. Invariant prediction of behavior is thus difficult at best. An explanation of motivation that can better account for varieties of behavior within different contexts seems called for.

In this book I shall attempt to use a particular theory of motivation, moral development theory, to explain political change. In doing this, however, certain difficulties must be surmounted, for moral development theory has its roots—and its widest application—in the discipline of psychology rather than political science. In translating the theory from one discipline to another, three metatheoretical requirements must be met. First, in order to argue that political thought and action have psychological roots, political actors (leaders and led) must be defined as an independent variable. Second, the theory must offer an explanation for the relation between collective and individual constructions of meaning, showing how both psychological and social structures of development are at once both determined and determining. Lastly, a theoretical language or vocabulary must be created that can relate political phenomena to psychological variables. Only when all of these requirements have been met can moral development as a theory of motivation make a contribution to our understanding of how individual and collective determinations structure the dynamics of political life.[9]

Chapter 1 describes moral development theory as it has been articulated by its leading proponents and suggests some modifications based on further research by other scholars. In particular it presents a model of the socialization process showing how various psychological and social strands affect development. This chapter is largely a theoretical exercise.

The second chapter shifts the focus to organizations, the social structures in which people live and work and the environment for important aspects of moral behavior. I attempt to show, with examples, how organizational structures have changed over time, giving people more scope for moral behavior, and how each of these advances has stimulated productivity and demands for further change.

Chapter 3 presents a vocabulary of rights, which translates moral development terms into categories that have traditionally been the language of political demands. Different categories of right are shown to be rooted in different aspects of moral growth; these aspects can be differentially reinforced by socialization practices. I then show how elites within organizations espouse particular conceptions of rights in order to define and legitimize different forms of rulership with different patterns of reward. Understanding the way that modern organizational practices can favor one type of right over another clarifies why particular rights are favored in different societies. These dissimilarities are perhaps the most dramatic differences among modern political systems. Finally, the rights that people enjoy within modern societies are shown to encompass only partially the underlying range of possibilities.

The fourth chapter shows how purposive behavior, as well as basic social changes, can lead to a perversion of the rights that legitimize elite status. In the process of change the obligations of elites may diverge from the expectations of followers in a manner that is perceived as violating customary or expected rights. Examples of both leader and follower behavior within organizations that stimulate perversion are given.

In chapter 5 demands for rights, motivated by moral concerns, are presented as a major factor stimulating change. Since expectations of right and obligation have a psychological basis, powerful emotions aroused over their violation serve as a motor for political expression. Because of this, however, the modern world is in tension, indeed, to some extent polarized, due to the threats to rulership that are implied by demands for rights.

The analysis is continued in chapter 6, where the role of organizations in political change is discussed. The factors that stimulate domestic change are shown to have explosive consequences internationally, for the organizations of different societies now increasingly operate globally. Destabilization is most likely in contexts where the outside organization's pattern of right and obligation varies from the local one. In such cases the potential for outrage is high indeed and may develop into a whirlpool of hate and revolutionary fervor.

Lastly, in the conclusion, I suggest how changes in socialization practices and organizational structures can peacefully resolve some of the tensions of political change. If fulfilled these changes can lessen the dangers that inhere in the present situation and lead to a world where the potential of all people can be realized.

In the ancient myth Theseus slays the Minotaur and escapes with Ariadne, the daughter of King Minos. Caught in the unfathomable mystery of Minos's palace, the hero eludes his fate with the aid of thread that Ariadne has strung as a guide through the labyrinth's strange and twisted passageways. Fleeing from the past to an unknown future, the two struggle with the complex and frightening difficulty that faces them.

This book is an essay about the process of change in the modern world, a process that often seems like a dark journey through a labyrinth. What the future will be is not a central question. I will have fulfilled my hopes here if I can set clear but one or two of the clues that, like the twine of the myth, are needed to find the way.

We live in the midst of a great civil conflict, a war between the present and the past but also a war between differing conceptions of the future even as that future takes shape around us. For some the conflicts of our century have created the deepest pessimism, a belief that the forces that have been unleashed carry the seeds of ultimate destruction. For still others change, though bringing with it problems of monumental proportions, is still cause for the profoundest optimism, for a belief that the greatest creative potential will be set free, leading ultimately to a way of life that will bring unparalleled prosperity and fulfillment to all. In truth, no one knows what lies at the end of the ordeal of change. But that we must seek a way through the labyrinth to whatever destiny awaits us is inescapable.

1. Moral Development

Nearly everyone agrees that some notion of morality is necessary for understanding the behavior of people and the nature of societies, but there has been wide divergence historically in its definition. What is one person's good has often been another's evil. Values that have been cherished as essential for the maintenance of the social order have often, at the same time, relegated outsiders to the pale. In fact, an enormous thicket of contradictions surrounds concepts of morality. They form a seemingly impenetrable barrier that has been the object of unending assault by moral philosophers.

The list of those who have discussed morality is long and illustrious. It includes from past millennia Plato, Confucius, Christ, the Buddha, and Mohammed. More recently, among others, are names like Locke, Rousseau, Jefferson, Kant, Mill, Durkheim, Dewey, and Gandhi. Each in his way was concerned with the consequences of behavior for the welfare of others, with the nature of a moral being, and with the appropriate limits on the need to respect social rules.

In contemporary times still other thinkers have added to the rich store of knowledge regarding morality. John Rawls, the eminent political philosopher, has devoted himself to the study of principles of justice.[1] B. F. Skinner, the famous behavioral psychologist, has stated that good and bad have no meaning in and of themselves. From his standpoint, definitions for goodness and badness derive solely from the positive or negative influences that people experience during learning.[2] Edward O. Wilson, speaking as a leading scholar in the controversial field of sociobiology, has advanced the proposition that altruistic behavior (which he feels is an essential component of moral behavior) may be genetically controlled.[3] In his formulation altruism has survival value; its presence in the makeup of people is important for the continuation of mankind as a species. Thus, while altruism may take many forms depending upon particular social conditions, its presence is not accidental but is said rather to be an attribute that is shared by all.

Within the discipline of psychology the concept of morality has been addressed by several distinguished schools. Psychoanalytic theorists, in the tradition of Sigmund Freud and others, have placed great emphasis on the tug of war between a moralistic superego and the ego and the id. Although it has been difficult in a rigorous scholarly way to verify how myriad individual tugs of war within the personality are reflected in very large-scale social events, popular psychology has not hesitated to make these connections. In a different mode, social-learning theorists, while not unmindful of internal needs and drives, emphasize the way that the environment affects individuals. They see social influences as the major factors prompting the development of moral stances. Because they believe that moral orientations are related to these influences, they focus on learning and tend to underscore the distinctive characteristics of different socialization processes. Echoing B. F. Skinner's conceptions, moral behavior is said to be a type of response where the individual avoids anxiety by actions that are in conformity with the requirements of a previously learned code of behavior. Since emphasis is on cultural differences, morality is thought to be relative in the sense that the values that relate to moral behavior are different for different societies.

Despite the undoubted importance of the contributions made by these schools of psychology, it is cognitive theorists who have staked a preeminent claim in the field of moral development. Relying heavily on the work of Jean Piaget and Lawrence Kohlberg, these thinkers leave aside Freudian personality variables and downgrade the importance of social influences; they place emphasis on the internal construction and reorganization of cognitive structures as the basis for the development of moral orientations.

Cognitive development theorists believe that during growth there is a correspondence—but not an exact correlation—between cognitive change and a person's capacity for moral reasoning. They feel that moral judgment develops with age in an invariant, irreversible stage sequence. Because these stages reflect a process of cognitive development that is a common human attribute, any given level of moral reasoning is said to be possible in any culture. Knowing the social environment is important only for explaining the variance in moral judgment that remains after the intellectual variance is removed and for understanding the opportunities for role taking that exist. From a theoretical standpoint, these social influences are secondary to understanding the cognitively related process of development.

Cognitive development theories of moral development are concerned with judgment, not behavior. A particular idea underlies the assertion of universal culture-free stages of development. Because all people are members of the human species they share the same type of cognitive structure. Analyzing this structure gives insight into the processes of thought that change during development according to universal laws; analyzing structure thus tells one how a person thinks about his or her beliefs. On the other hand, it is also possible to study the content of moral beliefs. Content, however, must be separated from how a person thinks, for the content of beliefs reflects external influences. Content, therefore, may differ among people according to particular experiences and general cultural influences.

For cognitive development theorists the small child is said to be in a primitive stage of moral reasoning that reflects the self-centered nature of the child's reasoning processes. Piaget referred to this type of thinking as egocentrism, and he termed the form of moral orientation that is associated with it as heteronomy, where rules are deemed to be good per se because they emanate from adult authority. As children grow they become increasingly able to see themselves in relation to others. Gradually egocentrism gives way to forms of cooperation and to a capacity for mutual respect. Children thus come to understand the needs of others in relation to themselves and thereby develop an ability to think in terms of egalitarianism and reciprocity. Piaget termed this later mode of thinking the morality of autonomy; it is one where the older child relates to others—and thus behaves—in terms of self-imposed rules.[4]

Subsequent work by others has never fully verified Piaget's ideas. The original formulations, however, were elaborated by Lawrence Kohlberg, who set forth a six-stage model of moral development that is linked theoretically with changes in cognitive ability. According to Kohlberg, the development process involves an invariant sequence of growth from an early obedience and punishment orientation to a final, rarely attained stage of conscience or principle orientation.[5]

The six-stage model has been extensively analyzed and used by many moral development theorists. It is divided into three general levels with two stages at each level. At the first general level, called the preconventional, the child interprets notions of goodness and badness—or right and wrong—in terms of punishments and rewards and what will satisfy his or her own desires and needs. At this level children unquestioningly defer to power for its own sake; they also behave toward each other very much in terms of mutual advantage. The child does what is necessary in order to satisfy his or her own needs. The second general level is called the conventional. With age the child has had more opportunity for role taking that enhances a social perspective and moves the child from a self-perceived unquestioned position at the center of the universe.[6] At the conventional level the expectations of the groups of which one is a member are thought to have a rightness in and of themselves. Conformity and loyalty to these expectations are the sine qua non of moral judgment. The child tries to please or help others and thus gain their approval. Rules and respect for authority and maintenance of the social order for its own sake are valued goals. The third general level is termed postconventional, autonomous, or principled. At this level principles involving moral values are valid apart from the authority of groups. At the apogee of development principles of distributive justice (equity or equality of consideration) and commutative justice (reciprocity or equality in exchange) are internalized and reasoning is in terms of these principles rather than social standards that have been agreed upon by society.[7]

Kohlberg tested his theory in a number of societies and in all of them found these levels of moral reasoning, although there were marked differences in the degrees of adherence to any given stage and in the rates of change from one stage to another.[8] One finding of considerable interest for political scientists is that few people in any society move beyond the conventional level, and many remain at the preconventional level. Any large-scale social activity (such as a revolution), therefore, will have participants who are at different levels of moral development.

The number of people who are at the postconventional level is distressingly small. Kohlberg's cross-cultural data, referred to above, make this point dramatically; his findings have been verified by others using different tests. Robert R. Holt gave a national probability sample of American youths Loevinger's Sentence Completion Test for assessing ego development, a test which he states is moderately well correlated with Kohlberg's test. Only 15 percent of the respondents were at a level where behavior is controlled by well-internalized inner standards, and only 5 percent were at levels similar to Kohlberg's postconventional level.[9] Recent findings also indicate that the shift from the conventional to the postconventional level, when it occurs at all, is not a transition that can occur early in life. A span between the late twenties and early thirties is the earliest that the change takes place.[10]

Kohlberg's pathbreaking efforts have earned him deserved admiration. Criticisms, however, have mounted and have usefully provided corrections and additions to his ideas. For instance, with his heavy emphasis on the relationship between cognitive growth and moral reasoning, Kohlberg is said to have slighted the role that emotion plays in moral orientations. Morality, critics say, is not just judgment; it is also a feeling, especially the ability to empathize with the needs and aspirations of others and to sympathize with their frustrations, pains, and hurts.[11] Kohlberg did not address how empathic feelings develop (or do not develop), yet their development is just as important for a truly moral concern as is the development of cognitive structures.

Without empathy as a central component, Kohlberg's scheme appears to "load the dice" in favor of Western liberal tenets of individual freedom and autonomy and against systems that emphasize community sharing and cooperation. In fact, of course, Kohlberg's stages posit a progression from a relatively uncritical acceptance of group standards to personal reflection about and acceptance of a set of guiding principles that may or may not include community-related values. A large part of Kohlberg's difficulty in making this clear was due to his emphasis on cognitive factors and his deemphasis of variables such as empathy that are integral to cooperation and sharing as well as to values of equality as an aspect of justice.

Carol Gilligan, in line with these criticisms, has gone further by suggesting that Kohlberg's theory ignores a critical moral development theme or voice. For those who speak with this voice, identity "is defined in a context of relationship and judged by a standard of responsibility and care" whereas for others "the tone of identity is different, clearer, more direct, more distinct and sharp-edged," radiating "the confidence of certain truth."[12] Empirical testing (in the United States) by gender revealed these two moral ideologies. Men, seeking separation and autonomy, justify moral solutions by an ethic of rights while women, for whom attachment is important, validate their solutions with an ethic of care.[13] Gilligan believes Kohlberg's work is flawed because he simply overlooked the fact that people can approach moral questions from the perspective of a framework different from the one he had developed. Sharing and cooperation, which must take place within a web of relationships, are equally as valid criteria of moral maturity, she asserts, as is an ultimate autonomy that justifies itself in terms of principle.

Gilligan's arguments find a measure of support from others. Davies avers that life itself is aggregative and collaborative and that cooperation has deep-seated organic tendencies.[14] Kegan, noting along with Gilligan that developmental psychologists have generally favored a conception of growth as increasing autonomy or distinctness, believes the yearning for inclusion is equally strong. He states emphatically that there are two processes at work in individual development. On the one hand is the yearning to be independent, autonomous, and distinct. On the other is the desire for integration, attachment, and inclusion.[15]

Kohlberg's theory, then, has been questioned as having too limited a conceptualization of moral development. Just as important, it has also been criticized as positing too rigid a degree of coincidence between forms of moral reasoning and changes in cognitive ability. James Rest, for one, using different tests, has made the point that individuals develop not through an invariant sequence of stages.[16] Rather, depending upon circumstances, people retain an ability to reason at all stages although there may be a predominant mode of reasoning. Rest's ideas make clear the common-sense observation that people's judgments and behavior do shift, depending upon circumstances, as great literature often portrays. This finding is an important one for political scientists, especially in cases of social breakdown (e.g., war, mob actions, conditions of shortage) where right and wrong may take on a coloration different than in normal circumstances. Emler, summing up criticisms of the notion that invariant logical development is the sole foundation of moral thought, rather briskly states that "The idea of a rational, autonomous conscience, untouched by history and circumstance, personal biography and social structure, or even by the natural history of the species, has the ontological status of the tooth fairy and the Easter bunny."[17]

Even the stages of development themselves have been questioned. Emler questions the logical and empirical validity of stages four, five, and six; others report empirical support for the first four stages but not beyond.[18] Still others have wondered whether the six stages are not too complex a construct. Could not the idea of development, they ask, be more adequately handled with a tripartite or even simpler division?[19] Recent reports indicate that shortly before the end of his life, Kohlberg reduced his stages to five in number.

Last is an oft expressed concern about the relationship between moral judgment and moral behavior. Because of the emphasis on cognitive structure and adherence to a formulation of a congruence between changes in this structure and the manifestation of moral orientations, moral development theorists have hesitated to go beyond investigating the rationale for behavior, the ways that moral judgments change and develop. Although a recent review of moral reasoning literature indicates considerable support for the hypothesis that moral reasoning and moral behavior are statistically related,[20] there is in the literature often only an implicit assumption that particular kinds of moral judgment will be translated into related forms of moral behavior. Such a stance is not one that political scientists can take. As the old saying "the road to hell is paved with good intentions" suggests, judgment itself cannot be the sole area of interest. While the thought of a Gandhi or a Himmler is clearly important, their actual behavior is the stuff of politics.

In sum, while moral development theory has excited the attention of many and has good claims to at least partial empirical validity, it has been constructively criticized in a manner that suggests that a more expanded—and perhaps less ambitious—definition of moral development is called for. I propose now to do this, retaining as valuable the notion of stages of development but integrating the cognitive aspects of moral development more fully with social learning and personality variables.

Components of an Alternate Theory of Moral Development

The highest level of moral competence, which I shall also call mature morality, has characteristics involving altruistic awareness, empathy, and personal responsibility. Altruistic awareness, following the lead of Kohlberg and Piaget, is the consistent ability to view situations in terms of the needs and claims of others. For instance, viewed in terms of principles of justice as fairness, mature moral behavior consists of acts that would be acceptable to any individual within a particular context where every person who is involved in the context does not know in advance which particular role he or she will play.[21] Altruistic awareness is the ability to apprehend the related goals of others and to adjust to their needs on the basis of a *cognitive* ability to determine an outcome that maximizes each person's opportunities.

Empathy, in contrast, is the ability *emotionally* to take the place of other people. Kohlberg, with his emphasis on judgment rather than behavior, argues that empathy is a "precondition for experiencing a moral conflict rather than a mechanism for its resolution."[22] This viewpoint, rather than minimizing the need to consider empathy, makes clear that without it altruistic awareness would not come into play to provide a cognitive solution to a moral problem. For this reason empathy is as critical a component in the resolution of moral dilemmas as are the other components. In its highest form empathy is the ability to sympathize, to feel the emotions that another person has along with a desire to minimize any distress that the other person may feel.

Personal responsibility is the ability to form judgments independent of situational cues, most particularly those that come from groups or authority figures; it involves qualities of will and rectitude. Personal responsibility implies that judgment will not be influenced by whether others are known or unknown. Although in normal circumstances judgments may conform to social rules and customs, in other instances they may be opposed to them. Personal responsibility assumes self-governance, but this quality is distinct from egoism. In morally mature behavior personal responsibility is always linked with altruistic awareness and empathy. Prompted by sympathy, judgments are made in terms of internalized standards that encompass concern for the goals and feelings of others.

Is immature moral judgment and behavior, or what is commonly called just plain immorality, the reverse image of mature morality? The answer is yes in the sense that immorality is characterized by a perception of the self as the center of social activity and by an inability to recognize the claims of others. There is also an inability to empathize and feel sympathy and a reliance on situational cues, especially those that are related to rules, the dictates of social custom, and the pronouncements of authority figures.

The Moral Development Process

All people have an affective response capability, a cognitive development capability, and an autonomus response capability, which are related to empathy, altruistic awareness, and individual responsibility respectively. These internal capabilities develop neither in a vacuum nor in a random manner. Rather, the external influences that an individual experiences during childhood (and throughout life) play a decisive role in the development process. Of these influences the critical ones for moral development are affective manipulation, morals training, and autonomy training.

The form and intensity of affective manipulation, morals training, and autonomy training (as well as the inherent capabilities that they act upon) differ for every individual, even for members of the same family, as stories of brothers and sisters who are saints and murderers portray. Despite individual variation, however, people in one group or culture do generally share common experiences with regard to these influences and as a consequence have distinctive values and behavior patterns. As noted earlier these outcomes make up the content and mode of expression of moral beliefs, the particular forms that different societies have for expressing moral sentiments.

With regard to affective manipulation, certain anxieties are associated with particular forms of manipulation. For instance, if physical punishment is frequently used, fear is likely to be the response that guides behavior. If a person has been exposed to what are called love withdrawal punishments, that is, to being ridiculed, ostracized, or rejected, then the anxiety is one of shame, and behavior will be directed toward attempts to minimize this possibility. Or, individuals may experience induction training where they are taught to feel the kinds of emotions that their behavior arouses in others. In this kind of learning what results is a desire to avoid those actions that will make others feel bad.

Research suggests that mature morality is not fostered by physical punishment and is also unassociated with love-withdrawal techniques of discipline used alone.[23] In these instances individuals who are excessively fearful of authority or who have anxieties about being humiliated or ostracized may attach undue importance to the views and opinions of others, especially authority figures, such that an ability to assume personal responsibility for choices is minimized.

Mature morality is positively associated with induction techniques of training. In this case empathic feelings involving concern for the welfare of others develop. In its most mature form empathic feelings include whole groups or classes, including people who may not be known personally. Of particular concern in comparing societies is the degree to which particular types of discipline elicit or retard a capability for empathy. Where empathy exists, we assume that one learning condition for the development of mature morality has been met. Where, on the other hand, the characteristic patterns of feeling are fear, shame, or guilt, we assume that learning conditions favoring mature morality have not been met.

A second major external influence is morals training, an aspect of learning that is found in one form or another in all societies. Anthropologists have done extensive field work examining patterns of interaction within families and the values that are imparted there; others have studied schools, peer groups, sports teams, and so forth, and whether learning is formal (e.g., exhortation or indoctrination) or informal (e.g., a proverb mentioned in casual speech). Whatever the locale or form of learning, societies are not neutral with regard to the values imparted to the young. The object of morals training is to insure socially approved behavior and to inculcate a consensus with regard to those values that will unify and preserve the social order. These values not only concern the desirable ends of social life (justice, for example) but also acceptable ways that people should behave (aggressive, accommodative, etc.).

Individuals cannot reflect on the validity of values until they have the cognitive ability to understand firmly a particular set of values. The ability to accept or reject values, however, is also dependent on the freedom to choose. Many forms of learning involve indoctrination, where personal responsibility regarding value orientations is deemphasized. In this case the stress in morals training is on the one right way to do something, and those who do not believe this, or who do not act in accordance with what is said to be the right way, are automatically deemed to be less deserving than others.

In any social system some values are more emphasized in learning than others. If, for instance, cooperation is heavily stressed, then cooperative behavior will be deemed a prime virtue. Yet in viewing morals training one must keep in mind that the way that a value like cooperation is taught may not be conducive to the development of the highest levels of moral competence. If cooperation is stressed only with regard to particular groups and individuals, say the family or coreligionists, then the widest possible circle of people for whom altruistic awareness applies will be unrealized.

Historically within communities some people have often been labeled as outsiders—deviants or strangers—and have, as a consequence, been treated miserably. Sociobiologists have hypothesized that people may be genetically inclined to divide others into friends and enemies, to fear strangers, and to manifest altruism very much in proportion to the strength of their relationships.[24] Other work, however, suggests that sense of community is not fixed in terms of group size or group composition; certainly the development in the modern period of nation-states implies that sense of community need not be restricted to small-scale linguistic or tribal groups.

The feelings that people have about group membership have not been a central feature in recent moral development literature. Nevertheless, both the strength of these attachments and the level at which they are primarily operative (e.g., family, organization, religious group) are of central importance, especially in autonomy training, the third major external influence.

The significance of feelings about community for an understanding of the way that people relate to each other has long been noted. Political philosophers from Aristotle to Michael Walzer have stressed the importance of community as a good where people are linked to each other by acts of proportionate reciprocity.[25] Others have pointed out how collectivist tendencies are at least as natural and strong as individualistic ones. People, it is suggested, have two fundamental motives, one toward autonomy but also an equal one toward affiliation.[26] In fact, the two are—paradoxically—highly interrelated as Piaget suggested in his seminal study of moral development.[27] Autonomy develops, he averred, by learning how to cooperate in group play in terms of mutually accepted rules.

A fixation of identity on some particular group, however, will retard moral development. Very small children, of course, are not aware that they belong to many of the groups of which they are members. It takes a while for a child to learn that he or she is American, Chinese, or Nigerian. In fact, in the earliest stages of growth children tend to perceive reality in terms of themselves, that is, in a self-centered manner with emphasis on personal needs and wants. If in the process of overcoming self-centeredness there is, in the end, only a transference of this centeredness from the self to the group, then the development of an autonomus capability will be impeded;[28] just as important, there will also exist boundaries that limit altruistic awareness and empathy.

As attachments to large-scale social entities develop, a person does not, of course, forget or ignore smaller groups such as the family or the work unit and may even have a special affection for them. Also, these groups are extremely important as loci for the interplay that gives meaning to most moral behavior. However, what happens in autonomy training is a shifting of the reference point for the validation of behavior beyond groups such as the family to larger groups such as the nation, or, for some, to all mankind, the community of all persons.[29] As a result there develops an ability to act without an exclusive need for emotional support from others who are familiar. Where behavior involves people who are unknown, a person must be guided by a set of internalized principles that are thought to be right in and of themselves. Behavior in terms of such principles involves personal responsibility; it is manifested autonomously without the need for reference to or dependence on a specific group of people. Principled autonomous behavior by itself, however, is not morally mature. Putting principles into practice without reference to the needs and feelings of others bespeaks a lack of knowledge of the ambiguity that is so much a part of human relationships. Only when personal responsibility is joined with altruistic awareness and empathy is there a truly mature moral orientation and a merging of autonomous and community concerns.

Stage Aspects of Moral Development

Cognitive development theory holds that during growth people become morally mature by stages. These stages have been verified in a number of societies; the proofs of their existence have bolstered claims that moral judgment capabilities are related to common cognitive structures.[30] There is at least partial truth to this assertion. Moral competence, however, is not solely associated with cognitive structure. Rather, it is a more complex manifestation of human personality that includes feelings and a quality of will.

Just as mature morality is dependent on more than cognitive change, so also is the stage characteristic of moral growth related to more than age-related shifts in internal capabilities. For certain external influences that people experience are universal aspects of learning that are sequential and cumulative in their impact. Affective manipulation, for instance, begins at birth. Parents, by a variety of facial movements and sounds, convey to the child from its earliest moments their notions of right and wrong. Praise and stroking or certain forms of withdrawal of nurturance (or failure to provide it on demand) have emotional importance for the child and very early become triggers for particular patterns of behavior. It is when the child begins to learn language, a manifestation of cognitive development, that training begins to include overt value injunctions. At this point affective manipulation is attached to verbalized morals training with the result that particular value injunctions become associated with feelings. Of course, it is only with increased age and further cognitive development that chidren are able to relate values to each other and to understand their relationship to social life. With age children also learn about the groups of which they are members. They early acquire knowledge of the family and somewhat later of the neighborhood. Only when they are older, however, do they slowly develop an awareness of larger groups and an ability to apply values in depersonalized relationships.

Developing a mature moral competence is a complex and lengthy process that is still little understood despite centuries of analysis. Clearly, mature morality is related to capabilities for intellectual development, self-governance, and empathic feelings. These capabilities are acted upon by social environments; the complex and interrelated influences are experienced in a lengthy and complicated learning process. It is small wonder that the factors that affect moral development have proven so difficult to unravel and are still imperfectly comprehended. What is clear, however, is the close relationship in moral development between psychological and social variables that extends well into adulthood and indeed throughout life.

Figure 1 shows schematically the moral development process. In distinctive combinations depending on culture, external influences prompt the development of internal autonomous, affective, and cognitive response capabilities. These capabilities as they develop determine a person's moral competence or capacity to express altruistic awareness, empathy, and personal responsibility. Moral competence, in turn, guides moral behavior, which influences the social environment in which socialization takes place. There is, thus, a feedback loop; although this loop is admittedly diffuse and long term, there is no compelling reason to doubt either its existence or its importance.

Moral Development and Society

The study of the relationship between the moral citizen and the moral political order was for centuries the central focus of philosophical inquiry. The characteristics of desirable behavior that were set forth, however, were subjective and were asserted rather than empirically observed. In the modern period, therefore, those who

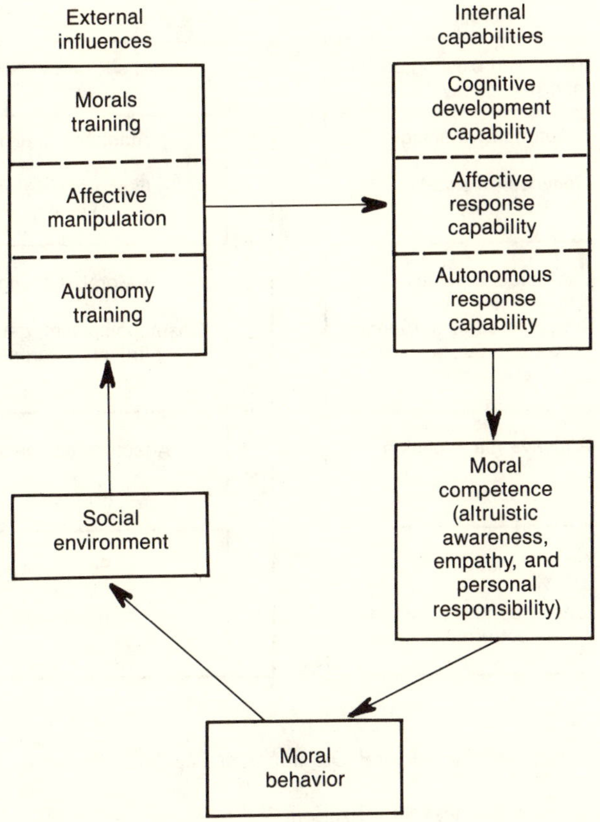

Figure 1. Moral Development Model

Source: Richard W. Wilson, "Political Socialization and Moral Development," *World Politics* 33, 2 (January 1981), 163.

study behavior have tended to put aside these conclusions as unproven. Yet modern scholarship, while increasingly sophisticated and riogorous with regard to its understanding of the form and dynamics of actual behavior, has been deficient in relating its conclusions to the nature of the good society and the making of the good citizen. Moral development provides the opportunity for an end to this divorce. Its focus on desirable ends is matched by insistence on theoretical models that can be subjected to empirical verification. The assertion by political philosophers of the desirability of a just social order can now be wedded to a concept of moral growth that is

Actual	Ideal
Historical and existing social and political systems	Ideal social and political system
Autonomy training (Reliance on situational cues)	Autonomy training (Reliance on internalized values)
Morals training (Group centeredness; reduced altruistic awareness of outsiders)	Morals training (Cosmopolitanism; generalized altruistic awareness)
Affective manipulation (Fear, shame, or guilt)	Affective manipulation (Empathy)
Feedback (Adherence to prescribed patterns)	Feedback (Flexible)
Mixed moral orientations	Mature moral orientations

Figure 2. Actual and Ideal Moral Development Feedback Patterns

Source: Wilson, ''Political Socialization,'' 176.

grounded in concrete, verifiable social psychological experiences.

There has never been and there is not now any social and political system that has universally fostered mature moral orientations. As a consequence, all societies have an admixture of people at different levels of moral competence. Figure 2 shows the feedback loops for societies as they actually are contrasted with an ideal form. The two patterns are the end positions of a continuum and show how the influences that are associated with either mature or immature moral competence are related and mutually reinforcing. Actual societies have socialization influences that, in varying degrees, foster immature individual moral competence as well as morally imperfect societies; alternately, an ideal society has socialization influences that enhance mature moral competence and the existence of a moral social order. In neither case, of course, is the feedback loop impermeable to change.

In the ideal pattern a person does not exclusively identify with a particular group. Rather, what develops is an attitude of cosmopolitanism where all others are perceived as legitimately within the sphere of moral concern. Cosmopolitanism requires judgment (and behavior) in terms of internalized values; it requires personal responsibility. Morals training involves exposure to value contradictions. Altruism is stressed but not in terms of some predetermined mode of behavior or toward some particular group. The outcome, therefore, is awareness of the feasibility of various forms of altruistic behavior. In affective manipulation, induction techniques of discipline teach the child to relate to the feelings that others may have as a result of his or her actions. From these experiences empathy develops. Learning does not fix a particular form for the expression of altruistic awareness and empathy; rather, stress is on experimentation and on progressively understanding which forms are most appropriate for given circumstances.

The socialization experiences that enhance morally mature behavior can be contrasted with those that foster immature moral competence. In this case learning patterns reduce the capability for personal responsibility, altruistic awareness, and even-handed empathy. Stress is on membership in a particular group and on the lower worth of others who are not members of the group. Emphasis on loyalty to a group and its leaders is coupled with anxieties about ostracism and rejection. The outcome is ethnocentrism, a concern for one's own group and its particular values, and a reduced capacity for personal responsibility in the face of group demands and requirements for conformity. Morals training takes the form of indoctrination. Loyalty is stressed. Values are taught as unchallengeable and alternative value orientations as unacceptable. Affective manipulation stresses physical and/or love-oriented techniques of discipline where the emotional outcome is fear, shame, or guilt. In learning no flexibility is allowed with regard to altruistic awareness and empathy; rather, their expression is permitted only in terms of approved group forms.

If, in pure form, there has never been a society with a majority of citizens with mature moral competence—and, I believe, there never will be—there is still in the modern world movement in many places toward this condition. The shift is due to a number of factors, none sufficient in and of itself to cause change. For instance, for political reasons there may be efforts by authorities to break down small group loyalties in favor of the nation as a whole. Such training, in fact, is common in modernizing nations and is historically one of the first steps toward more cosmopolitan attitudes. Or, within some families, there may be changes in methods of affective manipulation. Physical and love-oriented techniques of discipline, for instance, may give way to emphasis on induction training. Although indoctrination of moral values is quite common worldwide, values that permit disagreement and stress the desirability of experimentation with regard to what is "good" in social interaction may come into existence. Any and all such changes foster shifts in patterns of learning and thus gradually induce the emergence of more moral individuals and more moral social and political orders.

2. Organizations

The experiences that shape moral orientations come not from some amorphous entity called "environment" but from more intimate contexts. There is the family, which is critically important in childhood and continues to be influential in later years. There are also school and friendship associations. In many traditional societies these groups were all that really mattered. For modern men and women, family and friends are still highly important. But they have been joined by larger-scale, formal organizations that entwine the lives of people from the highest levels of citizenship to the mundane events of daily work.

In modernized societies the most significant social activity is within and among organizations. Parent-teacher associations interact with school systems, school systems with boards of education, and boards of education with local governments. Corporations interact with consumer groups and also with government regulatory agencies. Political parties vie among themselves for leadership and court the votes of ethnic groups, religious organizations, farm associations, and labor unions. These organizations, of course, are not equally important, and membership and position in one or the other (or in a combination of them) help determine whether a person has high or low status. In myriad areas of life, from politics to jobs and even to families, people live in organizations and interact with others in terms of organization.

Organizations are situated in societies in different ways. Some, such as a political party or a church, may dominate society. Others may be an arm of government, such as the army or a national bank. Some organizations such as corporations may exist relatively autonomously. Still others are deviant, such as the Mafia or a secret revolutionary party. Organizations can be thought of as miniature societies. Although they reflect the values of the larger society, they are social units themselves with their own forms of hierarchy, distinctive methods for getting things done (appropriate for different goals), and often even specialized rules and vocabulary. These patterns coalesce to form modes of operation that differentiate organizations from each other.

Despite dissimilarities in organizational objectives and procedures and in the influence of the larger environment, modern organizations are the product of social, economic, and political change and share attributes that are functional for their operations in the contemporary world. As a consequence, there are broad similarities in the influence that these organizations have on their members' moral behavior. What these influences are and how they came about are the subjects of this chapter.

Groups and Their Influence on Moral Behavior

Kohlberg claimed to have found evidence of moral development by stages in a number of societies.[1] Although he stated that it is only the rate of development that varies cross-culturally, the differences in response patterns among the societies that were tested—the United States, Taiwan, Mexico, Turkey, and the Yucatan—are striking. At age sixteen respondents from isolated, traditional villages in Turkey and the Yucatan are still giving predominantly stage 1 responses whereas in the more advanced social contexts of Taiwan and Mexico the responses at the same age are largely at stages 3 and 4. In the United States, in contrast, stage 5 statements are the largest category by age sixteen, followed closely by stages 4 and 3. Although in all of these societies all stages are in evidence (an important point for Kohlberg), the differences are nevertheless startling, even when account is taken of criticisms of Kohlberg's definition of moral maturity, of his scoring procedures, and of the cultural biases (about property especially) that inform the moral dilemmas used in his tests. Political scientists, at least, cannot fail to take note of these large variations.

Differences among groups in their moral response patterns have also been found by others. Aronfreed has presented evidence showing that internalized moral orientations never develop to any significant degree in some non-Western societies.[2] Stephen Chilton has suggested that political cultures limit "the cognitive levels of feasible social action"; there must be, he states, an average cognitive advance for a population before cultural change can take place. In other words, cultural change—including change in moral development patterns—will not occur without a prior shift in the general cognitive competence of a population.[3] This conclusion suggests that societies, historically and at the present time, will differ in their most frequent or modal moral stage.

Such findings about moral development differences are disturbing for those who would like to see all people everywhere as essentially the same; they are not, however, anomalous. Differences in moral orientations have been found to be class-related in the sense that middle- and working-class children differ in the extent and speed of developmental shifts in moral thought; change is exceptionally small for the working class in comparison to the middle class (even when intelligence, which is highly related to moral development, is factored out).[4] Hay found highly significant differences by educational level in preferences for principled considerations.[5] Such findings suggest, at the least, that different social influences have an important effect on moral development. Following the previous argument these would include, for lower-class children, the greater amount of physical punishment that has been noted for them (which would depress their rate of moral development) and, for the better educated, the greater emphasis on cognitive training, especially the development of abstract reasoning skills, that comes with increased education (which would enhance the rate of moral development).

In a somewhat different vein Garbarino and Bronfenbrenner found confirmation in a comparative analysis for the hypothesis that high scores on political pluralism are positively associated with mature moral orientations. Their findings indicate that the greater the support for sociopolitical pluralism, the less likely it is that individuals will have an authority orientation.[6] In fact, in the United States, the better educated (who are more likely to have higher moral competence than the less educated) are more consistent in the application of abstract principles of democracy than others.[7] In a carefully designed study Emler, Renwick, and Malone found a strong relationship between political orientations and moral judgment with the differences between stages 4 and 5 corresponding to a conservative/radical distinction.[8]

There are, of course, no historical cross-cultural data on moral development. The data that are available, however, strongly suggest that differences in the external influences that affect moral development have indeed changed over time. It does not seem unreasonable to suppose, therefore, that differences among past and present populations in education levels, punishment techniques, and degrees of inclusiveness of group life would correlate with differences in moral orientations. The reasons for wishing to know, even speculatively, whether this correlation exists are clear. Showing over time how changes in social influences have brought about changes in moral competencies (and vice versa) can lead to a better understanding of the variations in moral development that have been noted cross-culturally in the modern world. To the extent that these variations also coincide with historical differences in organizational practices one can begin to develop more informed judgments about how organizations have affected moral competence in the past down to the present time.

Patterns of Influence in Traditional Life

Hobbes was right when he said that life was nasty, brutish, and short, but he need not have restricted this to the state of nature for it applies perfectly well to many aspects of traditional life. Although societies differed in many important ways, about 85 percent of all people everywhere lived in small, relatively isolated communities and were engaged in agricultural pursuits. To put it bluntly, they did not live well. Life consisted generally of dawn-to-dusk labor. Mortality, especially among infants, was high. Living conditions were primitive in small windowless dwellings with dirt floors. Food was monotonous and sometimes in short supply, and sanitation was crude. It has been estimated that the nineteenth-century German peasant had an active vocabulary of about six hundred words.[9] To the extent that this level of ability applies to other traditional societies, we can infer that social interaction did not involve the niceties of philosophical discourse although, of course, all people, peasants included, asked the great questions about life and death and the vagaries of fortune. In short, existence in general was impoverished and arduous and placed severe restraints on what people were able to do. It was not this, however, that was the harshest aspect of life.

There reigned, it must be said, a general savagery. To be sure, there was cooperation within families, which were economic as well as procreational units. But even among kin within the same village, exploitation of the weaker could be sharp and unrelenting. Still, families did provide some buffer against the outside world, and family solidarity was marked at all levels of society. Partly as a consequence, intense local orientations predominated. It was not unusual for a person to travel no more than ten miles from home throughout life. For such people the others who mattered—and they mattered a great deal—were in close proximity and well known. Their opinions and feelings were of paramount importance and were reinforced by local custom and the dictates of local authority.

Education was virtually nonexistent. This does not mean that people did not listen to stories, pay attention to the words of religious leaders, learn carefully the roles of their parents, which they would one day follow, and imbibe the rules that guided life in general. But the imponderables of existence were often best explained by superstitious beliefs, which in their darker forms included forces of horrifying and malignant malevolence (werewolves, banshees, and the like). There were village schools in places but, overall, learning the three Rs in even rudimentary form was unknown, especially for females.

Exploitation through kinship units was the pattern at every level throughout society. There was, additionally, an elaborate hierarchy of power that extended from the lowest levels of the peasant village to the uppermost levels of government but included only a very weak middle sector. Despite these webs of interaction there was little collective consciousness over wide geographic areas. The policies of the center were largely extractive and regulatory.[10] At times the "taxation" of the population could hardly be distinguished from robbery or extortion; it was a constant source of grievance. In Europe in the late Middle Ages, for instance, the papacy was the greatest financial institution. Abuses in its fiscal system, which had been minor in the thirteenth century, became a flood by the fifteenth, affecting virtually everybody and contributing mightily to the rise of reformist movements. In China exploitation of the peasants was always more severe as dynasties declined and taxes increased.

There was, to be sure, an ultimate framework of meaning that commanded people's loyalty (to king, religious leaders, nobles, and superiors generally) and justified—as it always does—economic transfers among classes. This framework also legitimized the rule of females by males, of younger generations by older ones, of guild apprentices by their masters, and, in the wide areas and many guises where it existed, of slaves by masters. In addition there was in places rule by particular ethnic or religious groups with special forms of taxation for those in less favored categories. Such was the practice, for instance, in the Ottoman Empire.

Overall there was an institutionalized disregard for individual dignity. Aggression against the lower orders was an accredited form of action. Punishments, invariably physical, were often severe, including public torture executions and flogging for breaches of payment, etiquette, and so forth. In China a favorite method of discipline was to force the offender to wear for a specified number of days a large wooden collar or cangue, which prevented the face from being reached by the hands. Physical mistreatment lasted down into the nineteenth century (and in some places into the twentieth) for slaves, soldiers and sailors, industrial workers, serfs, and the like.

This sketch of traditional life is clearly too harsh a description for some people in some places. Chinese peasants at the start of strong dynasties, for example, had a better existence. There were also countervailing values of benevolence and charity that mitigated the worst aspects of life for many. Festivals, too, gave periodic relief from hard work and fostered communal solidarity. Unfortunately, however, what has been sketched is too mild a description for the lives of others. Black slaves in the West Indies, for instance, suffered unbearable repression. The orphaned, widowed, and diseased, among others, often fulfilled destinies of a bleak and harrowing nature. Life could truly be nasty, brutish, and short.

In a climate where there is a low level of societal trust and of identification with a larger community, where punishments, often public, are physically severe, where formal education is virtually nonexistent, and where kinship boundaries are an effective limit for most obligations, one can confidently expect generally low levels of moral competence. In traditional societies—and in some areas of the modern world, such as the villages in Yucatan and Turkey that Kohlberg studied, where many traditional values still exist—neither morals training (in a societal sense), affective manipulation, nor autonomy training were of a nature that fostered mature morality. The behavior of individuals and groups that is noted in the records confirms this assessment. Organized life, often diffuse and unstructured by modern standards, was characterized by open aggrandizement and piratical behavior; the buccaneering ethic of the Viking was scarcely masked. Mistreatment and degradation were common. Harshness was a fact of life, and few buffers existed to prevent it.

The Coming of Change

Capitalism did not begin with the Reformation or even with the Renaissance. The thirteenth century was rich in creative thought and technical innovation in both industry and transport; this progress had its origins in the twelfth and even earlier in the eleventh century. Spanish and especially Italian bankers pioneered developments in business techniques (such as the creation of deposits) which spread slowly northward in succeeding centuries along with the center of gravity of financial and productive power.[11]

By the time of the age of Elizabeth in the sixteenth century, particularly in the later decades, the English had grown prosperous. Along with the ruination of the old feudal nobility by the democratization of land ownership and the concomitant rise of new men there were continued efforts at many levels in society to break down the particularism of protectionist interests. Sweeping changes designed to reduce costs occurred in fundamental industrial techniques in mining, transport, and manufacture. Oriented toward profit rather than artistic craftsmanship, the English became fiercely productive. On the eve of the English civil war in the mid-seventeenth century, Great Britain and Sweden together produced as much iron as the rest of Western Europe. It was used for the rollers, boilers, stoves, and tools that went into dyeing and carding wool and cloth and in brewing, soap boiling, and sugar refining. Also in demand was coal. In the years 1631–1640 the annual output of coal in Britain approached two million tons, an astonishing figure since the rest of the world combined produced only one-fifth as much.[12]

Other significant changes were also afoot. In the sixteenth century efforts to reform the Catholic Church burst into full-fledged schism. While cause and effect are difficult to unravel, scholars, especially since Max Weber, have viewed this period as formative of values and social forms that are still important. Among the most deserving of attention are those that derive from Calvinism, that sturdy branch of the protest movement that demanded from its adherents wholehearted participation in a ceaseless struggle to create a new type of human community. Believing that the true aim of man was not personal salvation within the existing political order, Calvinism imparted to its followers a different view of politics and an extraordinary organizational impulse. To achieve their goals men and women from all walks of life were called upon to glorify God by labor and strife and to reveal their inner virtue by personal responsibility, discipline, and asceticism.

As one searches for the origins of the modern world it is clear to an increasing number of scholars that the English Calvinists, the Puritans, played a pivotal role. The civil war in England in the mid-seventeenth century which they did so much to instigate—and which they won—has been rightly viewed as a major bridge from the past to the present. Partly obscured by different forms of speech and by a religious fervor whose modern counterpart is economic and political, the gleam of a new age nevertheless shines through.

The Puritans had a deep sense of covenant making, binding people in new forms of association (e.g., the Mayflower Compact). Friendship, government, church, partnership in business, and marriage were voluntary associations that were covenantal in character. Their world view, involving a collectivist discipline never marked by respect for privacy, was one of brethren rather than kinfolk, of congregation. A holy commonwealth bound by religious discipline was to take the place of traditional forms of order. This commonwealth was to be subordinate to the church, for the Puritans imagined each congregation as a commonwealth in miniature in which individual households, each dominated by a godly father, were bound by covenant.[13] A mutual recognition of dignity and equality was demanded of everyone, and, indeed, the new sorts of organizations that came into being among justices of the peace, city aldermen, and members of Parliament were, like the congregations, based upon these very principles.[14]

It is in families, however, that one sees most clearly the principles of Puritan organization. Marriage was thought of as a social estate, a trial ground for salvation. The family, conceived of as a microcosm of all human society, was to be transformed into a voluntary alliance for virtue and goodness. As there is a covenant between God and man so also was there to be a contract of mutual obligation within the family. Although wives were expected to be dutiful, helpful, and subordinate, the family was perceived as a joint enterprise founded on free mutual consent.[15] Compared with wives in ancient Rome, the Middle Ages, or even most of England at that time, the Puritan wife had a relatively enviable position. Her husband, although clearly the head of the household, could not strike her or command her to do anything contrary to the laws of God. This limitation on authority was a remarkable step away from more traditional patterns.[16]

In Puritan society all inferiors were expected to fear their superiors, to be obedient, faithful, and reverent. Discipline could be severe, as in Cotton Mather's epigram regarding children, "Better whipt, than Damn'd."[17] Nevertheless, in an age when tolerance was not even thought possible, the attempt was made to institute the laws of God, even in pecuniary areas. As Calvin noted, a pious man was to give to his brethren all that he could. The good Christian, according to the Puritan Richard Baxter, must not extort or make money at the expense of others. Servants and laborers must not be defrauded, nor should usury be so high as to prevent a borrower from making a reasonable gain.[18] That these ideals eroded over time and were subtly sidestepped in many areas should not blind one to their actual force in daily life. Good works were lauded, hierarchy was not treated as natural in the medieval sense, and no man, pope, king, or bishop, could claim to have a special mediating role between God and men. Good behavior determined status. The political order was one in which the participants had specific duties, enforceable at law and in conscience. Such sentiments no doubt underlay the effective refusal by the House of Commons in the seventeenth century to permit the Crown to collect new and heavy taxes from the mercantile classes.[17] With the exception of the United Provinces there was no parallel for this type of political opposition in continental countries—to say nothing about taking off the king's head, which in 1649 during the civil war was the fate of Charles I.

Clearly, with the Puritans a great change had taken place in the influences that shape moral competence. Through the idea of covenant a unity was perceived between the individual, the family, and society that broadened immeasurably the scope of community concern. Punishments, although still physically severe, became increasingly imbued with guilt feelings, with special emphasis on not failing in one's religious duties. Within the family the new ideal of a happily married couple included a stress on work and love together rather than work being a burden and marriage a boring responsibility.[20] Energy was released, not solely because of a "protestant ethic," but because of an organizational climate that gave people a new sense of their worth. As recent work on achievement indicates, productivity varies in accordance with different types of influence on group members.[21] Getting more out of others is related to participative practices (i.e., allowing others to feel that the enterprise is in real ways a joint one) as well as to an emphasis on getting the job done.

Participation and getting the job done were certainly goals that the Puritans stressed. In England, however, the collectivistic aspects of Puritanism slowly gave way, except in families and congregations, to wholehearted individualistic business enterprise. Alongside the discipline of faith was the discipline of work, which found an outlet in voluntary, self-initiated economic behavior. Even the intense social discipline of the Puritan theocracy of New England eventually retreated from the regulation of prices, limitations on interest, and fixed minimum wages.[22]

Other changes also occurred. The notion of covenant, of relationships freely and voluntarily entered into, was formulated as contract law toward the beginning of the seventeenth century. These laws allowed greater flexibility and innovation in economic action. In the area of education, new ideas modified previous practices. Learning for everyone, even if only in a rudimentary sense, began to be stressed as an ideal, for how else could the dutiful child receive the Godly guidance needed for inner direction? From this basis, combined with the increasing emphasis on worldly pursuits, learning, especially in the scientific area, acquired a heightened prestige. This was a factor of decisive importance for the rise of industrialism.

The End of the Traditional World

The fierceness of continental wars combined with peace at home did much to stimulate the early English industrial revolution of the sixteenth century.[23] One should not, of course, assume some particular British genius for development nor overly emphasize the role of Protestantism, for despite war and exhaustion notable gains were also made in the sixteenth to eighteenth centuries in Southern and Catholic Europe. It is true that after the peace of Westphalia in 1648 Central Europe did not quickly recover even the moderate prosperity that had existed in some areas prior to the Thirty Years War. Indeed, in England itself, the civil war also put a stop to development, and although there was some recovery after the Restoration in 1660, not until 1750 did the rate of industrial output become as rapid as in the period 1540–1640.[24] Some real gains, of course, were registered. In the first decade of the eighteenth century the steam engine was invented and coke was substituted for charcoal in pig iron blast furnaces. On the whole, however, the Puritan eruption probably delayed the later Industrial Revolution[25] while at the same time being essential groundwork for that event.

On the eve of the French Revolution France overtook England in per capita production of iron although it remained greatly behind in coal production and in output generally. In 1780 English iron production was little more than a third of France's. What happened thereafter, however, had no historical precedent. Output in England doubled between 1785 and 1797 and then doubled again by 1805. By 1840–41 output was three times that of France, having registered a twentyfold increase in the space of fifty years.[26]

Other changes also reflected—and spurred—the increased emphasis on productivity. The Benthamite Reforms of the 1830s and 1840s, the Prescriptions Act, the Inheritance Act, the Fines and Recoveries Act, the Real Property Act, and so on helped to institutionalize and protect new beliefs about property.[27] These acts, embodying utilitarian concepts, favored the interests of that breed of men whose lineage extended back two centuries to the Puritans with their emphasis on duty, hard work, and commitment to a calling. Their activities at this time, however, were not hampered by the restrictions that had previously worked to mitigate the lot of the poor. In preceding centuries there had been an effort by government, violated most cruelly in the enclosure movement, to insist that ownership was limited by the rights of the community and the obligations of charity. By the nineteenth century many decades had passed since these traditional economic ethics had appealed to the consciences of men. Instead, promethian energies were released; new men were given sanction to create and build unhampered by any need to consider the welfare of others. From the growth of wealth, production, invention, and scientific knowledge these people believed that the general progress of humanity would ensue. That was sufficient. Established churches and aristocracies were frowned upon, government regulation of the economy was disparaged (as were any attempts to organize unions), and the efficient, enlightened, and especially untrammeled right to the use of property was heralded. Here indeed was the birth of an achieving society par excellence.

The Creation of a New Social Arrangement

The drive for efficiency places a premium on the development of elaborate machines and plants. But machines do not pay unless large amounts of goods are produced and unless labor can be purchased—freely—at a cost that does not undermine the ability to obtain raw materials, process them, and sell the finished product at a profit. All factors must be in scale for long-term investments in plant and machinery to be realized. Rewards for workers and owners alike must derive from the sale of something, making the ethic of profit imperative. As Polanyi has pointed out, the new emphasis on profit as a social good involved a change from the economy being embedded in social relations to one where social relations became embedded in the economic system.[28] What was required was a change in attitudes about people. If everyone was not equal (and they were not), everyone must still be equally free to sell their labor as a right and as property. These emerging ideas about the place of individuals in society came to be applied in many areas. The French Code of 1791 stated "Everyman condemned to death will have his head cut off." Here was an advance indeed (over torture and dismemberment) for the code truly meant "everyman."[29]

The miseries of the Industrial Revolution, the brutal exploitation, the breakup of families, and so on cannot be minimized, and they called forth passionate cries for change (not least from Karl Marx). In viewing organizations, however, this period, oppressive of workers as it was, set the stage for the full coalescence of earlier trends. Values of austerity, devotion to an occupation as a calling, and individualism, among others, have been noted as having roots in the Puritan tradition.[30] What occurred during the Industrial Revolution was the mutation of these ideas into an industrializing ethic along with a decisive separation of the work organization from the household and an enormous increase in its size. This development in Western Europe and North America stands in sharp contrast to organizational patterns in other parts of the world. So rapid was the advance of this new type of social structure that, beginning about 1875, there emerged in North America and Western Europe employee societies where large organizations increasingly dominated life. Moreover, these organizations built upon themselves, merging continuously in a pattern that led both to increased size of organization and to a general pervasiveness of the bureaucratic work style.[31]

The lure of the modern organization (military, commercial, etc.) lies in its capacity to multiply output many times over traditional forms of endeavor. This is done through a structure that places maximum stress on efficiency, discipline, punctuality, obedience, and attention to repetitive tasks. A number of characteristics differentiate the contemporary organization from its predecessors. Max Weber, for instance, suggests that modern bureaucracies are characterized by specialization of function, calculable and formal rules and regulations, a clearly defined chain of command that insures the coordination and quality of the sequential and interdependent tasks performed in the division of labor, and, perhaps most important, the elimination of purely personal, irrational, and emotional elements from human interaction.[32] Predictability of operation (i.e., dependable role performance) combined with hardheaded rationality are the underpinnings of modern organization.

Are these characteristics of modern organizational life really something new? The Byzantine and Chinese empires, after all, were governed by organizations that had many modern features. In the Chinese case, for example, the imperial bureaucracy was staffed on the basis of merit, and elaborate precautions were taken to insure the secular orientation of its members. Although not nearly as specialized as today's organizations, the traditional Chinese governmental system had bureaus for defense, foreign affairs, judicial matters, and so forth. Yet this bureaucracy, impressive and relatively efficient as it was, was still qualitatively unlike organizations of the modern world. The most significant difference was the very tiny proportion of people who worked within the bureaucracy and lived according to its rules, whereas in modern times virtually all people have become bureaucratic. Today, in advanced societies, most people spend part or all of their lives working in bureaucratically structured organizations; even when they do not work for such organizations they are, as consumers and citizens, intimately affected by their operation. No member of a modern state escapes the influence of corporations, the military establishment, the police, health organizations, labor unions, and a host of other bureaucracies. Lindblom, for instance, using the *Encyclopedia of Organizations in the United States*, notes that 256 pages are needed to list national business associations (by far the largest category), 17 for labor organizations, 60 for public affairs organizations, and 71 for scientific, engineering, and technical organizations.[33] America, clearly, is interwoven with organizations. Concomitantly the machinery of government has become more complex and pervades ever more regions of private life. Indeed, the whole concept of efficient, rational, and pervasive political authority, so similar to the concept of authority in modern organizations generally, has been set forth by one scholar as defining political development.[34]

The values of bureaucratic organization have become part of the mentality of everyone. There has, for example, been a pronounced growth of secular attitudes and a corresponding reduction in importance of customary myths and beliefs. One important feature of secularization has been the substitution of the notion of merit for traditional determinants of worth. A marked increase in education, at least partly related to a need for technological expertise, is another characteristic of organizational life. As the rate of change accelerates, technological innovation causes, and is the result of, increased capabilities in the use of knowledge. Perhaps nothing reflects this so much as the increase in literacy rates throughout the world and the vast increase in all types of educational facilities in all countries. In the United States, for instance, at any given time, three out of ten people are involved full-time with some form of learning, making education the major activity within this society.

This new pattern of life has also called forth large concentrations of people within urban and suburban areas. In traditional societies the proportion of people living and working on the land was approximately 85 percent or greater. In the present-day United States the farm population now constitutes less than 5 percent of the total; ever larger numbers of people who work in or in support of complex organizations live in urban areas connected by high-speed transportation facilities. Interdependence among the urban, semi-urban, and rural portions of the population is absolute. Most people have no control over even as basic a product as their food but rely on complex organizations to grow, harvest, and distribute these commodities. The same is true in virtually every other area of life from transportation to clothing, heat, and energy, and even, to a great extent, entertainment and ideas.

Interdependence among organizations is also increasing. The resources of one organization may be critical for the operation of another ten thousand miles away. At present the management of this interdependence is to a great degree accomplished by large-scale commercial corporations. These, however, are by no means the only ones; they are merely among the most visible. Whole areas of the world are interdependent in terms of military organization, political affiliation, professional association, or educational exchange. Doctors operating in European hospitals, for instance, now have virtually instantaneous access to medical data in the United States provided by organizations that specialize in transmitting medical information.

The modern organization is more than an economic, political, or social system though it is certainly all of these. It is a way of life and of thinking, and it has spread throughout much of the world without regard for ideology. Lenin was an avid organizer and industrializer. Soviet theories of organization sound a familiar note; they stress clear-cut goals and responsibilities, carefully defined lines of command and subordination, and a response to job demands that involves total devotion and spontaneity.[35]

The proportion of a population in organizations is highest in the Scandinavian countries;[36] in France in 1963, 38 percent of the work force worked in only one-fourth of 1 percent of all French companies, a striking degree of concentration but not at all unusual.[37] In terms of scale, socialist organizations tend to be even more huge and all embracing. China, which is economically less developed than the Soviet Union and Western countries, is nevertheless highly organized. State and party organizations are tightly interlocked, and the party has established a complex network of mass organizations that effectively blanket this large and populous nation.[38] In short, while not every society in the world has become truly organizational, none has been untouched by organization.

Organizations and Moral Competence

The ethos of the modern organization is a significant advance over that of traditional social structures where self-serving blatantly superseded empathy and altruistic awareness. In previous times buccaneering, often openly affirmed, was possible against outsiders and even toward low-ranking members of one's own community (e.g., peasants or workers). Self-serving involved personal aggrandizement through the use of power and, in addition, any other tactic that would insure an unequal grip on scarce resources. Unfair rent practices, the manipulation and control of markets, the payment of subsistence wages, and other like practices were all prevalent. The interaction context was generally small in scale; oppressor and oppressed quite often knew each other and were sometimes linked by personal bonds.

In modern organizations, in contrast, the stress on allegiance to the organization suppresses overtly clannish or self-centered acts; there is, in fact, an increase in efficiency and output from the release of energy that comes about when people are motivated by the possibility of greater benefits for all of the organization's members. Although privileges for subordinates are never obtained to the same degree as they are by those in leadership positions there is, nevertheless, frequently a spurring of subordinate enthusiasm (although this word should not be overly stressed) for the organization and its goals that contrasts sharply with the situation in previous centuries. Greater teamwork, larger size, and better-planned procedures make modern organizations more productive than their traditional counterparts. The larger scale of operation places a premium on functionally specific roles and on learning to identify with and acquire behavior patterns appropriate for large-scale group interaction. This is quite unlike traditional society where interests were best served in face-to-face contexts, where there was great emphasis on exclusive attachment to a small group, and where situational factors were highly important.

Organizations that stress allegiance to the organization's rules eliminate capriciousness. Punishments for infractions tend to be "bureaucratic," stressing demotion, dismissal, or public disapproval rather than physical torment. For the organization's members there are widely understood and approved patterns of behavior and a regularity of reward that minimizes the need for particularistic links with others. For the organization's leaders there is an enhancement of the reliability of subordinates because subordinate behavior is based on rules, explicit procedures, and a loyalty to the organization that supersedes self-interest.

By shifting loyalty patterns from a particularistic to a universalistic mode, modern organizations foster moral growth through a widening of group concern. Some scholars, such as Michael Walzer, have pointed out that moral competence does not require the transcendence of particularistic orientations.[39] Such a view is certainly partly true. No work in political psychology, with its emphasis on motivations, would fault the importance of understanding the crucial and lifelong significance of particularistic group ties for moral growth. Yet as the history of traditional China amply demonstrates, strong primary orientations, bolstered in the Chinese case by moralistic Confucian beliefs, were a major stimulant to continuous predatory intergroup relations. Walzer, of course, rightly understands the critical importance of a pluralism that modifies the potential insularity of purely primary ties. It was the development of intermediate-level modern organizations, a phenomenon that both reflected and stimulated enlarged and interconnected economies and political structures, that decisively altered the traditional motivational environment.

Modern organizations stress the need for education (indeed, they increasingly require it) and by doing so foster abstract reasoning skills. By their emphasis on explicit, regularized procedures they minimize the need for arbitrary physical punishments. Cooperation and teamwork are stressed and widely realized in practice. All of these influences minimize self interested calculations; they are, as was pointed out earlier, significant for prompting developmental shifts in moral thought and represent important advances over the experiences of traditional social life. It is my belief that these influences have been the essential ingredients for the enlargement of moral competence in contemporary societies.

Negative Influences of Organization on Moral Competence

There is a widespread belief that large organizations in government, industry, and the military are essential for the provision of benefits to all. There is also a widely shared belief that citizens who are morally mature are essential for the maintenance of a decent society. What is less clear is that there are aspects of organizational life and moral maturity that are in a contradictory relationship.

With increasing moral maturity the gap between what a person feels should be done and what that person actually does diminishes. What has been squeezed out, so to speak, is the influence of situational factors. People at higher moral stages are said to have an enhanced ability to disregard "quasi-obligations," to use Kohlberg and Candee's term, that are imposed by situational factors or by relationships with others; those who are at lower moral stages tend to interpret the rightness or wrongness of an action in terms of punishment, peer pressure, anxieties about status, reward, authoritative dictates, and the status of the person performing the act.[40] Although situational factors and moral maturity are not always in conflict, the morally mature person is able to resist situational influences when there is a conflict.

Membership in highly structured groups such as modern organizations implies a shared perception of reality, of the obligations that a member should honor, of the goals of organizational activity, and of the appropriate procedures for achieving these goals. The attitudinal bedrock upon which organizations build is a set of shared perspectives derived from relatively similar socialization experiences with regard to such things as time (one must not be late, absent, or interrupt tasks), activity (being attentive and careful), manners (politeness and promptness in carrying out instructions), speech (no insolence or idle chatter), body habits (cleanliness, no irregular movement or gestures), and sexuality (avoiding impurity and indecency).[41] These attitudes, which emphasize social discipline and are necessary for carrying out organizational tasks, at the same time strongly dispose individuals to pay attention to situational demands.

Within all organizations a powerful situational influence is the loyalty that is demanded of members, especially in the small-group contexts within which most people work. Allegiance is often freely given, related to feelings of security within the group context, a belief that the organization performs a socially useful function and a desire for recognition and acceptance by work associates. Loyalty is often accompanied by a belief that the organization is a mirror of and a guide for the best in society, exemplified by the popular paraphrase of a statement by a former American corporate leader and high government official, Charles E. Wilson, that "What is good for General Motors is good for America."[42]

Modern organizations, however, do not leave loyalty to chance. Most have relatively rigid shared core values and stress personal identification with the organization and these values. There is much yea-saying and reinforcement among peers. Japanese corporations are sometimes thought to be exceptional in this regard and, indeed, work-section personnel do identify with their companies to a very high degree. The pattern, however, is not unique to Japan. Thomas Watson, Jr., of IBM once said that the single most important factor in corporate success is faithful adherence to corporate beliefs (set forth, in IBM's case, by Watson's father). In 1940 IBM employees had these lyrics in their IBM song book: "We know and we love you, and we know you have our welfare in your heart" (the "you" in the song being Thomas Watson, Sr.).[43]

There are also powerful, if often latent, punishments that enforce respect for and acceptance of the organization. In the military during wartime, for instance, death may be the penalty for treason or mutiny. In some military and police organizations corporal punishment can be inflicted. In the modern Soviet Union, as in ancient Greece, banishment may be ordered for the nonconforming (although this behavior must usually be interpreted as political deviation). More generally a person may be fined, stripped of rank, or denied opportunities for advancement. Among work associates informal mechanisms of censure may arouse feelings of shame and guilt that motivate a person to increased allegiance. The result of both positive and negative pressures is a heightening of loyalty toward work associates and the organization. Guilt and feelings of disloyalty are aroused if organizational rules are violated. These feelings increasingly separate those who are members of the organization from outsiders; they reduce the possibility that moral sentiments can be universally expressed without consideraton for situational (i.e., organizational) factors. Within this context leadership can define what is appropriate behavior toward outsiders which, in some circumstances, can include exploitation, a denial of responsibility, and even atrocious actions.[44]

Leaders set forth an organization's goals and establish the rules that ordinary members must follow in order to achieve these goals. Good subordinates can minimize the threat of being punished by wholeheartedly supporting the organization's objectives, by living by the rules that have been established, and by believing in the values that legitimize the orders of the organization's leaders. Doing so reduces anxiety and assures rewards for one's self and one's family. Formal organizational theory accepts the notion that people give power to leadership in return for benefits. What is less recognized is that compliance with authoritative demands is, in fact, a generalized role expectation; the members of organizations expect, without any conscious deliberation of costs and benefits, that they and all others will comply with rules and directives.

Organizations are composed of members with diverse natures who work in a changing environment. No organization is ever the completely rational and impersonal mechanism of theory. Uncertainty and unpredictability surround the organization and beset it internally by disputes, imperfect communication among departments, and other sources. The prime function of leadership is to reduce uncertainty, and this is done by centralizing policy decision making, proliferating supervisory-level roles, maintaining strict control over internal procedures, and ensuring appropriate feedback. Promulgating rules of conduct and enforcing their observance through the power to reward and penalize become increasingly specialized functions as an organization becomes larger and more complex. Coordination, which is achieved basically through some mixture of explicit programming and by allowing feedback and adjustment, is furthered when superior positions are invested with legitimacy so that subordinates know which orders to follow.[45]

In short, in complying with rules and orders and in meeting requirements for organizational loyalty, subordinates develop habits of unreflective discipline and passivity. Situational cues for behavior become highly important. The response to thinly veiled coercion and the deprivation of responsibility is sometimes goldbricking and poor workmanship. More fundamental is a pervasive feeling of lack of autonomy and of means for self-expression.[46] The environment of modern organizations is a large step away from traditional patterns. Nevertheless there remain, as the cross-cultural data on moral development surely reflect, patterns of interaction that reinforce conventional moral orientations even in advanced societies like the United States.

Change in Modern Organizational Patterns

It would be wrong to leave this discussion of organizations entirely with the gloomy conclusion that although modern organizations are necessary for fostering widespread moral growth, they are also inherently flawed as instruments for the fulfillment of this task. Although it is fair to say that around the world most people in modern organizations have little control over their jobs, no part in decision making, and no scope for the exercise of initiative, there are important changes in some organizations that challenge any notion that this pattern is immutable. Although I shall have more to say on the subject of organizational change later, a few comments now on this subject are appropriate.

In the most advanced societies there has been a change in the last few decades in the nature of production activities. In this new pattern, variously called postindustrial society or the information age, the nature of work and the skills needed for that work have altered. In the United States in 1950, 65 percent of working people had jobs in the industrial sector while 17 percent worked in telecommunications, computers, and other businesses in the information sector (according to a Commerce Department study). In 1980 the figures were almost reversed with 60 percent of the work force in the information sector and only 13 percent in industry. Information has inundated all areas of life, including but not limited to factory management, law, art, agriculture, politics, warfare, and space. The need to understand and use information has drawn into advanced education larger and larger numbers of people. The information itself knows no boundary based on religion, skin color, sex, or brawn. Its most effective use is by anyone who can master the techniques of gathering, processing, disseminating, and acting upon it.

To be useful information needs to be manufactured, analyzed, and directed toward its users. No traditional agricultural community can handle the vast amounts of data now available, nor is the form of factory organization of one hundred years ago suitable, for the boss passed his orders down a relatively simple chain of command. Today the processing and dissemination of information requires many specialized skills and highly complex organizational procedures. Statisticians, librarians, and accountants interact with research and development teams and managers in intricate patterns with the aim of manipulating information more rapidly and accurately than ever before.

New needs and patterns of interaction notwithstanding, organizations overall tend to change slowly. Enmeshed in their own rules and decisions and protective of sunk costs, they tend to make incremental rather than sweeping changes. This does not mean, of course, that an organization cannot seek flexibility in its operations; in fact, large organizations are often quite flexible (and, not incidentally, the ones most likely to be computerized and thus capable of handling information more efficiently) as they are in a better position to experiment and have many kinds of specialists who insure a flow of fresh ideas to the organization's leaders. Moreover, if they have avoided upheaval for many years, such organizations tend to have power more widely shared than originally, heightening the probability that new alternatives will be tested. (Top-heavy organizations, by comparison, are not noted for spontaneity and full expression in their upward flow of communications.)[47]

To cope with changed circumstances some organizations, especially flexible ones, have experimented in job enlargement, job rotation, and job enrichment. Operating on the assumption that forms of management and decision making are related to performance and that high control from above tends to reduce the effectiveness of work groups, these experiments stress horizontal rather than vertical work-role differentiation and the development of open (i.e., not rigidly structured) interpersonal processes. These trends are stimulated and reinforced by the increases in information that are available through computers. Easy and relatively costless access to information reduces the need for task specialization that comes about when the most efficient communication method is through vertical tiers of supervisory personnel. The relaxing of external controls and the increase in functional differentiation does not, however, lessen the organizational imperative for task coordination. There must still be knowledge of and conformity to the work-needs of superiors, co-workers, and subordinates. As a consequence workers, who are no longer tightly supervised, must develop internalized controls in order to do the right thing at the right time.[48]

Many new organizations have undergone radical decentralization at the same time that they have intense (albeit often informal) communication among segments of the organization. A degree of autonomy is allowed, but there is also emphasis on a few shared core values and on internal competition, which motivates performance. Formal direction, rule, and committee-driven behavior is relaxed. In a structure called "matrix organization" temporary units—task forces, project teams, and so forth—honeycomb the larger organization for the purpose of carrying out special jobs. Since team leaders are hardly ever the same as the nominal administrative superior, formal authority tends to be diffused.

As a consequence of changes in information technology, organizational procedures have been adjusted for the purpose of achieving greater efficiency, reducing uncertainty, and enhancing profit. Although generally unintended, these new procedures have also altered the workplace in a manner that enhances the potential for greater moral competence. Other organizational changes, not necessarily at variance with these but motivated by different concerns, have additionally begun to modify the moral environment in a few organizations. These changes are more directly concerned with worker welfare viewed in both a material and a psychological sense.

It has been found that when a worker's say in his or her own job performance is restricted there develops a passive, alienated style of work with jobs viewed only as a means to consumption.[49] In the belief that greater participation could overcome these problems, efforts to increase a say in decision making and to provide a greater share in any increased profits have been part of a number of job-enlargement plans. It was felt that morale would improve with greater control over immediate jobs and with more money and job security. At the same time, however, survey data indicated that while 95 percent of employees mentioned a need to direct and regulate their jobs, 65 percent also stated that they preferred to be directed and 88 percent stated that they did not wish to have any responsibilities associated with their jobs.[50] Clearly, those whose primary aim was greater organizational democracy (increased justice, freedom, protection of interests, and equality) would have to structure an organizational environment that could account for nonsupportive values. How, in effect, can workers have a greater say about their jobs and rewards without a reduction of management prerogatives to define job objectives, set requirements, and enforce obligations?

In Western countries this general problem has led to various experiments in self-management and worker ownership. In one notable model the rights of ownership and property are divided, with workers and their managers having an unrestricted use right to capital while rent from capital assets goes to parties distinct from the enterprise.[51] In another model the workers themselves assume ownership (in varying degrees) and by election or appointment choose managers to regulate their activities. In both of these models worker input regarding the organization's operations is solicited and managers are subject to recall or dismissal.

Experiments with organizational democracy are not limited to one type of political system. With varying degrees of success they have been tried in Western Europe, Chile, Yugoslavia, North America, China, Japan, and elsewhere. In Japan, for example, where high productivity is noteworthy, there has been considerable experimentation with work patterns in the post-World War II era. Traditional emphases on hierarchy and on ideals of harmony and cooperation still exist and play their part. There also lingers from the past a suspicion of profit as a criterion of individual worth and a belief in the merit of working for society. But added to these values, which foster group solidarity and service, is great emphasis on disseminating information, on collective decision making at the work section level, and on better salaries and new amenities for everyone as the organization prospers. There is a constant emphasis on good human relations at all levels.[52]

In the United States some of the most noteworthy experiments in job enlargement and enrichment have taken place in worker-owned or self-managed firms. These range from companies with limited worker participation to those where work teams do virtually everything—hiring, quality control, disciplining, firing, and even janitorial tasks. Overall, productivity is greater than in comparable, traditionally managed plants, and absenteeism (an indirect measure of job satisfaction) is less.[53] There is also evidence that participation, when it is real, is habit forming.

At the least these new types of organizational patterns suggest trends that will promote moral psychological growth and maturity.

It should be kept in mind, however, that these patterns are absent in the great majority of organizations in the United States and elsewhere and that nothing (and certainly not advanced technology) predetermines their occurrence. No doubt the probability of their emergence is enhanced where customs and laws facilitate communication between leaders and led and where social relationships generally are relatively egalitarian. The existence of such customs and laws, however, is in no sense a guarantee of their reflection in organizational patterns.

Modern organizations are not static. Over recent centuries they have evolved from humble origins into institutions whose processes and values govern social life. Reflecting in their growth patterns both technological improvement and the demands of reformers, they are a crucial environment for the development of moral competence. As change has occurred this environment has offered possibilities for a reduction of ethnocentrism, fear, shame, and guilt, and rigid indoctrination. In the last few decades advances in information technology and experiments in workplace democracy have furthered trends toward a restructuring of organizational relationships. These trends, however, take place within a context of prevailing attitudes and situational demands that retard the possibilities for change. They also take place within frameworks of elite control and reward that are powerful and conservative. It is to this latter important topic that consideration now shifts.

3. Dominance

Just as individuals in modern societies are embedded in organizations so are organizations embedded in systems of rulership or dominance. Modern organizations are a bridge between the individual and the larger community. Differences among people—necessary, in terms of skills, for the functioning of large-scale, complex organizations—are transformed through the coordinating aspects of organizational structure into the basis of solidarity of modern societies.

Modern organizations set the tone of contemporary life. They are woven and interwoven throughout the larger society. An individual cannot be understood without knowing the organizations with which he or she is affiliated; so also are organizations constantly influenced by the societies in which they function. Modern organizations, however, are not bound to a particular political form. As Max Weber noted long ago, there is a high degree of similarity in bureaucratic structure regardless of whether a society is socialistic or capitalistic.[1] Others have affirmed these conclusions. Lindblom, for one, has stated that communism is but a new form of business enterprise, "more a technocratic or organizational revolution than a social one."[2]

Depending on size and function, an organization may strongly influence public policy on a wide range of issues. In the case of large government bureaucracies or the Communist party this linkage is relatively clear, direct, and straightforward. Organizations, of course, may have an impact on what happens in a society extending well beyond their own specific areas of concern. Budgetary decisions for military expenditures, for example, may affect policies regarding health care, education, and a host of other concerns. In modern societies organizational elites in general attempt to make their interests known to and heeded by government authorities. This type of interest articulation takes place regardless of the nature of a political system. Indeed, it is actively sought, for the leaders of modern polities are crucially concerned with coordinating a variety of activities in different sectors and for this purpose need to be aware of the diverse needs and interests of their constituencies. In socialist societies the Communist party, through the placement of its cadres in key posts in all major organizations, plays the crucial role in this regard. In other societies, such as the United States, various autonomous organizations engage in this activity (among others). Labor organizations, chambers of commerce, lobby groups (oil, agriculture, airlines, public utilities, banking) all perform this way. At some levels, such as local and state government, the relationship between interest groups and government may become so intimate as to skew public policy in favor of these interests at the expense of the public at large.[3] The outrage that occasionally spills over as a consequence should not obscure the fact that every modern political organization must know the needs of the major institutions in society. It is equally important to stress that from the necessity for coordinating diverse interests there arises, not always harmoniously, an interaction among the top elites of the major organizations. An Eisenhower may denounce the military- industrial complex, and the activities of this particular grouping may indeed have deleterious consequences, but the fact of organizational elite combination itself is no surprise. Nor should it be a cause of wonderment that these elites share certain viewpoints about society and their own role in it, solidified, in many cases, by similarities in background, education, and so forth.

With minor exceptions the elites of society are the elites of organizations. This is true whether one is speaking of artists, whose works or publications become known through organized channels, or captains of industry and the like, who are more formally placed in an organizational hierarchy. It is the institutional base that is important for elite status whereas the skills needed for leadership vary along single or multiple dimensions such as ideological expertise, administrative skill, knowledge of military operations, and financial acumen. Whether the position of dominance in the organization was obtained by election, appointment, or the ownership of property is clearly not irrelevant but pales in significance next to the fact of incumbency itself. That is what defines elite status.[4]

Organizations can exist with any form of ideology. What they cannot exist without is ideology. Regardless of the nature of a political system, none has been able to abolish ideology as a device for explaining the procedures and goals of organizations and for legitimizing control. Leaders especially take the ideology seriously for the justification it provides for the benefits they receive. They are also likely to be the ones who are most concerned about changes that undermine these justifications.

Status and Values

Some of the most important values in any society are those that legitimize differences in status. These differences can be noted among social strata as well as among individuals who are members of a particular stratum. Usually different statuses are referred to by titles such as leaders and led, patrons and clients, nobles and serfs, superordinates and subordinates. I will, instead, call those with higher status elite or dominant and those with lower status subordinate or submissive. The terms dominance and submission are widely used in animal studies but less so in studies of humans. They are appropriate, however, because they connote psychological attributes as well as power differences.

What an individual does in life is determined by a number of factors. Among the most pertinent are one's sex, innate disposition (aggressive, passive, etc.), birth order (first-borns are slightly more likely to succeed than later borns), and social class. In any society, traditional or modern, any of these factors may be significant. In addition, other factors related to the nature of society may be important. For instance, is a person's station in life determined from birth? Individuals born into slavery frequently had little hope of escaping servitude during their lifetime. Or is more leeway allowed? In traditional China, if a peasant child was exceptionally intelligent, was male, and had ambitious parents, it was conceivable, by the passing of appropriate examinations, to advance to the highest positions in the official hierarchy of government. In the modern period, of course, with universal education, such opportunities are even more common though many inhibiting conditions remain.

Social stability occurs when people do their jobs and receive rewards in terms of commonly accepted community standards. That is to say, societies are relatively tranquil when the values that establish personal and social goals and the ways to achieve these goals are widely shared and strongly held. People then work with the belief that what they are doing is legitimate and justified. The rules that govern the social order seem to be inherently right; those who dispute this rightness appear to be unquestionably wrong. The rightness of any specific rule, of course, is partly determined by the social and economic level of a society. The jobs that must be done in a traditional community, for example, are vastly different from those to be performed in a computer-oriented society. Correspondingly, the rules that govern behavior in these two situations, and the techniques for their enforcement, are also different. When conditions change, when new, large organizations linked by computer equipment come into existence, then the rules and techniques that guide behavior also change. This process, which many in the world have now experienced, is difficult and disruptive. The old rules, which once seemed inherently right and were associated with social stability, no longer appear valid while new rules, promulgated in a period of social instability and personal anxiety, appear fragile and untested.

The quality of dominance is the ability to exercise control over limited resources such as wealth, force, or knowledge. In societies this inequality is sanctioned by formal rules (laws) and by more general values that legitimize preferential access to these resources for elites. Those who are subordinate, on the other hand, accord correctness and enhanced worth to those who are dominant. During childhood all people learn how to be submissive; they experience a kind of diffuse and informal coercion that effectively inhibits tendencies toward self-assertion.[5] In later life the behavior patterns associated with submission can be activated under the appropriate circumstances. Moreover, values that legitimize hierarchy, strongly acquired in childhood, continue to be bolstered by elites who use their control over resources to mobilize support for the major symbols that buttress a social order (e.g., the monarchy in England). Changes in dominance values are thus usually resisted even when their maintenance is prejudicial to many people, for change threatens group solidarity, organizational procedures, and the stable functioning of society. In normal circumstances people behave toward superiors in work, politics, and social life with submissive patterns that are felt to be legitimate, are deeply internalized, and are often unconscious. As a consequence, the values that support dominance and submission often seem to be intrinsically correct.

In practice dominance is usually justified by a number of criteria.

In one society it may be religious power combined with high social status. In another it may be economic power combined with military prowess as well as being male. The possible combinations are large and often vary among the subunits of a society, a fact that has been extensively recorded in many detailed anthropological studies. However, although combinations are generally the rule, dominance systems have at their core one preeminent set of values. This simplifies analysis, for although actual systems may comprise a mix of forms, there is one value dimension overriding all others that girds dominance and on which less central values depend.

Dominance Values and Moral Development

The core values that justify dominance have at their heart a moral psychological dimension. Without this moral component rulership can be maintained only by resort to coercion. In chapter 1 it was noted that moral maturity consists of a combination of altruistic awareness, empathy, and personal responsibility. What one sees in modern nations is a lack of symmetry in the importance of these competencies. Different socialization experiences seem to be the major reason for this, reflecting an underlying dichotomy in psychological growth.

Robert Kegan has noted two processes of individual psychological development, one favoring autonomous, independent growth and the other integration and attachment.[6] The importance of this finding for understanding the salience of different moral competencies is made clearer by looking at the work of Carol Gilligan.[7] In one of the best-known critiques of Kohlberg, Gilligan faults him for failing to note, and theoretically to account for, marked differences in the moral development patterns of American men and women. Kohlberg, she states, drew his theoretical conclusions from data drawn from a male sample. Subsequent tests showed that females tended to exhibit an inferior development pattern (according to Kohlberg's scheme) compared to men, largely ceasing to mature past a conventional level of moral reasoning. Gilligan suggests that what Kohlberg failed to do was to perceive two equally valid development patterns. Both of these can be stated in postconventional, principled terms with the merger of both being ultimately required for moral maturity.

American males, says Gilligan, stress in their moral development an ethic of autonomy, a theme that is the ideal in American society. Calling this, in places, the ethic of rights, she notes that those who favor this mode of moral reasoning emphasize individuation and the capability to formulate moral judgments independent of formal rules or the dictates of authority figures (that is, American males favor what Kegan calls autonomous, independent growth and hence tend to justify moral solutions in terms of rights or principles in a way that fulfills Kohlberg's definition of postconventional moral reasoning). For females the pattern is quite different. Their emphasis in growth is on the protection of relationships, on nurturence. Gilligan calls this the ethic of care or responsibility. Because of the importance that is placed on the particular character of relationships, those whose development is prompted more by the ethic of care (Kegan's integration and attachment) test at the conventional moral level according to Kohlberg's ideas. It is important to be clear about the concepts "care" and "autonomy" because the terms "responsibility" and "rights," which are paired with them respectively, receive different and fuller treatment in this essay. In Gilligan's words, the ethic of care is the "responsibility to discern and alleviate the 'real and recognizable trouble' of this world" while the ethic of autonomy is "an injunction to respect the rights of others and thus to protect from interference the rights to life and self-fulfillment."[8]

Gilligan's work has been a milestone in moral development literature. Like Kohlberg, however, her conclusions are arrived at from data drawn from an American sample, and she makes no claims beyond that. Kohlberg's cross-cultural data (noted in chapter 2), however, showed for his Chinese sample from Taiwan a higher overall level of conventional moral responses than was the case for Americans.[9] This seems suspiciously similar to the gender differences in American society that prompted Gilligan's inquiry. In fact, socialization data from Chinese society suggests strongly that Gilligan's ethic of care is one that is heavily emphasized in Chinese childhood socialization and is generally favored by both males and females.[10]

An ethic of care places special emphasis on altruistic awareness and empathy. It promotes concern for relationships and the maintenance and strengthening of social ties that bind people together. In Chinese society one pithy way to express this ethic is in the phrase "filial piety," a formulation that is as binding on superiors as it is on subordinates. In traditional China it underlay the designation of officials as *fu mu guan*, or father-mother official, while in contemporary China the counterpart is the ideal of the selfless and caring cadre. In the United States, by contrast, the ideal is one of autonomy and the stress is primarily on personal responsibility and independence and only secondarily on altruistic awareness and empathy. Protection for subordinates comes less from the caring qualities of leaders than from provisions established in custom and law that insure redress against the failures of those who lead. In both the Chinese and American cases the predominant value has a moral root. Yet in both cases the particular value emphasis (and it must be stressed that this emphasis is only a tendency and not an absolute quality) is only a partial fulfillment of the full range of possibilities.

Although the contention needs further elaboration, Gilligan's work suggests that socialization influences in modern societies stress moral competencies unequally as ideals. On the one hand are those cases where socialization reinforces norms that emphasize empathy and altruistic awareness (care and attachment); on the other are those where socialization stresses norms of personal responsibility (autonomy and independence). The question that then arises is how these different moral perspectives justify dominance. I shall turn to this question before returning to the issue of the relationship between developmental characteristics and the dominance patterns of modern organizational elites.

Rights, Obligations, and Dominance Patterns

Rights

The tasks allotted in the division of labor may be highly unequal, but people rarely question deeply the reasons for this. Although political philosophers universally have asked questions about authority and subjection, their origins, basis, and proper domains, the nature of justice, and the rights and obligations of subjects and rulers, few ordinary people concern themselves with such matters.[11] There is, perhaps, more than a hint of false consciousness in the support that usually undergirds prevailing values, testifying eloquently to the powerful effect of socialization processes. No doubt fear of reprisal and of disrupting group solidarity also play their part.

It is not the case, however, that people have no expectations regarding the social systems in which they live. Nor is it the case that elite justifications for dominance flourish in a vacuum independent of and unrelated to the prospects of the led. Although historically often quite limited, some expectations (thought of, usually, as customary) were held to be appropriate and justified. Among others, these included physical security, assistance in times of crisis, the right to inherit land or occupation, and redress for wrongs. The nature of these expectations varied in type and degree from area to area but always existed (except in unusual circumstances such as social catastrophe). Although there was little comprehension of "right" in the modern sense, a violation of expectations could arouse deep resentment and be the basis for social unrest or rebellion.

In the modern world, in the last two hundred years, there has been a translation of expectation into the notion of right. Modern people have rights in a way that traditional people did not. There has come to be an inviolable quality in the notion of modern expectations, a conception of them almost as property, a possession that is (or should) inhere in the human condition, to be acquired, held, and defended without need for justification.

American Chief Justice Earl Warren once observed that "Ever since Hammurabi published his code to 'hold back the strong from oppressing the weak,' the success of any legal system is measured by its fidelity to the universal ideal of justice."[12] This statement about law expresses two aspects of rights: they embody an ideal of justice and, to be operative, must (following Bentham's utilitarian precepts) be clearly articulated, preferably codified, and enforced by sanctions. In some conceptualizations rights can, indeed, be thought of in legal terms as traditional legal rights, nominal legal rights, and the positive legal rights of specific classes of people or individuals.[13] A right, however, as modern people use the term, passes beyond the notion of legal entitlement to include metaphysical, moral, political, social, and rhetorical qualities. Rights embody the enjoyment of possibilities usually established by appeal to natural law or to some body of transcendent moral principles, the violation of which constitutes a grave affront to justice. Rights thus function as means to ends; they secure integrity and assure the opportunity to develop individual capacities.[14]

On August 26, 1789, thirteen years after the American Declaration of Independence, the French Assembly, meeting at Versailles as a consequence of the financial collapse of the government, issued the Declaration of the Rights of Man and Citizen. Article I declared that "Men are born and remain free and equal in rights." In the years that followed, this dictum was more often violated than honored. The idea prospered, however, becoming by the mid-twentieth century the concern of governments everywhere and even a basic guideline in foreign policy (e.g., President Jimmy Carter's emphasis on human rights as a criterion in U.S. foreign policy decisions).

Shortly after World War II, on December 10, 1948, the United Nations General Assembly (the USSR and its allied states abstaining) voted to establish a Universal Declaration of Human Rights. The articles of the declaration establish, inter alia, the right to be free from torture and from arbitrary arrest or detention, the right to own property and to have freedom of opinion and expression, and the right to take part in government and to be able to work and obtain an adequate standard of living.[15] At least a portion of the thirty rights enumerated in the Declaration were reemphasized in the Final Act of the Helsinki Conference (August 1, 1975), where in Section VII the participating states agreed to respect human rights and fundamental freedoms, including freedom of thought, conscience, religion, or belief.[16] Liberal democratic states have subsequently made much of the violation of these particular rights by Communist countries. The latter, for their part, have responded in kind. The Chinese, for instance (who were not signators of the Helsinki Agreement), have with others railed against bourgeois property rights and the opposition by rich countries to the UN-sanctioned right to development. They bitterly resent charges by outsiders of abuses of human rights, calling these allegations unfriendly interference in China's judicial and administrative affairs; the Chinese, they contend, uphold UN human rights goals regarding an end to discrimination against women, protection of children, taking care of the old and the handicapped, elimination of illiteracy, and promotion of science and technology.[17]

What is to be made of this plethora of rights and of the contentious charges by various parties regarding their violation? Clearly, some states regard some rights as more "right" than others. While all seem reluctant to renounce their adherence to rights in general, what is emphasized in each case is often quite different, making nonsense of the notion—as stated by the United Nations—of a universal declaration, equally emphasized and equally binding on all of the world's peoples.

Preeminent among the goals that modern men seek are two rights that are analytically distinct. The first of these is "freedom from" (negative rights)—the desire to be free from restraints and exactions imposed by those in positions of dominance.[18] The asserton of "freedom from" is frequently directed against the ideological authority wielded by a dominant group—that is, against the power of that group to establish norms for the rest of society and to enforce their observance. In their simplest form negative rights affirm the right not to be robbed of life or liberty. Originally termed natural rights, these claims aroused and justified men in their struggle against various forms of intrusion and oppression. Only later did these rights become legal in the sense that they were given title and were secured and administered by authority.[19]

Negative rights do not speak to the problems of distributive justice. These are embodied in assertions of "freedom to" (positive rights)—the desire for access to a fair share of the goods of society. Included in the notion of a fair share is the right to participate in public affairs, to be admitted into the realm of decision making with regard to social goals. When people champion "freedom to," they call for a redistribution of resources (wealth, food, clothing, transportation, shelter, education, medical care, etc.) and for a redefinition of the evaluation of social classes (worth, reputation, honor, eminence, etc.).[20] "Freedom to" is usually asserted against dominance groups that uphold an unequal distribution of power and resources.

Concretely, there is sometimes confusion regarding which category of rights people are seeking in a given circumstance. Is the right to hold free elections, for example, a positive right, a fair share, or is it a negative right, freedom from restraints on political participation? The distinction is difficult to draw and is not made easier by the fact that modern, large-scale social systems recognize, in varying degrees, both categories of right. The question can only be answered by asking of whom the right is demanded and among what general category of claims the particular demand is located. Against dominant groups that uphold an unequal distribution of power and resources, claims, including being allowed to vote freely, are for positive rights, in this case the right to be admitted into the realm of decision making. Against dominant groups that establish norms for the rest of society and enforce their observance by censorship and restrictions on public expression, a demand for free elections is one for negative rights, for freedom from restraints imposed by those in positions of authority.

In one of the most famous and important tracts on the subject of rights, Isaiah Berlin discussed the differences between the positive sense of liberty answered by the question "by whom am I ruled?" and the negative sense of liberty that embodies the absence of interference with individuals beyond some recognizable frontier.

Those who espouse the first champion an ideal of positive self-mastery by classes or people and wish to place authority in their own hands. Those who espouse the second believe that "there are frontiers not artificially drawn, within which men should be inviolable. These frontiers are rules so long and widely held that their observance has entered into the conception of what it is to be human."[21] In Berlin's opinion, the negative sense of liberty—of freedom from—is the most true and humane ideal since it involves the consciousness of individual rights. A social structure must be guided by the principle that not power but only rights are absolute.[22]

Rights and Obligations

Curiously, duty to the community was listed as a right in the Universal Declaration of Human Rights voted for by the UN General Assembly in 1948. The confusion, of course, stems from the fact that duty is an obligation, not a right. Obligations and rights are inseparably linked but are analytically distinct. Rights can be thought of as entitlements that are enjoyed or sought; obligations embody the motivations that insure the fulfillment of the claims of others.

The importance of particular obligations is a function of the way that the components of moral competence are related to values that regulate behavior. Altruistic awareness, empathy, and personal responsibility are generally not manifested with equal intensity. Since each obliges different aspects of moral behavior, their relative salience is important. The values of altruistic awareness, for example, stress understanding the goals of others and the ways that goals can be mutually realized in a reciprocally beneficial manner. Knowing rules or—at a higher (postconventional) level—principles of reciprocity is thus valued. Empathy is generally associated with values that stress active caring (e.g., aiding, nurturing), although it can, less typically, involve not intruding on others. In like manner, personal responsibility is usually related to individualistic values that sanction autonomous volition (e.g., standing on one's own feet, making up one's own mind). It can also pertain to the commitments of individuals as members of groups. At the individual level, then, different obligations are related in a probable manner to different moral psychological competencies. At the group or social level, obligations are social ideals that are normative in nature.

If this reasoning is persuasive, then a relationship between the definition of moral maturity that applies to individuals and the obligations that are the moral bases of social systems can be posited. At the individual level obligations are related to psychological attributes; at the group or social level these obligations embody values that are supportive of the rights that people enjoy or seek. To be more precise, at the group level an obligation is a deontological value compelling commitment to the fulfillment of a right. At the individual level that commitment is powered by the psychological attributes that comprise moral competence. Obligations, therefore, are norms and values at the social level that are acted upon in accordance with the strength of different aspects of individual moral competence. When conceptualized in this way obligations link the vocabulary of moral psychological development with the political vocabulary of rights and obligations.

Associated with the positive right of "freedom to" is an obligation to foster its development and to protect its existence when it has been extended to others. A person who promotes freedom to—access to common goods—is one who is altruistically aware of the goals of other people and who empathizes with their feelings. In Gilligan's terms such a person's moral judgment is infused with the ethic of care. Obligations stress the strengthening of social ties and support fairness within the group. For those who strongly support this category of obligation, individualism can be a selfish evil.

The right of "freedom from," on the other hand, is associated with an obligation not to interfere in the affairs of people in a manner that violates their ability to live according to their own principles. It is an obligation that calls for restraint, moderation, and prudence in social relationships. Those who believe strongly in this category of obligation support for themselves and others what Gilligan calls the ethic of autonomy. A person who champions freedom from is one who preeminently assumes personal responsibility for his actions and who permits others to assume responsibility for theirs. To impinge on the possibilities that a person has to direct his or her own life is considered by those who favor this category of obligation as an unwarranted intrusion on individual choice.

The positive right of freedom to is balanced by what can be called "obligation to," while the negative right of freedom from is linked to a duty that can be termed "obligation not to." The right to a fair share of the rewards of society goes with an obligation to ensure that these rewards are made available to others, while the right to be free from interference goes with the obligation not to place unwarranted restrictions on what other people wish to do. Together these obligations involve individual responsibility for one's actions, governed by altruistic awareness of the goals of others and empathy for their feelings.

Although the full acceptance of all three responsibilities is pre-eminently a characteristic of personal moral maturity, obligations can clearly be articulated as laws or rules—or, less formally, as shared folk orientations. In any known society only some individuals have ever fully supported both categories of obligation. The likelihood of this becoming more general can only occur when both types of obligation are widely honored in society and are buttressed by the sanctions of law. Charles Fried has suggested the way that these obligations become interrelated. According to him the negative right "to choose how one will relate to, contribute to, and cooperate with one's fellow men, a liberty to develop some and not other capacities, in short, the liberty to determine a life plan, to choose one's self" can also be thought of as part of the fair share that an individual has as a member of society.[23] Morally mature individuals who understand and empathize with the needs of others for a fair share also adhere to social norms that regulate the processes that guarantee choice within social structures. Individuals have a positive right to the satisfaction of needs, but mature morality with its basis in altruistic awareness and empathy assumes that a person will be entitled only to a just share of society's goods, tangible and intangible. Schemes that seek a just and moral social order by assuring fairness cannot, therefore, at the same time violate the "fair share" of personal responsibility, or autonomy, that is equally an individual right.

Obligations, Rights, and Dominance Systems

Obligations are responsibilities taken on in families, schools, job settings, local politics, and, in fact, in every social context. The violation of obligations by a parent, for instance, may affect other family members just as much, or more, as a lack of responsibility on the part of a local political boss or work manager. There is, in a sense, a seamless web of obligation among all members of a society, at all levels, and in all contexts. In another sense, however, those who occupy dominant positions have a special responsibility with regard to obligations. Because of the control that dominant individuals exercise over the most important organizations in society, and because they are often looked upon as exemplars of acceptable behavior, a failure of responsibility within the dominant strata can have severe repercussions throughout society.

There is a complementary relationship between those who are dominant and those who are submissive. Coercion, although sometimes an aspect of dominance, is usually dormant or masked.[24] To underline a previous argument, differences in wealth and access to resources are justified in terms of the services that the dominant are thought to provide. The institutions of rulership (courts, assemblies, etc.) moderate the naked authority aspects of relationships. Those who are dominant are in a position to manipulate symbolic supports that bolster their own status and retard suspicions of aggrandizement. Feelings of group solidarity welded by shared goals and values operate to internalize constraint and to legitimize the existing social system.

Those who lead society are never a homogeneous order. Especially in the modern world, dominant status is enjoyed by groups that have skills in areas such as military operations, resource management, intellectual endeavor, and bureaucratic administration. There are, in addition, other forms of dominance involving relations between the sexes, the generations, ethnic and religious groups, and a number of other cross-cutting cleavages. Furthermore, societies often combine the characteristics of several dominance forms in varying degrees, or manifest different forms of dominance toward different groups. Within large-scale social units, there is always a multiplicity of interests and abilities among the dominant as well as among the subordinate.

These caveats notwithstanding, the major goals of society are always related to a cluster of values (which embody a particular distribution of rights and obligations) that legitimize associated patterns of dominance. In other words, the balance—or distribution—of rights and obligations is noted ideologically by a set of values that is determinative of a particular pattern of dominance. Upheld by the strength and cohesion of the dominant strata, these values establish the decision rules of a polity, the rights that people have regarding these rules, the range of resources that are available to elites and nonelites, and the degree (and type) of autonomy that is allowed individuals and groups. The values justify the monopoly that the dominant maintain over certain goods and their access to rewards in other areas as well.[25]

The ways in which the dominant and subordinate are expected to behave, the resources that are available, and the degree of autonomy that is permitted are determined by the rights people have.

These rights are realizable in accordance with the obligations that others in society—especially elites—have to honor them. Dominance values are embodied in the particular obligations which elites assume. Just as rights and obligations are related, with rights depending on obligations for realization, so also are obligations and dominance patterns related, with the pattern of obligations determining the nature of a dominance system. Hence, the rights people have, and the rights they do *not* have, reveal the obligations of elite groups and the dominance pattern of any particular society.[26]

Elite status in organizations and society is justified by the values (ideology) that apply to the particular balance of rights and obligations that exist. The balance may be quite stable over time, as was the case historically in China, or it may be relatively unstable, as has often been the case in modern times. The balance can be noted in the ways in which dominant and subordinate individuals and groups view particular values. For instance, in the United States a high percentage of people believe that the interests of business organizations coincide with the interests of the average person (in 1981, 57 percent agreed with the statement "What's good for business is also good for the average person"[27]). This indicates moderate support for business organizations and, by extension for the general type of leadership that exists in these organizations (which does not imply, of course, that businessmen as such need be highly admired). Other cultures would show different patterns. An interesting example of differences among people was revealed in an analysis of the writings of three men, Adolf Hitler, Barry Goldwater, and Lenin, with regard to the frequency with which seventeen different values were mentioned in their works. Two of these values, freedom and equality, had characteristics that permit us to redesignate "freedom" as negative rights and "equality" as positive rights. For Hitler both of these rights were in last place. For Goldwater, negative rights were in first place but positive rights were in second to last place. In contrast, Lenin placed negative rights in last place while positive rights were in first place.[28] For the Japanese the emphasis is on obligation itself (and on empathy), revealed by a dominance pattern where debt and repayment (rather than explicit reference to rights as such) infuse the values of dominance and submission.[29] In all of these cases the values noted reveal the type of obligation that elites acknowledge (and, for the Japanese, the strength of obligation) and hence the dominance pattern that is likely to exist.

Forms of Dominance

In his well-known work *Politics and Markets*, Charles E. Lindblom notes that there are currently two major types of systems in the world: those with central authoritative planning with subsidiary use of prices, and those with consumer sovereignty market systems.[30] The distinction between these two systems is best noted in Lindblom's later discussion about two different visions of how men conceive of and organize problem solving in modern societies. The first vision, called Model 1, derives from an optimistic view of man's intellectual capacities and calls for an intellectually guided society dominated by those who are wise and informed enough to rule in accordance with a comprehensive theory of social change. These people know correct solutions and know how to organize society. Their vision has led to the first of the two major systems mentioned above. The second vision, called Model 2, derives from a more pessimistic view of man's intellectual capacities. For these people there is no such thing as a comprehensive theory of social change because there is, fundamentally, a mismatch between intellectual capacity and the complexity of the social world. Since rulers are not competent to know what is correct, dominance is best exercised by allowing individual volition to indicate the preferences that people have with regard to what they need and want (despite the fact that people may be misled about their preferences and not know, in fact, what they really do need and want). This vision has led to the second of the two major systems mentioned above.[31]

The two visions that Lindblom mentions coincide strikingly with systems where positive rights (Model 1) or negative rights (Model 2) are emphasized respectively. As descriptive of all existing systems, however, these two models are incomplete in that they do not encompass the broad range of societies that support neither positive nor negative rights. Nor do these two visions encompass yet another possibility, perhaps forever unattainable but nevertheless the goal of many modern people, of a society that honors both negative and positive rights.

In Model 1 societies dominant status is based upon knowledge of and adherence to ideological principles that uphold a goal of communal well-being. This system of dominance may be referred to by the Platonic term of *guardian*. In contrast, the emphasis in Model 2 societies is on enhancing personal choice. Specific rewards are shared unequally, but there is emphasis on increasing total resource productivity through individual action. This type of dominance system, which glorifies individual initiative and volition, is *entrepreneurial.* The third form of dominance obtains benefits for its adherents by the exploitation of certain categories of home groups (such as peasants in traditional society or the Jews during Nazi rule) or of conquered foreign peoples (as in colonial regimes). This form of dominance is *predatory.* The final type of dominance may be termed *moral.* In this case, rulership is committed to the maximum enhancement of both individual well-being and autonomy.

Figure 3 sets forth schematically the ways in which obligations and associated rights are related to moral, guardian, entrepreneurial, and predatory dominance systems. Although set forth in the familiar x-y axis form, the figure is a theoretical device for ordering variables rather than one of empirical utility. Measurements along the axes, for instance, are indeterminate. Moreover, in a real-life sense, since all dominance systems contain some admixture of both positive and negative rights, the zero point on either axis would not be at the intersection of the axes but closer to the negative pole of each. In only rare cases is a person absolutely and entirely without rights (e.g., the condemned).

When those in dominant positions recognize and carry out obligations to assist others to obtain their fair share, and also refrain from repressive acts, the dominance pattern is located in the upper right quadrant where there are positive values for both of these obligations. In this quadrant, both negative and positive rights are balanced with their appropriate obligations. Behavior is motivated by altruistic awareness, empathy, and personal responsibility.

In the lower right quadrant, there is an obligation to assist but much less of an obligation not to interfere. Positive rights are furthered by the responsibility to help people attain a fair share of public goods, but negative rights are often violated as there is less obligation not to restrict what people might wish to do. Altruistic awareness and empathy with regard to the community as a whole are emphasized, with less regard for personal responsibility. Leadership places heavy emphasis on the criteria for obtaining a fair share within the community but is relatively unrestricted in its ability to direct the lives of citizens and to establish the criteria that define deviance.

In the upper left or entrepreneurial quadrant, negative rights exist and are balanced with the obligation not to interfere in the lives of citizens. Positive rights, however, are accorded less value as less attention is given to the obligation to assist others to obtain a

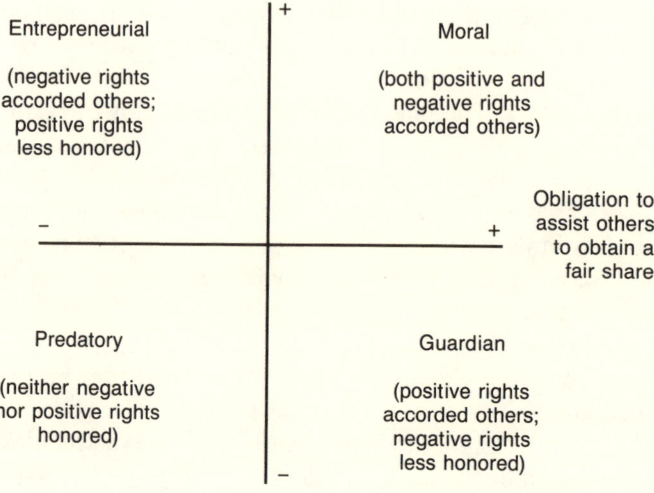

Figure 3. Forms of Obligation and Related Dominance Patterns

fair share. Personal responsibility is more highly touted than altruistic awareness and much more so than empathy. In contrast to the guardian system, the emphasis is on autonomy—the self or small group—rather than on the whole community.

Predatory dominance is shown in the lower left quadrant. Toward low-ranking members of one's own society (workers and peasants, for instance) there is scant obligation to accord either positive or negative rights. Elite behavior is little motivated by altruistic awareness, empathy, or personal responsibility. Toward enemies or conquered peoples no obligations may pertain. Genocide may occur internally, and foreign foes may be delivered to the same fate to which Carthage was by Rome.

By determining the value cluster (or ideology) that is most significant for legitimizing a particular dominance system, any society can be placed relative to others on the grid of figure 3. For the present purposes, it is not necessary to do this; nor, in fact, is sufficient empirical evidence available to make these calculations with exactness. Nevertheless, based partly on income inequality measures and reports of police intervention in private lives,[32] it is not difficult to make approximations of where societies would be located. Hong

Kong, for instance, would be roughly in the middle of the upper left quadrant. The Scandinavian countries would be toward the far right of the same quadrant while the United States would be between them and Hong Kong. China, Cuba, and the USSR would be located variously in the lower right quadrant. South Korea would be located in the upper part of the lower left quadrant (as would Britain in its early industrializing phase in the first decades of the nineteenth century). Other less developed countries would also be located toward the peripheries of this quadrant. More firmly located there would be Idi Amin's Uganda, Pol Pot's Kampuchea, and, of course, Hitler's Reich and its conquered territories.

The Ideal Characteristics of Dominance Systems

Predatory Dominance

There is a story, told to a chilling climax, of a village where each year one person was selected by lot for sacrificial death.[33] As the time drew near, tension in the village mounted. A sickening and pervasive fear chilled each heart. People gathered and waited. And when it became known who the victim was, an indescribable relief swept over the others, a joy that neither they nor a member of their family had been chosen. Free for another year! But what of the victim? For him or her there was wrenching fear, a knowledge of imminent doom, an outcast from the group which before had nurtured but now killed. Such, indeed, in literary form, are the images of the many united against the one or the few, of blood and terror, of expiation to the gods, of a purifying of the social whole. And, in fact, the historical record, even accounts from the present time, are filled with stories of luckless people who in one way or another were tortured or killed for the benefit of others. Yet such treatment is only the extreme form and masks the daily pain and humiliation meted out to ordinary people, those who may not even be aware that they are the perpetual victims of society. These individuals are those whose humiliation and subjugation legitimizes power. Their lot in life makes visible the values by which some maintain themselves in elite positions while others are relegated to lesser roles that sometimes include even the ultimate one of painful death itself.

Who are these victims, these people against whom systematic discrimination is practiced? They may be some caste or class that has been stigmatized, some untouchable group from whom all others shy. They may be individuals who are said to be deviant, the nonconformists, the crazy, and retarded. Women in traditional societies, especially those from the lowest strata, were frequently treated as chattel and fulfilled their lives of misery in humble silence. Or the victims may be some racial group, those who by some feature do not look like the acceptable ones. Or they may be those who believe in different gods. Or those who, by some accident of history, speak a different language. Whatever their origin, they have often been silent in their own victimization.

Those who are victims need not always come from within society. Prisoners of war have often served as the grist for grisly rituals. History is replete with stories of raiding parties that have brought back the heads, ears, and other bodily parts of those who, for one reason or another, were not able to defend themselves successfully. Slaves brought from foreign lands are an outside group that lives within society, often held at arm's length and treated as dray horses for the needs of their owners.

All victims are people who are looked down upon in terms of the central values of predatory dominance. Yet to say that they are undervalued is to speak only of their persons. Although in some cases their lives can be put aside at the whim of their masters, in one very real sense victims are highly valued. For their presence, dead or alive, affirms the core values that justify dominance. The insatiable desire among some headhunting tribes to display grisly trophies of triumph was only a way of providing visual evidence of the prowess of the collector and of his right thereby to an important position in society. The victim was thus highly esteemed and might even have been honored by the conqueror, for his existence, mute though it had become, was the source of power for its possessor.

A dominance system based upon predatory values is common among primitive peoples as well as in many modern societies, as the histories of Nazi Germany, imperial Britain, or many present-day South American countries clearly show. In these societies a number of socialization influences act to retard moral psychological development. Core values, for example, grant status to individuals in terms of their ability physically to subjugate others. This may, of course, not always involve firsthand use of the sword, whip, and club but there must be a readiness to use such weapons to force acquiescence by others. The character traits that are highly valued are aggressiveness in the face of threat, insensitivity to the physical pain of others and a predilection, or at least a willingness, to use physical force to obtain one's ends. The learning process whereby these abilities are acquired sets great store on rulership per se, noblesse oblige, the white man's burden, and survival of the fittest. Morals training exalts predatory virtues with emphasis upon the glory of battle, the legitimacy of killing, the cultivation of machismo, and the desirability of suppressing feelings of empathy toward victims. Physical punishment, to toughen the learner, is the accepted pattern (e.g., British public school training in the nineteenth century), and the fear that the learner experiences is expected to be transmitted later to the victim. Group orientation is highly ethnocentric, with the values of one group, that of the predators, placed above all others.

It is well known that even in the simplest societies some aspects of inequality exist (by sex and age, for instance). It has been suggested, however, that a degree of choice has always existed between reciprocal and predatory solutions to status tensions arising from the division of labor. Competition among societies and the temptations of higher civilizations have, it is averred, "pushed" societies toward predatory solutions.[34] Further pushing is presumed to occur from the fact that leaders find their role desirable only when the total resources collected by them produce a surplus for the leader. How disproportionate collections are made (according to rules regarding taxes, donations, extortion, etc.) defines who is a have and a have-not.[35] Followers, for their part, although their resources may be virtually robbed from them, find their lot preferable to outright harm and, under normal circumstances, are mollified by the promise of stability and solidarity in exchange for their loyalty and resources.

This historical pattern of elite aggrandizement was not, I think, ever seriously open to general discussion by the members of society. Certainly at the dawn of agricultural societies, about ten thousand years ago, both the proto-agricultural societies and their nomadic hunter-gatherer adversaries fashioned predatory solutions to the problems they faced. Hunters trained and organized themselves to acquire forcefully the agricultural output of others while the agricultural societies developed fighting bodies to protect themselves from nomadic bands and from each other. To the extent that responsibility for a group's competitive edge fell increasingly into the hands of a few people, this power could be used not only to protect the group but also to further personal advantage. And once this power became institutionalized in the roles of kings and nobles it became increasingly difficult to dislodge these elites from their positions of prominence. Dominance became justified in terms of the group's ends, and rules were formulated to insure that these goals were sanctified.

Values and behavior reflect the underlying reality of the division of labor that emerges in the struggle for resources in any given period of history. There is, however, no simple link between environment and values and behavior. Thus, in the earliest of the ancient agricultural societies, the values and behavior of Meso-Americans differed greatly from those of Babylonians or Egyptians, and these in turn differed from those of the Chinese of the Shang and Zhou dynasties. The diversity is exceptionally broad. Yet in all cases where statist organization took place one notes the rise to dominance of groups trained for military activities, of an allied class of priests responsible for the sanctification of military dominance values, and of mechanisms, often protobureaucratic, for the regularization of commercial activity.

One other pattern that developed at that time was also shared. The labor of an overwhelmingly large proportion of the people, those who were involved in agricultural production either as peasants or as free farmers, supported the small group of rulers, aristocrats, priests, and merchants. Although there was a degree of mutual sharing within the family or village, the lowly had few rights in society as a whole. In that larger context the higher organizations of society, primitive though they were, were extractive and victimizing.

Human beings can get what they want in goods and services by individually or collectively making the goods themselves, by stealing, or by forcing others to make goods for them.[36] The predatory solution is the third of these. But the economic transfers of that early time were not effected by markets but were rather an integral aspect of noneconomic institutions—political, religious, social, and kinship organizations; clan, totem, sex, age group, custom, and ritual governed life. Kings or chiefs acted for the community. Exchange among groups was essentially a collective activity, under the direction of the chief, and intertwined with obligations of kinship, magical ritual, and so forth. Gift giving and ceremonial distribution were pervasive elements in primitive economic life.[37]

The evolution of primitive societies into larger and more complex social entities involved a heightening of the prestige factor for elites (displayed through prestige wealth) and a transformation of the territorial base from village to city to region, with villages in the latter stage feeding staples (tax or tribute) into the redistributive organization of the central palace. This expansion invariably involved warfare (and the growth of a war-making group) and the progressive institutionalization of slavery, replenished and augmented from the ranks of the defeated. These last performed the meanest and lowliest tasks and served also as a source of prestige for their owners.

Slavery (although sometimes a debated issue, as in ancient Athens) was the ultimate proof of economic subordination and, correspondingly, of predatory virtue. In historical Polynesian societies, for instance, warfare among neighboring islands was endemic while internally the sacrifice of slaves was carried out for a variety of purposes. It is known, for instance, that slaves, often chosen at random, were ritually thrown to their deaths under sliding hulls at the launching of war canoes or were buried alive under the postholes of temples. To improve the prospects of success of the sacrificers, these slaves, whose personal feelings were a matter of indifference to their masters, fulfilled the necessary role of sacrificial victim to the gods. Yet in a more basic sense the death of the slave was a reminder of the power of the dominant, of the ability of the powerful to work their will upon others at their whim. Such an ethic, of course, also underlay the need of the Spartans perpetually to terrorize the Helots of the Peloponnese.

Perhaps nowhere in historical times has the predatory system been more clearly manifested than in Aztec Mexico. The Spaniards under Cortez, themselves harbingers of new and rigorous forms of dominance, were met in Tenochtitlan, the present Mexico City, with terrible sights, ones which they knew would envelop them if they failed in their enterprise. At the top of the Aztec religious pyramids were stone altars to the gods, and on these slabs victims had their beating hearts ripped from their bodies. According to contemporary accounts, the rooms that enclosed these funereal premises were caked with blood and reeked with death. The bodies of the victims, once dispatched, were unceremoniously rolled down the pyramid's side, there to be taken and cooked in a cannibal rite. Who were these people and who were those who ate their flesh? The victims, executed by the thousands, were prisoners of war, captured in the unending series of attacks the Aztecs carried out against their neighbors. Indeed, the wars themselves often occurred precisely to obtain these captives; Aztec tactics emphasized not the annihilation of a foe but his capture alive. Once returned to Tenochtitlan, the victims were caged and fattened and at the appointed hour went to their doom. Those who feasted upon the victims' remains were the very warriors, with their families, who had bested the enemy in combat. In one sense the feast represented the ingestion of the bravery of a fallen foe. In a more fundamental sense, however, the entire ceremony was a ritual enactment in the most terrible form of dominance by martial power and a proof to both victim and conqueror alike of the virtues of aggressiveness, insensitivity, and willingness to use ultimate forms of force and terror.

The great peasant societies that grew out of these more ancient forms (and whose residues exist in various degrees of completeness in many parts of the world today) inherited a number of predatory features. Aristocrats, usually basing their status in military organization, did not engage in productive labor but rather devoted their energies to extracting support for themselves from the peasantry. Although bureaucratic empires were more centralized than feudal societies, both maintained a strict distinction between aristocrats and nonaristocrats. Nothing was done for the mass of people, and, indeed, there was very little idea of labor for the public welfare or working for progress. For their part the peasantry were in no position to withhold their product or to demand concessions. Doing so might jeopardize the little security that was enjoyed.[38] At the societal level there were few buffers against warfare and tributary exploitation (in India, for example, rural villages were never in any real sense detached from the state). Within the villages relationships among kinship groups were also often highly inegalitarian, and only within families was there any persistent welfare orientation. Patron-client exchanges were based as much on power and exploitation as on any mutuality of interest. The vulnerability of peasants to even slight dislocations in their lives is revealed by their chronic state of undernourishment and their fear of starvation. In preindustrial Europe ordinary people spent 60–80 percent of their income on food (versus 22 percent in the United States in 1950), and they still did not live well even in the best of times.[39]

War was viewed as a natural state of man, and warfare, usually over control of land, was virtually continuous. Nobles had an exclusive monopoly of law and private rights of justice and enjoyed individual authority and property, at the highest levels making no distinction between their private patrimony and the state treasury. In Europe only the church, with a separate hierarchy, was an alternative to the profession of war. Personal valor was idealized but the hazards of the martial way of life were considerable. Between 1330 and 1479, 46 percent of the sons of English dukes met violent deaths.[40]

"The state," Walzer says, "is a tool that cannot be made without iron."[41] Modernity has made coercion and exploitation more controversial in some quarters but has not eliminated them. Workers, and even common soldiers, have been seen as social outcasts. Especially in the early periods of industrialization, elites continued to inflict injury by force and to see themselves as justly exempted from labor.[42] When military-industrial complexes spread from their homeland in Great Britain to other countries in the late nineteenth century, new possibilities for predatory dominance went with them.[43] Bloody rituals of an ancient nature were played out in the Second World War by Nazi Germany and imperial Japan. In Europe subject populations in the Slavic East felt the full brunt of contempt that was heaped upon them by a militarily aggressive Germany, especially by its politicized police and military formations of the SS. The shooting of civilian hostages, the torture of victims, and the wholesale brutalization of populations were raised to their extreme form in the death camps with the extermination of the Jews and others. But these acts all had a common thread—the need and willingness of the conqueror to prove to the subjugated that the denial to them of rights of any sort sprang from their lack of racial fitness as demonstrated on the field of war. In the Far East, countless Chinese and others fell victim to bushido, the samurai warrior code of Japan, which exalts martial virtues above all. Woe to the conquered, for by the very act of submission they exhibited their lack of worth. So strong was this feeling that a Japanese soldier would rather have died than become, as a prisoner, a living exhibit of deficient martial virtue.

Entrepreneurial Dominance

Dominance based upon entrepreneurial skills derives from a characteristic mix of learning influences. From a moral development perspective these represent an advance over predatory forms. Emphasis is on those socialization influences that promote an ethic of autonomy. The benefits for self and society that derive from liberty, in the sense of protection from authority, are highly touted. However, while individual attainment is emphasized, empathy for those who are less capable of asserting themselves is suppressed. Affective manipulation maximizes guilt regarding failure; these feelings are especially aroused by shortcomings in acquiring goods, status, or other distinctions that glorify the self. Morals training stresses the paramount virtue of self-expression and of personal responsibility for success or failure. Group orientation is rigidly ethnocentric, with a clear demarcation drawn between those who have been successful in acquiring rewards and those who have not. The former are accorded social worth while the latter are considered failures.

In the entrepreneurial dominance system the control of resources is the hallmark of the successful person. Control may exist over immobile forms of wealth such as land or minerals, but more typically it is calculated in terms of monetary power. The acquisition of mobile forms of wealth, of money, to such a degree that immobile forms can be obtained or dispensed with at will becomes the criterion by which dominance is recognized, and it is this aspect that differentiates this system from that where martial prowess is valued. For those with predatory skills may, in fact, control vast sources of wealth, but as a justification for dominance it is their martial prowess rather than control of resources that is valued. Thus in societies such as feudal Japan merchants, whose lives were spent in the acquisition of goods and wealth, were looked down upon and accorded low social status by their warrior overlords.

The entrepreneur is aggressive in seeking personal goals and skilled in the ability to assess the value of material things in relation to human wants. It is this particular aspect, the evaluation of resources as positive ends in and of themselves, that so frequently has led to dislike of the entrepreneur, for these traits appear to contradict any genuine concern for the community. Even the fearsome societies based on martial prowess usually justified themselves in terms of defense and security. In modern times it has required ever-expanding economies that increase the share for many others in society to change negative attitudes regarding acquisitiveness. And so it has come about that dislike is changed to respect and the entrepreneur is said to possess characteristics that are beneficial to society. He is, admittedly, acquisitive, but his profit orientation is presumed to create and develop resources that are useful for all. He engages in material display (houses, paintings, clothes, etc.), but such display, and the importance it is granted, is deemed necessary to motivate others to produce valued goods. Ideally anyone can become an entrepreneur and can share in the rewards that go with high status.

What were the origins of the entrepreneurial dominance system? Clearly it developed from predatory dominance or, more accurately, coexisted with that form of dominance for a number of centuries in a secondary position, its status criteria important only for sections of the population and its organizations subject to control by predatory state power. Only in the last century has this form of dominance become of primary and decisive importance in a number of societies.

European feudal monarchs and lords, while differing in respects from their counterparts in other parts of the world, partook like them of that overtly coercive characteristic of dominance noted for the predatory system. Yet the feudal division of labor, derived partly from the master-slave pattern of classical antiquity and partly from the communal pattern of the germanic tribal populations, had several unique aspects. The major one was the relatively autonomous existence of towns and an urban citizenry. The notion of an urban citizenry is classical in derivation, but the towns themselves existed freely due to the parcelization of sovereignty that characterized the feudal mode of dominance. Juridically the towns were like another world from the countryside, recognizing neither the control of the rural world nor its values. Towns were like frontier areas where serfs were free, talent could thrive, and a degree of latitude was allowed for the development of horizontal rather than strictly vertical social relationships (e.g., within guilds or universities). Rather than being centers of administration and consumption, as was largely the case in other areas of the world, these European towns grew as centers of production and as bulwarks against the smashing of resistance that the peasantry so frequently experienced.[44] Medieval agricultural productivity was high but was rivaled by the output of the towns. The growth of urban commerce reflected the general but slow commercialization of society. Communication among towns and villages increased with great political implications in terms of the links that formed among previously separate and distinct areas.[45]

The first break in the predatory pattern of dominance occurs, in fact, with commercialization. This is not a modern phenomenon. Phoenecia, the Greek city states, Rome, and Byzantium were all commercialized to some extent. Indeed, it was the concept of private property as an absolute right defined in Roman law that, when rediscovered, gave impetus to commercialization in medieval Europe. In most traditional societies inviolable private property does not exist. Nor is surplus purely economic in derivation; as suggested earlier, it is generated rather through extra-economic sanctions inherent in kinship ties, customary or religious obligations, and so forth. By contrast, private property in entrepreneurial systems is inviolable. Property can be held by a number of individuals and disputes about it do not have the zero-sum quality that they have in predatory societies (i.e., control of property decided on the battlefield). Rivals may both expand and prosper, although unequally.[46]

A reliance on prices and a small group (partnership or company) organization oriented toward private advantage did not have its first major breakthrough in Europe but in China. Although aspects of commercialization can be traced in China back to the third century B.C., market-regulated behavior became clearly noticeable there a thousand years ago. (In Song China, for instance, 60 percent or more of the total rural population were de facto small holders in their own right.[47]) It is difficult to posit any direct link between commercialization in China and that which occurred later in Europe, but it is clear that political-economic conditions on both edges of the Eurasian land mass had made this event likely. The Chinese, however, went no further than the beginnings. Custom and kinship remained powerful. Official ideology and popular belief frowned upon the accumulation of private wealth from trade or manufacture. The state monopolized key sectors of the economy, and legal prescriptions were essentially punitive. Moreover, there was a recurring pattern of harsh taxation that over time periodically undermined the soundness of the state.[48]

In Europe, on the other hand, with the Renaissance and the revival of Roman law, conditions were propitious for the growth of free capital. The economic revolution that began in Italy gave a powerful stimulus to speculation. By the sixteenth century Europe was in the midst of an economic crisis. In the words of Tawney, "Economic power, long at home in Italy, was leaking through a thousand creeks and inlets into western Europe."[49] There was an outburst of enterprise in mining and textiles, the rise of international commercial companies, economic imperialism on the part of Portugal and Spain, a revolution in prices, and a decline in the economic importance of Venice and the southern German cities. All this in the century following the dissolution of the Council of Basel in 1449 when papal power triumphed over the reformist conciliar movement and opened wide the gates of avarice, setting the stage for the Reformation.

In England, long before the Reformation and the confiscation of monastic estates, the question of land revenues had become acute. In 1430 the monasteries and the church as a whole owned 25 percent of the land while the crown had 6 percent. The income from the ecclesiastical holdings was about three-fourths as much again as the average annual income of the crown.[50] During the Reformation in England under Henry VIII the crown acquired these vast estates through confiscation. Henry in his wars with France and his daughter Elizabeth in her Irish war met their expenses by unloading on the market the huge fund of agrarian land that had been acquired from the church. This property found its way into the hands of the lay landed ruling class whose numbers and wealth grew correspondingly.[51]

Unlike the aristocracy on the continent, there had been a gradual conversion to commercial activities in the English countryside since the fifteenth century in wool farming and in investments in the rural cloth industry. But it was the growth of land speculation and prices that was truly significant in bringing about change. Land investments could not be secured and protected (and standards of living maintained) without improving agricultural techniques and rationalizing social relationships. Traditional land-use patterns were altered by the enclosure of common lands; traditional social relationships between lord and tenant were changed by rent racking and increasing fines. The abolition of feudal tenures, wardships, and purveyances removed obstacles to the free purchase and sale of land and opened the way to long-term rational estate management.

The first account of enclosure was written soon after 1460, and official opposition to depopulation began with legislation in 1489, followed by a stream of criticism and further legislation regarding this matter for nearly two hundred years.[52] This opposition by high officials and clergy infuriated landowners, who fiercely resisted (illegally defying the statutes) in the name of private property. During the English civil war in the seventeenth century these tendencies were hastened rather than retarded. Crown lands and the lands of many royalists were confiscated; there was a general foreclosing on mortgages, this being essentially an expropriation of the property of the more extravagant sections of the aristocracy and gentry by the new commercial class. The end of social feudalism was furthered during the revolution by better policing by the army, the disarming of a turbulent gentry, and the shifting of fortresses.[53]

The English civil war marked in bloodshed the crisis in dominance values that had taken place with the commercialization of society. Old justifications of social worth no longer applied; the established church was in a state of moral dilapidation, and by

Elizabeth's time only half of the aristocracy had fighting experience.[54] Commercial activities had expanded to the point that by the early part of the seventeenth century London, where there was a great concentration of trade and manufacturing, was the most dominant capital city of any country in Europe; by the end of the century England had something like a single internal market. In the countryside a yeomanry of well-off rural wage laborers existed alongside the peasantry. The privileged had no fear of a jacquerie and consequently no stake in a strong central, coercive government.[55] English absolutism fell afoul of the alternate interests of commercialized gentry, the commercial interests in the city of London, and the new commoner classes in both the city and the countryside.

Despite changes in Europe as a whole, merchants, traders, and financiers had little prestige or influence except in England and Holland. The citizenry who counted, of course, were never more than a few thousand in any country (even down to the eighteenth century). With Puritanism, however, ideas about private property were articulated by people who refused quiescence and instead boldly thrust themselves into the mainstream of social life (and political life as well during the civil war). At the level of ideology Puritanism was a major response to the economic crisis of the time, identifying social ills (in religious terminology) and sanctifying status obtained by disciplined labor in a calling rather than by predatory military valor. The Puritans advocated stringent self-control, but they rejected the established church and state as agents of regulation. Traditional restrictions on economic enterprise were shouldered aside. Property was thought to be a minimum condition for salvation, for success in a calling was said to accord with the will of God. Economic expediency was thus given ethical sanctification. Bad habits were the enemy, not riches that were acquired for the greater glory of the Almighty. Sloth was more dangerous than covetousness, and enterprise more praiseworthy than tending to the necessities of the poor. The unscrupulous especially hailed Calvin's doctrine of the legitimacy of moderate interest. As a tract of 1673 noted, "It took with the brethren like polygamy with the Turks."[56]

Individualism in religion led logically to an individualist morality (i.e., an emphasis on negative rights) and from there to a disparagement of the significance of the community as compared with personal autonomy. John Locke systematized these ideas in his theory that "the State which interferes with property and business destroys its own title to exist."[57] "Free subjects," declared a Committee of the House of Commons in 1604, "are born . . . to the free exercise of their industry."[58]

The monarchy was restored after 1660, but by that time many of the old feudal nobility had been transformed into a group that justified dominance on the basis of property unalloyed by military pretensions. The day of the industrial and financial elites of our own time still lay ahead. Political rule as such did not yet lie in the hands of the "middle class" bourgeoisie, but economic power did. Much more important, the justification for domination by property had been established to flourish fully in its own good time.[59]

For the entrepreneurial personality to succeed, a minimum amount of social interference is required. There must be laws to protect contracts and to insure social stability so that acquisitive activities are unimpeded, but additional regulations that restrict individual actions in the name of community values are anathema. Government is tolerable only when it is limited. Freedom, being essentially indivisible, means freedom from state regulation and freedom from any ideology that posits mandatory values. Elites value a social system that places minimum constraints on the exercise of individualism. Those in dominant positions perceive that a certain amount of well-being for others is required in order that social peace will be maintained. But there is resistance to any steps that will genuinely eliminate the gap between those who have acquired rewards and those who, for one reason or another, have proved less capable in this regard.

The fundamental tenet of the entrepreneurial system is the primacy of individual volition, and as long as there is no challenge to the importance of individualism per se the values that people hold with regard to religion, politics, sex, and so on can be personally determined. Elites will not use their authority to suppress idiosyncratic beliefs; indeed, since individualism may be expressed in many areas of life, its manifestation can be permitted in many divergent or diverse forms. The central liberty, however, the cornerstone of all others, is the liberty to engage in economic activity free of government control. It is this liberty that guarantees freedom of thought and expression, of religion and movement, and of relief from obnoxious interference by others. Thus, for instance, an individual (e.g., Jim Jones) may freely organize and lead a religious cult that has practices repugnant to many other citizens. Being a supporter of the Communist party, however, while legally permissible, is considered threatening and dangerous since it openly challenges the basic premises of the entrepreneurial system.

Individualism in its ideal form is expected to be tempered by the altruistic awareness of the needs of others. Personal responsibility in relations with others is stressed, but even more so is the virtue of self reliance, of not unthinkingly accepting the decisions of others, and especially the requirement to accept the consequences of one's own actions.[60] As practiced, this view of moral responsibility frequently results in a heightened emphasis on negative rights and a relative denigration of obligations to insure a fair share for others.

The consequences of entrepreneurship, then, are the reduction of the possibility that all people in a society can be genuinely equal. The emphasis on personal gain and on social worth based upon success in entrepreneurial activities reduces the capacity for even-handed empathy and altruistic awareness. As such, the entrepreneur sets in motion patterns of dealing with others that reduce the moral potential of society. For although the results of personal choice in many areas are often noteworthy, it is also true that a lack of material equality is the lot for a broad spectrum of society; such unevenness can, at times, be very marked.

The entrepreneurial society, however, organized around principles of liberty and equality, does not operate according to the rigid class distinctions that characterize many predatory societies. The entrepreneur claims privilege on the grounds that his dominance is functional for society as a whole. In modern entrepreneurial societies the common welfare is often touted. Individual merit, as the basis for privilege, is said to insure that the best will lead for the benefit of all. And indeed, the importance of the owners of capital has been steadily diluted in the twentieth century by the rise of those who claim success and income on the basis of occupational achievement.

Has this meant a fundamental change in the entrepreneurial system? The answer, I think, is no. Acting, it is said—thanks to the competitive mechanism—in the public interest but drawing strength from the notion that management rights of independence from regulation derive from their role as agents for the owners of private property, those who oversee the operations of large commercial corporations, state bureaucracies, voluntary associations, political parties, and, in fact, virtually every large organization in the entrepreneurial society have gained enormous semi-autonomous power. These new entrepreneurs are linked with the older group by common values. At root there remains the idea that those who control resources must have freedom in determining their allocation. Society, as John Locke conceptualized, is still a joint-stock company, not a community united by mutual obligations. The government is a convenience to maintain limited liabilities. Subject only to very general legal and customary restraints, owners and managers should be free to act in their own self-interest as they see fit. Because the general welfare derives from competition, affective neutrality (if not outright indifference) to nonowners and nonmanagers is perfectly permissible. The disciplining of those without resources in state and enterprise is justified on the basis that such people have not shown the zeal, inventiveness, and risk-taking qualities that are necessary to sustain and expand the general welfare.

Who are the victims in this system? In the seventeenth century they were preeminently those who were seen as slothful and without a calling. Because misfortune was clearly the punishment for sin, rogues, vagrants, and especially beggars, the "rotten legges and armes" of society,[61] should be forced to work for their own spiritual health. In the nineteenth century they were men, women, and children who worked in the dismal factories and mines of Europe and America. They were those who, from ignorance, poverty, lack of aggressiveness, youth, or being female, had failed in the struggle to acquire possessions. Their rags and poverty were held up as the justification for their lowly status and as an example of the sin of their lack of acquisitive skill. In modern America their descendants as victims are migrant workers, ghetto blacks, those on welfare, the helpless elderly, or the dispossessed of Appalachia. Such people are a burden, it is said, begrudged wards of the state, for they have not the "get-up and go" to make something of themselves. The degradation of their lives manifests clearly their lack of worth and even more clearly the superior consideration that is owed to those whose more comfortable existence reveals the virtue of entrepreneurial skill.

In its pure form the entrepreneurial dominance system is one without empathy for those who have failed in the acquisitive race. It is not, however, a closed society, and by its emphasis on individual achievement it may foster brilliant accomplishment in the arts and sciences as well as in business itself. But it requires as subordinates people who have failed and for whom the price of failure is exploitation by others. For both the dominant and the submissive the most characteristic emotional quality is guilt, a feeling that one has not lived up to a set of ideals, a sense of self-failure in the eyes of either a deity or a self-imposed notion of the good. It is a society where guilt is assuaged by the control of more and more resources and where comparison with the less fortunate provides visible proof of worth. It is a society haunted by a fear of imperfection, where inner peace can be obtained and maintained only by constant individual exertion on the treadmill of material success.

Guardian Dominance

In the guardian model, influences that affect moral development are also markedly improved over predatory forms. The ethic of care is emphasized and attention is focused on cooperation and concern for others. At the same time, however, socialization fosters conventional moral reasoning (i.e., adherence to the dictates of authority and to norms). In the learning process, for example, the guardians serve as models. Subordinates emulate the behavior of leaders and determine their success by comparing themselves with other group members. The importance of knowing who is within one's group is thus accentuated. Ethnocentrism becomes pronounced since outsiders, by definition, are people who, for one reason or another, live outside the "fairness" guidelines set by the guardians. Morals training denies that people are capable of true individual responsibility, for moral values are defined as the particular rules and norms of the group; moral indoctrination is the most characteristic method of morals training. Autonomy training for the young is muted and individual responsibility is subsequently minimized. People are taught that moral dilemmas should be solved not by personal responsibility but by reference to those values that have been set forth by the guardians. Individuals are motivated to conform by the use of shaming techniques of discipline where threats of group ostracism and ridicule are brought to bear; these techniques are thus a highly characteristic form of punishment in learning.

Guardians believe that their knowledge of desirable social ends and of the means to arrive at those ends is greater than others. Whether religious or political, this form of dominance is related to a set of beliefs that have, as a basic feature, a description of how people should live. Derived from an analysis of mythological, supernatural, or historical events, these descriptions contain reasons for society's woes and ways whereby these shortcomings can be corrected.

Ideally the dominant person is a true believer, virtuous in pursuit of a moral social order, although, in fact, there may be many whose adherence to doctrine is but a means to less noble ends. The ideal characteristics of guardian leaders are strict adherence to ideological prescriptions, intolerance of moral imperfection (which is to say, intolerance of behavior that is proscribed by the ideology), ability in the use of the ideology in daily life, and skill in perceiving and articulating the ideology's applicability to general life situations. The basis of guardian authority is the assumption that the characteristics of the good social order and the good citizen are both knowable. That is, there is an assumption that right thinking and right conduct are matters that are within the grasp of everyone even though in practice they may not be universally attained. Morality can thus be objectively observed, verified, and taught to others. Internal evaluations of right and wrong have external consequences; sooner or later they are manifested by actions that can be measured against the ideals of the ideology.

Since the ideology itself is beyond question, it is the duty of the dominant to insure that other members of society believe and behave in accordance with its precepts as interpreted by those who occupy the highest positions in guardian organizations. Individuals fitted for leadership are the masters of learning; they are said to be those who best exemplify correct thinking and conduct, and it is this quality that gives them the right to direct others. Ideally the guardian holds his position of responsibility not because he controls or possesses economic resources (indeed, he may be expected to have fewer resources than others) and not because he controls coercive power (which, in fact, he frequently wields), but rather because he has a sacred trust to act as a guide to the good and proper life.

A guardian in his modern guise, however, is not divorced from the hurly-burly of social life. He is not a lonely, withdrawn ascetic or a guide whose actions are meant to be mere passive reminders of what constitutes right thinking and right behavior. Rather, the guardian is expected to lead by example and exhortation and to devise policies that will bring society closer to the ideals of communal purity that the guardian himself exemplifies. Consequently, the guardian has a duty to intervene in the lives of others. Individuals who fail to make an effort to manifest right thought and conduct must be pointed out and brought to the attention of others. This implies that group condemnation can and should be mustered to bring pressure on people who, for one reason or another, fail to do what is considered proper.

If what constitutes the good is knowable, then this good can be set forth in explicit codes, and these codes can be imparted to people by appropriate forms of indoctrination. Controlling the learning and communication environment, then, becomes exceptionally important, for it is by control of this environment that moral precepts are set forth. Although rulership is legitimized by reference to ideological codes (as it is in other systems of dominance), it is the tight control of information and learning that is the true basis for the dominant position of the guardian.

Where guardian authority is the basis for governance all social actions and conditions have ideological implications. Interaction among friends, for instance, can be scrutinized in terms of ideological content; behavior in a family that reflects some traditional attitude can be examined in light of the new criteria. The notion that individuals have a right to be free from this intrusion into the personal aspects of their lives is banned. Where attitudes or behavior are found that do not meet the requirements of doctrine, they must be changed or destroyed, for their continued existence is a fundamental threat to the guardian system. For the guardian himself, his position is one of the elect. Yet, being certified as knowledgeable about right conduct and thinking implies the existence of others who have not reached this level and the probability that there may be those who, in fact, are failures. To assume otherwise would be to suggest that the guardian dominance system is illegitimate and that status based on guardian authority is improperly constituted. But this cannot be, for although correct behavior is knowable, perfection is a goal that is not obtainable by all. Consequently, all members of the group must be labeled individually in terms of how well they emulate the ideal.

Like the entrepreneurial dominance system the guardian society, one of the two major ideal types in the modern world, has an ancient lineage submerged in the predatory dominance of traditional societies. It is interesting to note that just as entrepreneurial dominance in its modern form can be traced back to the Puritans so also can guardian dominance. It should come as no surprise that in this first of the truly modern revolutions the seeds of both guardian and entrepreneurial dominance can be found. In its original impulse the Puritan movement sought to create a society where "godly order would be the rule and sin not a possible activity."[62] There was much emphasis on unremunerative work and on accumulating no more wealth than what was needed for a modest life. Discipline in the army was severe. Sinners were driven from the holy commonwealth while Puritan leaders observed, investigated, and, when necessary, punished others.[63] Eventually these aspects of Puritanism declined in favor of negative rights, but in the heyday of the Puritan movement they were powerful indeed.

Forms of guardianship that are analytically similar but socially different from Puritanism can be found in the Chinese tradition; these have had a noticeable affect on modern Chinese life. Confucianism, with its tradition of humane concern, held as a basic tenet the need for a moral government to provide for basic economic needs. Officials in the bureaucracy were recruited by examination that tested moral qualities rather than technical competence. Informed judgment guided by the ethical teachings of the past was more to be desired than government by regulation. In the modern period both the Nationalists and the Communists have derived their authority from absolute moral truths and have sought to oust evil men from the polity. This was true even during the 1930s when capitalists were presumably an important, influential group. In fact, as recent research has shown, they were stymied as a political force and never able to develop independent power.[64]

Modern guardian systems are the quintessence of organization although with weaknesses in the areas of leadership succession and internal conflict resolution (partly alleviated by meetings, discussions, and purges). Since the goal of these societies is less distributive justice in the material sense and more altering of the mode of production itself and destroying the division of labor (thus eliminating production for profit and accumulation), the need is for a vanguard political instrument or organization led by those with a theoretical understanding of basic issues.[65] For success to be achieved, disorganization must be strictly disavowed. Instead purposive, zealous, committed, and directed activity is required.

At the apex of organized life is the political party, which exercises control over the state bureaucracy and subsidiary organizations by its preemption of the right to set policy guidelines, its monopolization of the leading posts, its supervision of indoctrination, and its control over critical appointments and promotions. In this type of setting organizational matters dominate the daily life of both the rank and file and the leadership of the organization. Tightly disciplined, only those who function full time in a leadership capacity have real power, much the same as do entrepreneurs in the relatively autonomous organizations that they head.

The party is said to consist of advanced elements who lead the revolutionary masses. Even when professional and technical skills are required, ideological reliability and organizational loyalty are never missing as criteria for party membership.[66] As Deng Xiaoping in China noted, recruitment of cadres must be based on evidence of professional knowledge and adherence to the four cardinal principles—the socialist road, the people's democratic dictatorship, the leadership of the Chinese Communist Party, and Marxism-Leninism and Mao Zedong Thought.[67]

How are rights perceived under the guardian system that exists in modern China? Workers congresses, for instance, initially formed in 1957, tacitly abolished from 1966 to 1976 and revived in 1978, have the following powers: they can allocate housing; decide issues concerning worker well-being, including insurance funds and bonuses; issue rules and regulations for awards and penalties; discuss and examine directors' work reports and production and construction plans; criticize leading cadres regarding their qualifications and performance; and examine and discuss a factory's production principles and plans. They may not, however, make management decisions or elect leaders who are not formally approved by higher (i.e., Communist) authority.[68]

The rights, duties, and performance standards of party members are explictly set forth. The top two standards (of six) that members must meet are, first, a thorough grasp of Marxism-Leninism and Mao Zedong Thought and the policies based on them, and second, the ability to carry out the line, principles, and policies of the party. Their duties are to attend pertinent party meetings and read pertinent party documents; participate in discussions of party policies; make suggestions regarding the work of the party; make "well-grounded" criticisms of other members at meetings; vote, elect, and stand for office; present disagreements to higher levels "provided that they resolutely carry out the decision or policy [that] is in force"; and put forward any requests or appeals to higher authority. In meeting these standards and carrying out these duties, party members have the following rights: (1) conscientiously to study Marxism-Leninism and Mao Zedong Thought, (2) to adhere to the principle that the interests of the party and the people stand above everything, (3) to execute the party's decisions, (4) to uphold party solidarity and unity, (5) to be loyal and honest with the party, (6) to maintain close ties with the masses, (7) to play an exemplary vanguard role, and (8) to be brave and resolute in defense of the motherland.[69] Nowhere in this catalogue of confusion between rights and duties do negative rights appear, for the simple reason that they are not important for the practice or justification of dominance in China.

The new Chinese Constitution has stipulations stating that freedom of person, the personal dignity of citizens, the inviolability of homes, and the freedom and privacy of correspondence are all protected by law. These, combined with rights regarding the inviolability of socialist public property, prohibitions against exploitation, and guarantees of work, result in a social order that is thought to be, in essence, far superior to entrepreneurial dominance. The party, however, in sanctioning these rights, in no sense abdicates its privilege of enforcing its objectives and priorities on the Chinese people. As the political editor for the *Beijing Review* put it, "The stipulation that the Constitution is above all organizations and individuals does not contradict the leading role of the Chinese Communist Party."[70] The existence of some negative rights within the Constitution, therefore, in no way obscures the basic guardian nature of dominance in contemporary China.

The sacrificial victim in the guardian dominance system is the person who by accident, ignorance, or conviction cannot behave—or is said not to be able to behave—in accordance with the ideology. Some victims, however, may have characteristics beyond these. In the assessment of historical events, guardian ideologies frequently name some specific group as inherently incapable of living according to its precepts. Hence, those not of the same religion may be automatically stigmatized as heretics, witches, or infidels. Certain economic classes may be spoken of as incapable of living by an ideology's moral code. Even the people themselves may be thought of as prone to anarchy if divorced from the leadership of the guardians, and hence they require stern rule. Stalinism was ideologically justified because Stalin, the supreme guardian, claimed the right to impose the good of the working class on the working class.

The seventeenth-century religious wars in Europe spawned societies where many people were stigmatized as heretics for their adherence to Catholicism or Protestantism. The witch trials of Puritan New England sent old women to their deaths because of their supposed links with the devil. In the modern period bourgeois (and backsliding comrades) have been severely dealt with by Communists in Russia, China, and elsewhere because of their bad class mentality. Sometimes the hunt for victims reaches enormous proportions and great numbers of people are killed or otherwise badly treated in mass purges and Cultural Revolutions. In the revolution in China large numbers of people were brought before their fellow citizens, humiliated, degraded, sometimes killed, and in other cases sent for long terms to camps where an avowed goal of incarceration was the reformation of the character of the victim. The millions who have passed through prison camps in the Soviet Union and China are mute testimony to the status of victims in these two societies, people who for a variety of reasons are deemed to lie outside the bounds of moral consideration. Such individuals are said to be enemies of the state and as a consequence are thrust away from society in order that the purity of society may be maintained. Barrington Moore has eloquently described this:

> Since socialism is a workers' and peasants' state that belongs to the people, there are lots of people to explain . . . matters to workers and peasants and indeed to everybody who cares to listen. Furthermore just about everybody must care to listen. Woe to the person who stubbornly refuses to listen to the right noises or to try to make the right noises under socialism, since a socialist state is very efficient in its allocation of human as well as material resources. It sends human beings who prefer peace and quiet and thinking for themselves to listening to and making the right noises off to camps for reform through labor.[71]

It may seem anomalous that a social system that claims moral purity should degrade some of its own members. Yet, as with other forms of control, the logic of dominance demands the subordination of some in order to legitimize dominance for others. For how can moral purity as a criterion for dominance exist in a morally pure world? But, fortunately, the ideology points out the ills of the world and proclaims the duty of the guardians to root out evil. As a consequence, victims are brought forward; by the attribution to them of impurity the dominant affirm their own virtue and their continuing right to dominance.

The guardian society, like other dominance systems, is divided internally between the dominant and the submissive, between those who have social worth and those who are outcast. It is a society that champions altruistic awareness and empathy while in practice reserving these for the ideologically deserving. For the undeserving condemnation, even harsh cruelty, is appropriate. In an emotional sense these are societies where people at all levels suffer a fear of ostracism, of being ridiculed before others, and of being pointed out as lacking moral worth and therefore not deserving of social membership or status. Both the dominant and the submissive live with this fear of shame.

Moral Dominance

The last system of dominance that I will mention is the moral type. This form corresponds to what was referred to in figure 2 as an ideal social and political system. It is termed ideal because in its pure form this system has never existed, although some modern societies embody some of its qualities. Given the early childhood self-centeredness of individuals and the impossibility of eliminating all aspects of egoism, moral dominance may be forever unattainable. Indeed, many motivations (hunger, sex, etc.) important for survival have a strong inherent egoistic component; they can be modified in form and minimized as criteria of dominance but not totally eliminated. This does not mean, however, that dominance patterns cannot be changed. Predatory, entrepreneurial, and guardian dominance are not immutable. It is, in fact, the very knowledge that modification toward moral dominance is possible that lies behind so much of the struggle for rights in the modern world.

Moral dominance is a type of social existence toward which people strive and which, in part, is in the process of becoming. In this system the overriding quality of dominance is the lack of emphasis on the self, in terms of either martial valor, acquisitive skill, or ideological worth. Dominance, in fact, is synonomous with the act of supporting community well-being and enhancing personal choice for others. This concern for both the ethic of autonomy and the ethic of care is, I think, what Michael Walzer in his book *Spheres of Justice* had in mind when he spoke of "communities of character."[72] Dominance and submission lose their sharp-edged qualities; they merge subtly and imperceptibly into each other. Rulership in the state and in organizations becomes a matter of administrative service. The quality of this rulership and the rewards for it are subject to continuous assessment and approval by the ruled. Who then is dominant and who submissive?

In the moral dominance system the emphasis in learning is on superseding ethnocentric loyalties. Morals training stresses the virtues of cooperation and selflessness not just toward those who in some manner are closely associated but toward everyone. There is no a priori assumption of one road to the truth, nor can there be when all in society are given the right to assess the qualifications of citizenship. Above all the emphasis is on displaying altruistic awareness and empathy toward others without qualification and on being personally responsible for doing so. While fear, shame, and guilt may still operate, the effort in learning is to detach these feelings from reference to specific groups and individuals. Rather, stress is on consideration for the feelings of others regardless of who they may be.

In a moral dominance system there is no predetermined category of victims. This does not mean, however, that everyone is viewed equally but rather that the attributions of worth are made on an individual rather than a class or group basis. In every system of dominance, including the moral type, a normal distribution of moral competence means that there will be those who are egocentric. In the moral dominance system people who consistently fail to be personally responsible and to show altruistic awareness and empathy to others are viewed as failing to live up to their social obligations. The attitude toward such people, however, is restrictive rather than punitive. Restraint coexists with the conscious effort to eliminate, as far as possible, the social conditions that foster or permit amoral behavior.

4. Perversion

Centuries ago, Aristotle observed that systems of rulership "which have a regard to the common interest are constituted in accordance with strict principles of justice, and are therefore true forms; but those which regard only the interest of the rulers are all defective and perverted forms."[1] In its simplest formulation perversion is a violation of obligations. More precisely, perversion is a discrepancy between the actual distribution of rights and obligations in a dominance system and what people believe that distribution should be.

Perversion can take two forms. In the first case it involves the loss for subordinates of both positive and negative rights (a decline of opportunity relative to others, an increase in arbitrary arrest, etc.). The loss occurs from a decrease of corresponding obligations to assist others to obtain a fair share and to refrain from undue interference. Perversion of this type is likely to be experienced by broad elements of the population, including, at times, members of the elite. The second form of perversion arises from an increasing imbalance in the distribution of rights and obligations that characterize a particular pattern of dominance. Negative rights, for instance, and their corresponding obligations, may be progressively emphasized at the expense of positive rights. Or the reverse may occur. This situation (most easily noted in the entrepreneurial and guardian systems) involves a strengthening of one type of right and obligation—and a corresponding decrease in the obligations associated with the alternate right—in a manner that increasingly favors those elites who are best placed and most able to use this skewed distribution for their own advantage.

Perceptions of perversion have three forms, not mutually exclusive. First, rights and obligations may verifiably alter; second, subjective notions of what rights and obligations should be may change; third, confusion may exist, especially in times of rapid change, concerning appropriate obligations, leading to a belief that some in society are behaving wrongly. In the first case there is a relatively straightforward and shared recognition that previously held rights are being violated. Wealth may flow increasingly into the hands of a few people; elites may make unprecedented exactions on those lower in the social order; traditional rent practices may be discarded; new laws violating physical security or imposing censorship may be promulgated. In these and like cases, people begin to sense a deliberate failure of obligation and, in their minds, an illegitimate heightening of exploitative control.

The second condition that fosters a perception of perversion is subjective in nature. In the modern world this is an exceptionally frequent phenomenon. In this instance the dominance pattern is unchanged but people perceive it as perverted because of a discrepancy that has come to exist between the values that support the prevailing distribution of rights and obligations and the new values that people hold, frequently as a consequence of changes in internal or international factors. Feminist attitudes toward male dominance are largely of this nature, growing out of changes in women's work and child-bearing patterns. In Soviet society the increasing inefficiency of centralized decision making as economic growth proceeds has fueled an agonizing debate about granting greater autonomy in decision making to lower-level units. The granting of such powers, however, would constitute a significant increase in the importance of negative rights; therefore (as the Soviet Union is a guardian society) it is strongly resisted. The rigidity and overbureaucratization in this society are mirrored by covert and deviant (from the official point of view) activity throughout many sectors, indicating a pronounced discrepancy in values. In these and other cases people come to believe that the prevailing dominance pattern is inappropriate in comparison to the newer ideals that they hold.

There is, finally, a third perception of perversion that arises from confusion about appropriate obligations, a condition that is likely to be exacerbated during periods of internal or international change. People can hold conflicting values as, for instance, when negative rights are desired, but at the same time there is a belief that civic virtue can only be fostered by some form of guardian control. Or cooperation within an organization may be highly prized (with concommitant values of loyalty, affiliation, and solidarity) at the same time that there is a competitive drive toward individualistic achievement and a desire for special privilege.[2] The path that a person takes out of these dilemmas may place him or her at variance with other people's notions of right and obligation.

When perversion is limited in extent it is indistinguishable from deviance as that term is commonly used. Perversion decisively parts company from deviance and becomes a major factor in the victimization of members of society as the degree of avoidance of obligations begins to have systemic implications. It becomes definitely sociopathic as dominance patterns tend toward the extreme exclusion of a particular right or of both rights. Metaphorically this would lead in the predatory system to a Devil's Island society, in the entrepreneurial system to a Den of Thieves, and in the guardian system to an Ant Colony (enhancing rights to an extreme in the moral system would lead to the Kingdom of the Saints, a practical impossibility given the normal distribution of moral competence within any society). In fact, of course, although amoral people live within every dominance system and constantly undermine the balance of rights and obligations, perversion, when it occurs, almost never involves a radical shift. Rather, centripetal forces related to functional stability normally act as a brake against sudden and excessive perversion.

Perversion, often a multifaceted phenomenon, has three loci in the modern world: organizational elites, organizations and their members, and the system of organizations in society as a whole. For elites there are clearly always a few who will, if they can, impose disadvantages on others. The reason for this lies partly in inadequate moral competence (e.g., unconcern, intolerance), conjoined with competition in environments of resource scarcity (aggravated, often enough, during times when there are rapid changes in internal or international conditions). Such behavior involves the progressive avoidance of obligations toward those lower in the social order; some dominant individuals utilize their status to seek increased rewards of wealth or power. This type of perversion is often thought by ordinary people to be the consequence of deliberate malfeasance by dominant individuals although expediency and even lack of awareness may play a part. In the nineteenth century immoral self-interest was the view that was held of "robber baron" capitalists by many social reformers and workers. The late Shah of Iran, the Samoza family in Nicaragua, and the Gang of Four in China were also regarded in this way by many of the people in their respective societies.

Perversion by an organization is the consequence of activity by a large number of people not all of whom are elites. Some organizations, of course, are blatantly criminal in terms of society's values (e.g., the Mafia); the perversion of obligations and rights in this case is clearly marked. More subtle is the operation of organizations that have public trust but are in fact devoted to ends that serve only the organization's interests at the expense of all or a portion of the public. Member behavior in this case is often a consequence of leadership perversion and is entered into out of fear, ignorance, desire to conform, and loyalty to the organization. It involves, fundamentally, a lack of concern for those outside of the organization. Although the perversion may have been committed by only some members of the organization, outsiders frequently perceive the organization as a whole as engaged in wrongdoing. When Khrushchev, for example, denounced Stalin's crimes and released political prisoners, he acknowledged that members of the police organization had in general failed in their obligations. When the Lockheed corporation was accused of bribing Japanese officials, Americans and Japanese also denounced the corporation as a whole for illegal actions.

When people believe that many individuals and organizations are avoiding obligations on a large scale there may develop a sense that the system as a whole is perverted. This feeling is often accompanied by a belief that existing organizations are structurally inadequate for the needs of society and that the organization's members hold values that are no longer germane to society's needs. Often a sense of systemic inefficacy is heightened by crisis (war, depression, etc.) and by a failure on the part of the organization and its leaders to deal adequately with the crisis. Organizations may fail in this regard because they have over time become sclerotic or because their form and goals are no longer adequate to deal with new problems. In the nineteenth century, for example, when the Europeans assaulted many traditional societies, the military and administrative organizations of these societies collapsed, not simply from outside pressure or because they were moribund, which in some cases they were, but because they were perceived as inadequate for the new demands being placed upon them. In such cases, when responsibility and obligation are overridden by force of circumstance, self-interest, or even expediency to a degree that people begin to feel that the dominance system overall is characterized by a critical failure of obligation, or that dominance values that served the needs of people during an earlier period have failed or now illegitimately protect exploitative control, the result can be social collapse and revolution.

Having set forth briefly and abstractly the types, causes, and loci of perversion, it is appropriate now to enlarge upon this analysis with concrete examples. This will be done in the following three sections on elite perversion, organizational perversion, and systemic perversion.

Elite Perversion

Modern Organizations and Leadership

In modern societies the members of the dominant strata exercise their power through organizations. Dominance means control within an organization; it means being able to wield authority over the lives of those who work within it. It also means being able to use the organization to influence all those who in one way or another relate to it. Dominance in modern, complex organizations often acts as a brake against change at the same time that the organization's activities may disrupt established patterns and stimulate social transformation. Because the modern organization exists in the predatory, entrepreneurial, and guardian dominance systems, those who lead may have many common attributes (and feel a bond despite differences in dominance patterns—a Brezhnev with a Nixon, for instance). Of course, the values of a dominance system determine the form of the privileges that elites take for themselves. Yet the fact of aggrandizement itself is related to a similar level of moral competence that is shared by many leaders. It behooves one, then, to look more closely at elite behavior within modern organizations, for this is a major source of perversion in modern societies.

Certain kinds of work attract people with particular attitudes and skills.[3] The person who seeks leadership, for instance, must clearly have the ability to wield it in whatever form is required (e.g., ability in war or negotiations). Appropriate opportunities must also exist. Beyond these minimal conditions an aspiring leader—normally—must also wish to lead, to take responsibility and direct others. The leader must also have personality characteristics that mesh with the nature of the organization he or she heads (high tolerance for ambiguity, ruthlessness, etc.).

For reasons that are as yet imperfectly understood, some leaders may not develop the ability to express empathy or altruistic awareness or to accept responsibility for their actions. In the most extreme form these are psychopathic personalities, people who murder or commit other antisocial actions that are dissimilar to their behavior at other times. The periodic expression of psychopathology, which finds special opportunities in predatory societies, appears to vent powerful but repressed inner needs and demands. History, from Caligula to Ivan the Terrible to Idi Amin and Pol Pot, is replete with stories of this type of leader. Because of the fundamental absence of empathy toward victims this type of leader is often especially horrifying. More common than murderous or sadistic psychopaths, however, are elites who grow up in settings that reinforce ethnocentricism, guilt, and shame, and an inability to accept personal responsibility for their actions. In these cases, leaders behave according to widely accepted social customs that habitually oblige self-interested and even cruel behavior even when the leader has no special predisposition to behave in this way.[4]

A great part of the answer as to why dominance may become an end in itself (though frequently rationalized in terms of the public interest) has to do with the nature of leadership in modern organizational societies. Regardless of whether one speaks of modern large-scale military-bureaucratic, entrepreneurial- bureaucratic, or ideological-bureaucratic systems, each has a dominance system that is centered around an inner elite that has authoritative power for recruitment and promotion, discipline, and establishing goals. If there is not an absolute disposition toward oligarchy—toward extending authority, once acquired—there is certainly a tendency toward elite domination and toward the development in subordinates of feelings of awe regarding those who are powerful. The unequal distribution of power is matched by an unequal distribution of opportunity and rewards, which markedly affects the free will and personal autonomy of followers.

Inequality in terms of status, income, and authority is attached to different positions in a hierarchy. Rewards tend to be steeply accented and to cluster near the top. The perquisites themselves are part of the way in which the organization defines the authority that goes with different positions. Usually there is considerable tension and competition regarding the manner by which rewards are distributed along with anxiety about the merits of particular instances of inequality. People worry about the promotions of others and are prone to wonder whether their own rewards are equal to others at the same level. The overt tension and hostility that might arise as a result of these anxieties is modified in two ways. In the first place, tension is reduced by deference and by striving for upward mobility. In the second place, inequality in the distribution of rewards is usually justified by lauding the benefits that are said to be created for the organization as a whole by its leaders; greater individual reward thus carries a hint of superiority in achieving the objectives that are shared by all members of the organization. Andrew Carnegie put it well in his self-serving defense of accumulation of wealth by the competitive individual: "Unequally or unjustly, perhaps, as these laws sometimes operate, and imperfect as they appear to the Idealist, they are, nevertheless, like the highest type of man, the best and most valuable of all that humanity has yet accomplished."[5]

The obligation to comply with the directives of leaders is backed within an organization by rules that inhibit protest and constrain disorderly conduct. Rules establish rational procedures for the attainment of objectives; they enhance the organization's survival ability and bolster the legitimacy of the organization's dominance system. Lenin had this in mind when formulating his notion of an ideological-bureaucratic party: "The party link must be founded on formal, 'bureaucratically' (from the point of the disorganized intellectual) worded rules, strict observance of which alone can guarantee that we are kept from the willfulness and the caprices of the circle spirit."[6] (For Lenin there was clearly no alternative to organization. As early as 1904 he proclaimed, "in its struggle for power the proletariat has no other weapon but organization."[7])

Within a modern organization people are expected to obey the organization's rules, commend themselves to their superiors, be emotionally reliable, and above all be team players. If one is to hold securely a high position in the hierarchy it is important that everyone else in the organization, especially those with lower rank, not get out of line but obey the rules that pertain to their status. Any feelings of guilt about this can be stilled by reducing emotional and personal contact with those whose positions are lower. Empathy is dampened, and notions that others have a right to exercise individual responsibility are replaced by an emphasis on rules, conformity, and team play. Within this context opportunities arise for the blossoming of passions for power.

Many leaders, of course, do feel an obligation to their subordinates and strive to give them security, recognition, and evidence that their work has importance and significance. But the competitive drive for status reinforces intense personal attachment to superiors accompanied by detached feelings toward subordinates and compulsive concern about rank, symbols of prestige, and privileges. The quest for authority is often scarcely veiled. In a less refined manner Donald Frey, chief executive of Bell and Howell, put it this way: "In the crudest sense you could say it's a need for power."[8] Pragmatically, loyalty and conformity are exchanged by the upwardly mobile for privilege. Perhaps no one exemplified these traits better than the master opportunist Albert Speer, who as Hitler's minister for economic mobilization obtained rewards and position while harnessing technology to the criminal ends of the Nazi state.[9]

All too often in the modern world, personal judgment is suspended in favor of allegiance to the organization. Unfortunately, the dampening of moral competence that is thereby brought about is especially pronounced for those who seek advancement and the benefits that go with status. The opportunity to obtain those rewards that are sanctioned within a particular dominance system is most available to those who are able to manipulate organizational contexts for their own advantage. The stress on allegiance reduces the threat of having to share privileges with subordinates; it also silences any undue concern for outsiders that might dilute the organization's strength and efficiency. Modern organizations provide opportunities for self-serving for those who lead them. They ruthlessly condemn these patterns for subordinates.

Dominance and Privilege

But why shouldn't the leaders of organizations have privilege and reward? Where the values that gird hierarchy are widely shared, dominance qualities appear indispensable for the attainment of community goals. Indeed, in such circumstances, both dominance and submission appear legitimate.[10] The inequality that exists is justified by the presumed special and scarce characteristics the privileged are said to possess, for it is not the actual person who occupies a dominant or submissive position in an organization that is important but the values that legitimize these positions.[11] When defense of the community is of primary importance, for example, and military figures are given prestige and status to protect the common interest, then dominance by military leaders appears natural and justified and, indeed, quite worthy. Such also holds true when societies value the accumulation of resources or when the articulation of new values that are appropriate for new conditions seem particularly important. In these circumstances those who manipulate ideas or accumulate wealth may seem especially valuable and justly deserving of extra rewards in prestige and material benefits while those who honor different goals seem "foreign" and unworthy. There is, of course, no one kind of society nor any exact duplication from one to another of justifications for dominance and submission. What is similar is that status differences are treated as if they were due to different qualities of individuals.

Although some people who are ill qualified may become dominant, the stratum as a whole, and its justification for being, depends upon a large number of its members behaving according to values that are widely shared and strongly held. Dominance is then legitimate for all levels of society. In the learning of children there is then a built-in process whereby status is justified. Those who come to occupy high positions do so in terms of these justifications; those who do not achieve dominance accept their reduced station in life in terms of the very values that justify prominence for others. Within organizations the lowly accept subordination, lack of control, and monotonous and arduous (albeit socially necessary) toil as legitimate. The organizational ranks that grant awards to some at the same time mark the subordination (and sometimes the deliberate punishment) of others.[12] This is a phenomenon common in all societies although sometimes pregnant with the possibility of dissolution, as in the modern period.

Learning to be dominant means at least tacit acceptance of an unequal division of resources. As such, seeking to be dominant always involves the assertion of egoistic or particular group needs. This assertion is frequently accompanied, however, by a claim that those who are dominant legitimately have more worth than others and should, as a consequence, justly be accorded greater respect and privilege.

The fortunate (often unconscious of the dominance system that supports and protects them) are seldom satisfied with that fact alone. Just as distress is a proof of demerit, they wish to be assured that their good fortune is deserved and legitimate. Status measured by high income or by the right to make ideological pronouncements prompts comparisons of deservedness and the likelihood that scorn and aspersions of irresponsibility and the like will be heaped on those who might question the legitimacy of status differences. In this regard organizations play a critical role with their institutionalized mechanisms for reward and punishment. Managers feed upon the notion, rarely contradicted by close subordinates, that their power and position are the consequence of fine personal qualities (being smart, practical, sound, etc.), and that by leading the organization to fulfill its functions they have met their moral responsibilities within society.[13]

In its perverse form these attitudes allow leaders to persuade themselves that greed is enterprise, avarice economy, and bigotry truth. They allow wisdom to be scorned as antisocial and questioning to be stigmatized as disloyalty. In the United States John Z. De Lorean, himself tarred with suspicion, summed up the perverse consequences of this phenomenon as follows:

> It seemed to me, and still does, that the system of American business often produces wrong, immoral and irresponsible decisions, even though the personal morality of the people running the businesses is often above reproach. The system has a different morality as a group than the people do as individuals, which permits it to willfully produce ineffective or dangerous products, deal dictatorially and often unfairly with suppliers, pay bribes for business, abrogate the rights of employees by demanding blind loyalty to management or tamper with the democratic process of government through illegal political contributions.[14]

Aggrandizement justified by claims of superior social worth is hardly a modern phenomenon. While individual advantage was often limited in primitive and traditional societies by community sanctions, patrons claiming greater virtue (in terms of blood, education, etc.) undermined horizontal group organization by their power over coercion and taxation and their monopolization of positions that were vitally important to their clients.[15] The inequalities that existed were sizeable. In China at the end of the Qing dynasty, 10 percent of the rural population owned 53 percent of the cultivated soil; on average, gentry property was 128 times larger than a peasant plot.[16] In eighteenth-century France the nobles were certain that they contributed benefits to society that merited special immunity from taxes for themselves. Their attitude about their own worth and that of their subordinates was nicely summed up in letters written in the seventeenth century by Madame de Sevigne. On one occasion she went with friends to see a hanging; afterward she recorded that it was striking to see the condemned man trembling during the preliminaries of the execution, when he was only a common peasant. He groaned and wailed incessantly, causing some amusement among the ladies and gentlemen who had come to see the spectacle. Yet, as she said in another letter, the humbling of inferiors is necessary to the maintenance of social order.[17] For the aristocracy of a bygone day, peasants were low-ranking members of a predatory agricultural system whose exploitation was an accepted part of life, at least until the French Revolution.

Elite Perversion in Entrepreneurial Societies

In modern entrepreneurial societies one form of enrichment occurs as a consequence of pressure on government by trade and professional associations for special privileges.[18] Tax allowances, deferrals, write-offs for certain kinds of activities, exemptions that function as hidden subsidies, and protective legislation are all in this category. Together they amount to a diversion of resources, potentially available for community purposes, into the hands of elites. The claims that are made are not coordinated by the competitive mechanism of the market but rather are justified by special needs and worth. Success in competition, which is the general justification for privilege in entrepreneurial societies, is ignored or is cited only in the sense that special incentives are needed. The consequence is that the obligation to provide others with a fair share is progressively unheeded by elites relative to gains for themselves. (This is most clear when top executives claim high salaries while holding others to minimum increases, and sometimes to none at all.) Moreover, wealth, once acquired, is seen as inviolate, the reward for superior worth that is its own justification. It becomes a property that is passed by inheritance to children, who, by its mere possession, assume the same sacred mantle of worth.

In gross terms the distribution of income in the United States is clearly better than in most developing countries.[19] A close look, however, reveals that 0.1 percent of the population have an average individual net worth of $2,446,000, or about one hundred times more than the ordinary citizen. Another way of looking at it is to say that a third of all the financial assets in the country are owned by 4 percent of the adult population.[20] But is this pattern of distribution especially noteworthy or a cause for finger pointing? Are the values that support this pattern in need of change? After all, national myths notwithstanding, it is not the case that Americans at any level are particularly generous so why should elites not have a great deal more than common citizens? Welfare, for instance, is largely a government activity funded by taxes. Voluntary interfamily transfers altogether are only a tiny fraction of 1 percent of GNP, much less than the more than 1 percent of GNP that funded transfers to the poor at the end of the Middle Ages.[21]

Perversion was defined as a discrepancy between the actual distribution of rights and obligations in a dominance system and what people believe that distribution should be. It is interesting, therefore, that Americans do not hold values that are accepting of avarice and inequality. As Max Weber noted, capitalism is identical with self-conscious discipline and not with greed for gain.[22] Survey data show Americans to have a degree of hostility to money making and profits. They are suspicious of private concentrations of power in business and labor, believing both to be antithetical to the public interest. Businessmen are seen as driven by self-interest, people who put profit ahead of morality and who promote progressive activities only when it coincides with business self-interest.[23] According to a Gallup Organization poll, a large number of Americans have a very cynical view of the ethics of the nation's leaders in the professions and in business: 74 percent think that at least half of all business people pad expense accounts, 28 percent think that at least some of the business people in their own communities bribe or give favors to the police, and 64 percent think that at least half of all big company executives cheat on their taxes. Executives, while not nearly as negative about themselves as the general public, report considerable exposure to unethical pressures and temptations. These come, according to the responses, from various sources—40 percent mention superiors, 18 percent say suppliers, and 7 percent mention public officials. Some 47 percent of executives say they have also dismissed at least one subordinate for unethical behavior.[24]

Is there any substance to the public's inchoate sense of perversion? If one takes the attitudes noted in the survey data as a correct negative reflection of what the public believes the rights and obligations of dominant individuals should be, then the answer is yes. In fact, elite shibboleths about big responsibilities and service to the organization (to say nothing of the general welfare) are hollow in terms of the rewards and privileges that the dominant in entrepreneurial societies aggrandize to themselves. Wage stability, discipline, and living by the rules are clearly things that only subordinates are expected to honor. Incentives are needed for the man on top. In 1976, for example, Reginald Jones, chairman of General Electric, received a modest 24 percent increase of $120,000, bringing his pay to $620,000 per year. The chairman of General Motors, however, received a bonus that was larger than Jones's total remuneration.[25] Somewhat later, after Ford and General Motors had won four billion dollars in wage concessions from their workers (citing, as the reason, weak car sales), laid off thousands of employees, and won from the government protection from Japanese competition that cost consumers millions of dollars, top auto executives received bonuses of more than fifty million dollars from their boards of directors. Betsy Caldwell, the wife of Ford chairman Philip Caldwell, was asked whether he deserved a bonus of seven million dollars. She responded, "How can I answer that without sounding like Marie Antoinette?"[26]

These are not isolated cases. In 1977 only 5 executives in the United States earned more than one million dollars, but by 1983, 38 exceeded that amount and 18 made over two million dollars. By 1986, 220 of 634 executives surveyed made one million dollars or more in total compensation.[27] In 1983 the median salary (not including stock options) of the chief executives of the 100 largest industrial corporations was $655,000;[28] by 1986, according to one survey, the average chief executive's salary and bonus had jumped to nearly $830,000.[29] Between 1971 and 1981 the total compensation for senior executives in America's largest businesses rose 10 percent in real dollars while the economy as a whole was sluggish at best, and shareholders gains declined by 2 percent. In fact, in 1981, executive salaries had their largest increase in seventeen years, about 16 percent.[30] In 1986, however, the total pay of chief executive officers (including long-term incentive compensation) increased 29 percent, way ahead of that year's inflation rate of 2 percent and considerably higher than the 16 percent pay increase for labor leaders.[31] Japanese competitors, it might be pointed out, routinely pay their executives a fifth or less of what comparable American firms pay theirs.

How do the dominant in American society obtain these rewards? Certainly not from shareholders, who do not generally have the right to approve personnel decisions. Technically it is boards of directors who must give approval for increases in compensation. In fact, confusing management with entrepreneurship and administration with ownership, boards rarely challenge the recommendations that come from the very people who will receive the increases.[32] More subtle but not to be discounted is the status affinity (combined with the interlocking nature of many directorships) that directors feel for their counterparts in management.

Elite Perversion in Guardian Societies

Guardian societies have their own distinctive forms of elite perversion. One common example involving a violation of positive rights can be seen in the continuing denunciation in the Soviet Union of subelites who use their positions for private gain through the development of extralegal links with colluding compatriots. These individuals, who are said to have *blat*, are known to facilitate necessary economic transactions (and hence are often not prosecuted vigorously unless their behavior is extraordinarily flagrant) but act in a manner that is not condoned by formal ideological prescriptions.

As in entrepreneurial societies, however, the most serious elite perversions are by those who progressively emphasize the form of right that is the basis for domination. Concomitantly, they deemphasize the right that is less honored. In guardian societies, elite perversion of this type has meant an overemphasis on the correctness of positive rights and a deemphasis of obligations not to interfere unduly in the lives of others. The most blatant examples of this form of perversion can be noted at the very top of the social and political pyramid. Excoriated by the term "cult of personality," leaders like Stalin and Mao have been roundly condemned by their fellow citizens for so believing in their own ideological infallibility that they initiated policies with disastrous consequences. Given the relative lack of negative rights in guardian regimes, condemnation of elites by ordinary people is often private. When it suits the leadership, however, the errors of selected leaders can become public issues, as in Khrushchev's famous denunciation of Stalin's crimes.

Overemphasizing positive rights and deemphasizing negative rights was the basis of the condemnation of the Gang of Four in China. They have been roundly attacked (and sentenced) for having mobilized Red Guards to suppress and abuse those labeled as ideologically deviant. A stated goal of the Gang was to block the continuation of ideologically revisionist tendencies associated with "bourgeois rights," especially the right of unequal pay for unequal work. In the process of imposing restrictions on bourgeois rights, tens of thousands of innocent people lost their lives.

A particularly pervasive manifestation of guardian elite perversion is "bureaucratism." A political bureaucracy, legitimizing its rule by an elaborate ideology, is prone to spawn members who come to see themselves as representative of the power and prestige of the entire structure. Charged by ordinary people with arrogance and haughtiness, with impersonality and self-importance, such bureaucrats are condemned as interfering, arbitrary, and despotic. This form of perversion has not gone unrecognized by top leaders. In a list that is anything but parsimonious, Deng Xiaoping has described bureaucratism as

> a major prevailing issue that tarnishes the political life of our Party and state. Its harmful manifestations consist mainly in standing high about the masses; abusing power; divorcing oneself from reality and the masses; putting up a facade; indulging in empty talk; sticking to a rigid way of thinking; following conventions; overstaffing administrative organs; being dilatory, inefficient and irresponsible; failing to keep one's word; passing documents round without solving problems; shifting responsibility on to others; and even assuming grand airs as bureaucrats, reprimanding others all too often, attacking others in revenge, suppressing democracy, deceiving one's superiors and subordinates, being arbitrary and despotic, practicing favouritism, offering bribes, participating in corrupt practices in violation of the law, and so on.[33]

Even if this list were only partially correct, it nevertheless represents a comprehensive indictment of ideological-bureaucratic elite perversion.

Organizational Deviance

Why do some organizations engage in actions that violate rights? What factors cause individuals within organizations to behave in a manner that brings opprobrium to the organization as a whole? The answer to these questions requires a close look at group life in general and organizational influences specifically. Reference to situational variables is also necessary.

Loyalty and Conformity in Organizations

Pressure toward conformity, toward a moral stance that equates rule observance and living up to the expectations of superiors as the criteria of worth, is, as was pointed out in chapter 2, a pronounced feature of modern organizational life. Although not everybody is a conformist, conformity itself is a strain that has been persistently found in modern social life generally. It is reflected, for instance, in findings that reveal that nearly one-half of the respondents of a survey of American workers believed people should not be allowed to speak in public against democratic forms of government, and nearly 70 percent believed that people should not be allowed to speak in public against religion.[34]

Within organizations workers have been found to distort facts in order to protect a relationship with a superior.[35] The best explanation for such behavior is fear of consequences, of the penalties that might follow if the true facts were known. Losing one's job or demotion are penalties that repress a person's ability to speak up critically or, in fact, easily to leave a situation.[36] For the upwardly mobile, desires for higher status within the organization may also reinforce conformity to normative patterns and loyalty to superiors as the appropriate strategies for success.[37] In some cases, apathy, widely found by sociologists in working-class culture, may also strengthen these traits.[38] In addition, interorganizational competition places a premium on intragroup cooperation involving loyalty and conformity. To the extent that these behaviors further the interests of the organization vis-à-vis others—and thus stimulate greater interorganizational competition—there is likely to be even more (and certainly not less) emphasis on allegiant, cooperative, and conformist behavior.[39]

When conformity and loyalty become overriding, a situation may develop where the internal demands of the organization supersede the interests and needs of outsiders. In extreme cases these others may be reduced to a paranthropoid identity where, stripped of their humanity, they are no longer within the sphere of moral concern of organization members.[40]

In the last three decades a number of studies have shown the degree to which behavior can be modified when individuals respond uncritically to pressures for loyalty and conformity. In the 1950s, for example, Solomon Asch studied the effects of conformity. He reported that when a person was confronted by another individual who gave a report that conflicted with what the person actually saw, fully one-third of such people shifted their own statements to conform with what the other individual reported seeing and, in so doing, violated principles of honest and accurate reporting. When questioned these people said that they knew that what they were saying was untrue but felt that they could not go against social pressures.

An even more dramatic example of the way that situations influence behavior was revealed in an experiment that took place at Stanford University. There Philip Zimbardo and his assistants selected twenty-two college students and placed them in a simulated prison environment where they were randomly assigned the role of either guard or prisoner. The participants were placed in the basement of the psychology building for what was planned to be a two-week period. The experiment included providing appropriate uniforms for the prisoners and the guards, rules, the manipulation of privacy, depersonalization, and so forth. At the end of only six days, however, the experiment had to be terminated. The two groups of students had developed behavior patterns of a marked form depending upon which role they had been assigned. The so-called guards became highly aggressive and sadistic while the so-called inmates were excessively submissive and passive. Zimbardo concluded that within certain institutional settings behavior patterns such as passivity or sadism can be elicited with relative ease. The most important set of situational characteristics for eliciting such behavior is the presence of an authority figure responsible for consequences, the existence of dominant and nondominant roles, binding rules regarding proper behavior, and the remoteness of victims.

Of all the experiments involving modification of behavior, however, none was as disturbing as the famous experiment in obedience by Stanley Milgram. Milgram devised a laboratory situation where the subjects were commanded by an authority figure (a scientist) to inflict electric shocks on another person who was presumably learning random word pairs but who was actually a collaborator in the experiment. The object was to see whether people would, in fact, inflict high-voltage, painful electric shocks on another person despite moral prescriptions against needlessly hurting other human beings. When Milgram described the experiment to Yale undergraduates and to other professionals, they all agreed that giving painful electric shocks to another person was immoral even if commanded by a reputable scientist. Moreover, they predicted that only 2 percent or less of the general population would obey such a command. The now famous, chilling results of this experiment were that more than 60 percent of the subjects obediently administered high-voltage shocks despite the fact that they could see that their "victim" was in considerable pain. Although those in the experiment found obeying the scientist's orders personally distasteful, the situational context and the prestige of scientific ideology were such that moral considerations were put to one side with relative ease.[41] Interestingly, Kohlberg reported that in this experiment 75 percent of those individuals who were at the highest moral stage (according to his schema) disobeyed the orders to continue shocking the victim while subjects who were at lower stages showed a markedly different pattern: only 13 percent of these individuals disobeyed.[42]

A basic conclusion to be drawn from these experiments is that discipline, loyalty, duty, and conformity are among the strongest predispositions in behavior (even taking due account of the fact that the participants were in a tightly controlled and structured laboratory setting with restricted access to information concerning the total context of their behavior and the motives and truthfulness of the experimentors). The need to be responsive to a legitimate authority and to the perceived requirements of one's role in a given situation are experienced as sufficiently powerful imperatives that under structured conditions other moral principles may be accorded lower value. Moreover, in situations where there is a conflict with superiors, many individuals will suspend their judgment and rely instead on the dictates of authority. In short, it seems reasonable to believe that within structured contexts such as exist in organizations, situational influences may modify ideals concerning behavior in ways that actually strengthen the status of authority and reaffirm dominance values. Deference then becomes an expected and ingrained habit, reducing the real possibilities for acceptance or refusal of organizational rules and directives that subordinates might otherwise have.

Organizations and the Suspension of Individual Judgment

People at a conventional level of moral competence find conformity to rules and the expectations of others compatible with their beliefs about what a moral individual should do. For these people and for those at the preconventional level of moral competence, dominance has a compelling quality especially when the values that support it are believed to be true (as was clearly the case in Milgram's experiment where the aura of science played a crucial role). In addition, dominance positions are often filled by intensely motivated people, some of whom seek power within an organization as a means for eliminating low self-estimates through the control and manipulation of others. Their intense motivation is often sensed by their followers and awes them, reinforcing tendencies toward conformity and uncritical loyalty. All of these influences stimulate a division of the world into "we" and "them" and a lessening of a sense of obligation for outsiders. In some circumstances, when these patterns increase in salience, an organization can appear to "regress" in its treatment of others.

Conformity and loyalty can lead to a suspension of individual judgment. At the B.F. Goodrich Company there was an instance of falsification of data on tests for brakes that were designed and produced by the company for a military contract. One of the engineers rationalized the falsifications by saying, "After all . . . we're just drawing some curves, and what happens to them after they leave here, well, we're not responsible for that." The problem of falsification, however, was taken to the section senior executive for his advice. This individual declined to raise the matter with his superiors, saying, "Because it's none of my business, and it's none of yours. I learned a long time ago not to worry about things over which I had no control. I have no control over this." When pressed he went on, somewhat exasperated, "Look, I just told you I have no control over this thing. Why should my conscience bother me?"[43] Jeb Magruder said it best when discussing Watergate: "It is not enough to blame the atmosphere [Nixon] created. Instead, . . . we ignored our better judgment out of a combination of ambition, loyalty, and partisan passion. We could have objected to what was happening or resigned in protest. Instead, we convinced ourselves that wrong was right, and plunged ahead."[44]

Blind obedience and loyalty combined with fear were marked characteristics of Nazi death camp commandants. Colonel Hoess, who had been in charge of Auschwitz, was asked whether he had ever considered whether the Jews who were murdered were guilty or had in any way deserved their fate. Patiently Hoess explained that such a question was unrealistic:

> Don't you see, we SS men were not supposed to think about such things; it never even occurred to us. . . . We were all so trained to obey orders without even thinking that the thought of disobeying an order would simply never have occurred to anybody and somebody else would have done just as well if I hadn't. . . . Himmler was so strict about little things, and executed SS men for such small offenses, that we naturally took it for granted that he was acting according to a strict code of honor.[45]

When Lieutenant William Calley was asked at his trial why he had shot a group of civilians he invoked the fear of punitive authority: "Because that's what I was instructed to do, Sir, and I had delayed long enough. I was trying to get out of there before I got criticized again."[46]

Organizations and Moral Scale

Not all perverse organizational behavior, however, is the consequence of fear of superiors or blind conformity. Organizational actions that harm outsiders and are perceived as perverse are often not seen in that light by their perpetrators. The problem here is one of moral scale. This concept refers to the inclusiveness of the reference groups that people identify with and develop loyalties toward. As noted in Chapter 1, an enlargement of group concern is a feature of the moral development process. It proceeds from a perception of the self as the rightful center of group activity, to knowing and maintaining the social order for its own sake, to a belief that mankind as a whole is the legitimate focus for the realization of principles of justice. Without the broadest possible scale, moral competence is reduced by the restrictions on its applicability.

The groups that individuals most closely identify with and the degree of group inclusiveness are highly significant factors for truly moral behavior. It makes a profound difference if the reference group for moral concern is the family, the clan, a higher-level organization (commercial, military, religious, etc.), the state, or all mankind. Obviously, within societies the importance of these groups may shift historically just as for individuals their importance may change over a lifespan. The significance of the family in the early periods of life may be congruent with a societal emphasis on the importance of families. On the other hand, individuals may learn to shift the primary focus of their loyalty to organizations or to the state. This is not an easy or short process. Although we can acknowledge that having a concern for a group is an inherent human capability, we can surely also recognize the fragility and difficulty of reorienting group concerns from primary to more inclusive levels. For many people the highest possible levels of group identification are never achieved, with the consequence that the moral concerns of these people are focused on insiders while obligations to outsiders are reduced.

When the distinction between insiders and outsiders is institutionalized, then what is done for the organization is right while criticism from without is viewed as ill informed at best and usually motivated by hostility; criticism from within is viewed as virtual treason. As the luckless Jeb Magruder, who was convicted of crimes related to Watergate, said of his days on the White House staff, "I was given the impression that no one was just an adversary. There were only 'enemies' who were to be destroyed just as mercilessly as if we were meeting them on a battlefield."[47] In John Z. De Lorean's days in top positions at General Motors he observed how corporate management tended to view their own actions as right while the outside world was wrong. "It is always 'they' versus 'us,'" he said. "The press is viewed in a Nixonian sense as constantly carrying out a vendetta against the corporation."[48]

Within organizations there is a group definition of what is right, established often enough by leaders who are intensely ambitious and organization-oriented. At times these definitions may violate the standards of behavior of the larger society. At General Motors, for instance, it was known openly that a team spirit and personal loyalty to one's superior and to GM were all-important for promotion. In the Ralph Nader controversy about the safety of the Corvair, dissenters were told to "Get on the team, or you can find someplace else to work."[49] The president of Westinghouse adjured his employees to adhere to the antitrust laws not because violating these laws is a crime or against the interests of the public, but because "any such action is—and will be considered to be—a deliberate act of disloyalty to Westinghouse."[50]

Loyalty to an organization and to its leaders is often combined with an overriding sense of the moral correctness of allegiance and team spirit. Interviews of executives and their wives document their intense fear of being thought different. For these people constructive friendships mean relationships that can help one's career. There is, of course, nothing new in this, as Thorstein Veblen pointed out years ago when he showed that such attitudes have come to permeate all aspects of modern social life.[51] Jeb Magruder, again, noted clearly the intense allegiance that he felt in his White House days: "One of the most extraordinary things about Richard Nixon was his ability to arouse intense feelings of loyalty and devotion in the men and women around him." He spoke of his intense feelings of allegiance: "I had worked for this man for a long time, even before he was in office. I admired and respected him almost to the point of reverence, and believed in the goals he had set for himself, his staff and the country."[52] Magruder's assistant, Herbert Porter, explained to Senator Howard Baker why he had told a grand jury that money—which had actually gone to Gordon Liddy to finance the Watergate break-in—had been given for the more legitimate purpose of infiltrating student radical organizations. When Senator

Baker asked him why he had said nothing about his prior statements, which Porter clearly did not think were quite right, Porter responded, "In all honesty, probably because of the fear of group pressure that would ensue of not being a team player."[53]

An organizational definition of what is right can become deeply entrenched. At times these definitions coexist unconsciously with alternate views about social life generally. At other times an awareness of conflict exists but is brushed away by the overriding demands for allegiance. The myth of the human monster notwithstanding, immorality is usually a segment of behavior rather than a total personality; in other contexts the same individual may be highly respected, even a pillar of the community. What organizations do is to provide cues or directives for certain kinds of behavior, normative support for the actions in question, and apparent protection from retribution. For some individuals these are supports for kinds of behavior that in other contexts would be avoided. John De Lorean noted how the management of General Motors had given tacit approval for the underhanded means by which confidential Ford Motor Company cost reports had been obtained. These very same people, he observed, were outraged by the disclosures of Watergate regarding spying and intelligence gathering on ordinary citizens.[54]

Turning Outsiders into Victims

Above all, allegiance to the group means a denigration to some degree of outsiders, a reduction of their status to that of pawns or even, in the most extreme cases, of nonhumans. It has been found, for example that during combat group loyalty increases concomitant with a regression in moral concern for the enemy, allowing, in some cases, for participation in atrocities against them.[55] In Vietnam, where success was measured by the hardheaded rationality of body counts, Michael Bernhardt was the only member of Lieutenant Calley's company who refused to shoot civilians, firing but missing on purpose. Later he discussed the attitude of many American soldiers toward the Vietnamese.

> It has to do with the fact of communication . . . and these people did not appear to be communicating with the men in my company. Like I said, one of the aspects of humanity is the ability to communicate and since they lose this they sort of slide one level down on the human scale, not quite human and it makes them a whole lot easier to wipe out.[56]

Indifference combined with clear instrumentality have also been said to characterize the procedures of some American businesses; there is a willful production of dangerous products, the use of bribes, and illegal political contributions combined with demands for blind loyalty from employees and suppliers. When John Lientz, Union Camp Corporation manager, was asked about the possibility that heavy industrial underground water pumping needed for the production of paper bags in the Savannah, Georgia, area might one day dry up the area's water supplies he responded, "I don't know, I won't be here."[57]

The ultimate examples of how organizations deny rights to outsiders and reduce them to the status of subhumans are the Nazi death camps, the slave labor depots of the Gulag, and the systematic slaughter pens run by the Khmer Rouge in Kampuchea. It would be comforting to believe that the people who so cruelly dealt with the victims were uniformly pathologically aggressive and sadistic. Individuals with these traits did exist, of course, and certain organizations do attract people with particular emotional attitudes that are adaptative for an organization's psychostructure.[58] Brutalism and regression no doubt also played a part. But the fundamental traits of those who mistreated and killed were merely a heightened form of the characteristics that have already been discussed—allegiance, conformity, and an inability to see those who were designated as outsiders as having any integrity or worth.

One is rarely allowed intimate access to the minds of the members of such organizations, but some interviews have been conducted with former SS officers. Franz Suchomel, who worked at Treblinka where Franz Stangl was commandant from September 1942 to August 1943, described Stangl as a person who did not care about what was happening in terms of human life, but rather "what he really cared about was to have the place run like clockwork."[59] An inmate at Treblinka, Richard Glazer, was asked about the relations between the SS men who were members of the organization and their victims: "One must always measure whatever they did against the deep fundamental indifference they felt towards all of us. It was of course more than indifference but I call it that for want of a better word."[60] Stangl himself was interviewed years later during his trial in Germany. His wife had reported that he was a good and kind father who played with his children by the hour, teaching and working with them and making them toys. At one point in the interview he was asked, "There were so many children, did they ever make you think of your children, of how you would feel in the position of those parents?" It is reported that Stangl responded as follows:

> "No," he said slowly, "I can't say I ever thought that way." He paused. "You see," he then continued, still speaking with this extreme seriousness and obviously intent on finding a new truth within himself, "I rarely saw them as individuals. It was always a huge mass. I sometimes stood on the wall and saw them in the tube. But—how can I explain it—they were naked, packed together, running, being driven with whips like . . . " the sentence trailed off.[61]

Following the war Stangl escaped to Brazil. While living in South America he sometimes traveled. Of one such instance he reported as follows:

> "When I was on a trip once, years later in Brazil," he said, his face deeply concentrated, and obviously reliving the experience, "my train stopped next to a slaughterhouse. The cattle in the pens, hearing the noise of the train, trotted up to the fence and stared at the train. They were very close to my window, one crowding the other, looking at me through that fence. I thought then, 'Look at this; this reminds me of Poland'; that's just how the people looked, trustingly, just before they went into the tins . . . "
>
> "You said 'tins,'" I interrupted. "What do you mean?" But he went on without hearing, or answering me.
>
> " . . . I couldn't eat tinned meat after that. Those big eyes . . . which looked at me . . . not knowing that in no time at all they'd all be dead." He paused. His face was drawn. At this moment he looked old and worn and real.
>
> "So you didn't feel they were human beings?"
>
> "Cargo," he said tonelessly. "They were cargo." He raised and dropped his hand in a gesture of despair.[62]

Systemic Perversion

Systemic perversion encompasses elite and organizational perversion. It goes beyond these two, however, in that elite and organizational perversion can be singular occurrences whereas systemic perversion involves a pervasive loss of positive or negative rights and an erosion of obligations across a broad spectrum of social life.

The common theme in cases of systemic perversion is that those in authority generally have obtained an advantage that is not justified in terms of gains for the community as a whole. A schism then develops between the rights and obligations that people value in their private lives and those they see pertain in social life.

Monopolizing Privilege

Historically, strong groups or individuals have tended to use their positions to monopolize access to markets or power and to set the terms of exchange within society.[63] Over time these practices have often solidified into custom (as in the Indian caste system) or into regulations that are embedded in a matrix of law and administrative practice. These tendencies may be mitigated by countervailing customs and regulations that minimize distributional inequities. Because all societies have arenas of intense competition, however, no society is free of activities by subgroups to secure advantage for themselves. Such groups may be factions of nobility in traditional societies, combinations of bureaucrats and enterprise managers in guardian societies, or combinations of firms with economic interests in entrepreneurial social orders. Workers, too, may collude to maintain preferential wage scales and to prevent profitable transactions between employers and such groups as the unemployed, women, the less skilled, or immigrants. Sometimes troubled organizations, top heavy in leadership and slow to change, will seek protection (e.g., tariffs, fixed prices and wages) from government that will maintain a previously acquired advantage.

Modern organizations are characterized by their ability to engage in large, complex operations on a regular and continuing basis. They have highly efficient mechanisms for communication, control, planning, policy implementation, and legitimation.[64] Organizations attempt to insure their viability, their capability to function, by manipulating the outside environment to their own advantage, crucially by controlling their access to resources. Although this makes organizations in general appear to be striving for autonomy, this is, in fact, less the case for large organizations (those, for instance, that represent one-tenth of the income-earning capacity of a country), which are less likely than small groups to act solely in terms of narrow self-interest, narrowly defined. Being large, they have an incentive to weigh the effects of their policies on the whole society and to bargain with other organizations, sometimes in the interest of society as a whole.[65]

Unlike large organizations, smaller groups, factions, and cabals have little incentive to consider the needs of society but an intense interest in the way that rewards (material, political, prestige, etc.) are distributed. Mancur Olson, whose emphasis is on the way that income and wealth are distributed, calls these groups "distributional coalitions," organizations for collective action that represent only a narrow segment of society.[66] A good example are the guilds of medieval times. Reinforced by homogeneous social bonds, the guilds used monopoly and political power to enhance benefits for their own members, often at the expense of innovation and lower costs, which would have been beneficial for the rest of the population.[67]

Distributional coalitions do not favor the interests of the weak, poor, and untalented. Because they cannot obtain benefits for themselves unless outsiders are prevented from obtaining comparable advantage, they are always exclusive rather than inclusive, with barriers (social, educational, occupational, etc.) that control entry and with internal pressures to maintain homogeneity.[68] Over time, unless there is jurisdictional integration (a merging of autonomous economic units into large polities), free trade, and a competitive environment generally, distributional coalitions will increase in number, becoming a symptom as well as a cause of decline.[69] The dense network of self-seeking coalitions that eventually emerges is harmful, according to Olson, in that they make decisions slowly, impede the adoption of new technologies and the rational reallocation of resources, and increase the scale of bureaucracy and regulation generally.[70] Corroboration for these negative assessments comes partially from the reports of other academic economists who have served as presidential advisers in American government. They have noted repeatedly how optimal policies derived on grounds of technical efficiency are altered by the political machinations of small, well-organized, and powerful special interests.[71]

Avoiding Social Obligations

While distributional coalitions degrade economic efficiency, they are not individually an indication of systemic perversion. This occurs only when many groups, and especially those composed of people from the dominant stratum, act increasingly in their own self-interest. Such behavior, although often uncoordinated, can appear at times to be characteristic for large groupings in society. When one thinks of a social contract it is as a moral psychological bond that transcends particular differences and links all of the various members of a society. No such bond exists when resources and preferential treatment are possessed in accordance with the power of groups or strata. When rewards are distributed unequally merely because of criteria (race, sex, power, etc.) that have no intrinsic relationship to the resources themselves, then systemic perversion may arise. This happened frequently in traditional China where the wealthiest and most powerful stratum always had links with government, which could increase private income by as much as 50 percent.[72] In traditional Europe, where the poor and the wretched comprised (in the cities) about 13 percent of the population and where one-quarter of the population controlled at least three-quarters of the wealth,[73] the seigneurial class was often exempt in practice from direct taxation. Others also sought private advantage. The great merchant families from the sixteenth through the eighteenth centuries fostered policies of mercantilism through their governments that greatly favored their own interests at the expense of the rest of the nation. In class and caste societies, historically, different treatment always applied depending upon one's status. Each level represented a different degree of humanity, with the most human at the top. Harsher treatment was reserved for those lower in the social order; the more cruel punishments were usually only for those who were less human, slaves being generally the least human of all.[74]

As the historical record of Europe amply reveals, the impoverished condition of the lower classes was cause for frequent unrest and at times rebellion. The misery of the poor was only partly alleviated by ecclesiastical opposition to usury, speculation, and price gouging. Relief measures such as the Speenhamland system in England, which tied aid amounts to wage income, size of family, and the price of bread, also helped to alleviate the worst aspects of highly unequal distributions of reward. In some cases a margin of illegality was also tacitly permitted and was stoutly defended by popular disturbance if an attempt was made to enforce nominal rules or edicts.[75] None of these ways to alleviate misery, however, essentially disturbed the more favored in their quest for advantage.

Disparities among people in Europe at the start of the modern period were no doubt exacerbated by population growth, rural underemployment, and the steady flow of men, women, and children to the cities. (London, for instance, grew from 575,000 people in 1750 to 900,000 by 1801.[76]) Differences were marked in clothing, food consumption levels, health care, and by the growth of an explicit, coded, formal juridical framework that, while attempting to bring greater peace to society as a whole, dispensed essentially nonegalitarian punishments. The severity of the law increased; by the start of the nineteenth century there were 223 capital crimes in force in England.[77] Neither political nor economic policy favored the disadvantaged. Parliaments, for instance, traditionally largely represented landlords, and they did little to increase the security of tenure of the poorer agricultural classes.

For three centuries all the advantages in land sales were on the side of purchasers and against the tenants on the land who, to avoid eviction, had to provide written evidence of title (and if they refused and remained refractory were sent to prison). In Britain enclosures peaked during the first fifteen years of the nineteenth century, and the consequent political and social unrest would no doubt have been greater had there not been war with France and alternative ways to sustain livelihood by employment in the army and the city economy, and through relief. The last, however, was going out of style. The Poor Law Amendment of 1834 altered the previous system where the poor, for the sake of humanity, were to be helped. In England there was now to be no impediment to the accumulation of capital; no relief was to be given, for otherwise intense competition by the lower orders for low wages might break down.

The poor, moreover, were to be kept from any role in politics (hence the decisive rejection in 1842 of the Chartist petition, which had been signed by over three million persons). Democracy, it was thought, could be but a danger to property rights and the whole economic system as it then existed. This was the beginning of the notion of two nations in England, one comprising the impoverished and the other made up of those who controlled business, industry, and government for their own benefit.[78] Ultimately the state, under the prodding of reformers, did intervene to protect the downtrodden. Universal suffrage, trade union laws, antitrust regulation, and a host of other regulatory and welfare acts were passed to constrain the perversions of earlier distributional coalitions. Yet the ghost of older practices still haunts entrepreneurial societies.

Perversion and Dual Authority in Entrepreneurial Societies

The relationship of government to business highlights important ways in which dominance (through organizations) is exercised in entrepreneurial societies. It also makes meaningful why the distrust of universal suffrage by elites in the nineteenth century has been replaced by guarded affirmation. In entrepreneurial societies democracy exists in the public sector but not within organizations. As has been pointed out, democracy is also hedged by the influence that major organizations bring to bear on government for their own benefit. These actions minimize positive rights but are excused on the basis that unequal privilege is necessary to stimulate entrepreneurship, which, when successful in the competitive marketplace, provides rewards that eventually trickle down to benefit society as a whole.

The major reason why democratic procedures have a marginal causal effect on social and economic equality is that much economic activity takes place outside the scope of public control and comes to the attention of the public only when the private organizations that are engaged in economic activity seek public intervention for their own purposes.[79] Freedom from intervention by government (along with the right to make free contracts with other organizations and with labor) is the root value in an entrepreneurial society. This freedom brings with it, however, two different kinds of control, one by government officials (among the most important of whom are elected officials) and the other by business leaders. These elites collaborate in important ways on such matters as monetary or wage policies that affect society as a whole. The basis of their dominance and the constituency to whom they are responsible are different, however, for only the government officials are subject to democratic control while the business leaders are disciplined by the market and the general framework of laws.[80] Businessmen, as Tawney noted, don't have the power of the gallows, but they do have the power over whether bellies are full or empty, and this is power indeed.[81]

The degree to which business power can protect its own interests free of democratic control is impressive. In the United Kingdom, for example, despite a welfare ideology and an enormous increase in public expenditure, there has been no substantial redistribution of income in favor of the poor in the last three decades.[82] Nearly half of the American work force is essentially marginal, without access to the gains from productivity increases that accrue to the large corporations and organized labor. Tax practices, a subject of vigorous debate and efforts to reform, have highly favored powerful individuals and organizations. Most corporate tax, for instance, is absorbed by consumers. Taxes that are nominally progressive and equitable are altered by loopholes and exemptions, ideally to provide incentives for investment and growth in a competitive environment. In fact, owners and nonowners, rich and poor, have vastly different access to tax exemptions which in many cases have merely sheltered consumption income.[83] The consequence is that many costs, especially those in the public sector which are funded through taxation, are passed on to the less favored to bear.

In the United States business groups pay close attention to government, which in a general sense (but not across the board in every instance) has been supportive of their interests in terms of taxation policies and regulations. National government is big, and part of the reason for this is that in the last fifty years it has grown in order to underwrite the viability of large organizations. This support gives these organizations an advantage far beyond what might be expected in a neutral competitive environment. For instance, in May 1984 the Continental Illinois National Bank and Trust Company in Chicago, the nation's eighth largest, nearly failed. It did not because of an unprecedented decision by the government to guarantee—with billions of dollars—full repayment of Continental's creditors and depositors, thus stopping a run on deposits. This decision, of course, helped bolster the entire financial system and, by precedent, underwrote all depositors and creditors of every major American bank. Not incidentally it also thereby gave big banks a distinct advantage over smaller financial institutions.[84]

Does the public uniformly ascribe to the situation of dual authority between government and business? Surveys in America indicate no correlation between support for capitalism and support for democratic values. Americans make invidious statements about large organizations generally. But their very fears lend indirect support to the situation that prevails. Preferring smaller rather than larger institutions, the public fears state power—which in terms of organizational size is very great indeed—even more than business power. In addition, the public places labor unions at the bottom of the list on every poll of public esteem. In comparison to business leaders union heads are seen as corrupt, unethical, and autocratic and government officials as wasteful and inefficient.[85] By default, therefore, business comes out ahead.

Propensities for systemic perversion do not, of course, mean that systemwide perversion actually exists. Countervailing pressures from other organizations—the media, for example—may serve to minimize the growth and spread of perverse activities. Societal values may also limit the worst possibilities that inhere in coalitional self-seeking. Nevertheless, there remain in entrepreneurial societies, with their great emphasis on freedom from interference, powerful tendencies toward the enhancement of privilege and influence for some and their severe curtailment for others. That citizens may have volitions that serve not their own best interests but those of the elite does not make the condition less dire. As James Madison noted long ago in *Federalist* no. 10, "the most common and durable source" of disunity "has been the various and unequal distribution of property."[86]

A perception of inequity, of a maldistribution of resources, may not by itself lead to reform. It is when the control of resources carries with it the control of persons generally that people begin to believe that some in society have claimed a power that violates their obligations. When rulership in an organization becomes rule in society, and both, ultimately, become mutually reinforcing to the detriment of others, then people perceive perversion. This, I think, is what Robert Dahl had at least partly in mind when he stated that organizations have an impulse toward independence alloyed with an impulse toward oligarchy. He noted that this tendency is desirable in a minor degree but beyond that creates harm by stabilizing injustice, deforming civic consciousness, distorting the public agenda, and alienating final control over that agenda.[87] Even before an extreme point is reached there may be a marked skewing of the distribution of rewards (including political and social rewards as well as material resources), a reduction in opportunities for elite status (including a shift, in some degree, from status based on performance to status based on inherited social qualities), and a heightened protection of the rights and welfare of a minority at the expense of the majority enforced by the minority. These impulses toward oligarchy, of course, occur in different forms and to different degrees depending on the nature of a dominance system and the degree of intentionality that informs them. Overall, however, they often involve a failure to control abusive power (i.e., a violation of the rules and norms regarding punishment) and demands that run counter to or exceed collective notions of positive and negative rights. When power is beyond the easy reach of the public then organizations and their leaders can truly appear to be ominously beyond control. A Union Camp executive vice-president, for example, was asked if there were any limitations on the depletion of ground water needed for processing purposes; he responded, "I had my lawyers in Virginia research that and they told us that we could suck the state of Virginia out through a hole in the ground, and there was nothing anyone could do about it."[88] Clearly, this is power beyond the easy reach of the public.

Systemic Perversion in Guardian Societies

No one should think that guardian societies are beyond systemic perversion. Due to the centralization of power within the party, however, its form is in sharp contrast to the perversion that is associated with the bifurcation of authority in entrepreneurial societies.

Although there have been policies in the Soviet Union, China, and the Eastern European countries that have fostered limited entrepreneurship and private ownership, ultimate control of resources and people is openly affirmed to be in the hands of the party. In theory, control of money by individuals, necessary for consumption purposes, cannot become a private resource that carries with it political power. This strand of thought has been institutionalized into reverse discriminatory wage policies where those whose families had power in traditional society, or who have been otherwise stigmatized as politically deviant, may work without accumulating seniority or be more harshly evaluated when it comes time for wage increases, even in comparison with those who have committed ordinary crimes.[89]

In maintaining monopoly control the party always provides loopholes for the exercise of its power. In China, for example, the stipulations in the new constitution regarding negative rights have been hedged as follows: "Of course, the rights enjoyed by the citizens of a state are first subject to its social system and then to its economic, cultural and other objective conditions. Therefore, in a developing socialist country like ours, full implementation of the citizens' rights will take time."[90]

In guardian societies the coalitions that skew the distribution of resources are not autonomous organizations but factions within organizations, especially the party.[91] Direct aggrandizement of material resources is not generally the primary aim, although the behavior of the ruling Ceausescu family in Rumania suggests that avarice plays a part. Rather, what is sought is political power, which provides access to resources, especially in the form of perquisites (limousines and chauffeurs, special stores, country homes, etc.). Couched in ideological terms, which are not always pure rhetoric, factional disputes over power can be ferocious, with the most harmful consequences for ordinary people as in the purge period in the 1930s in the Soviet Union or the Cultural Revolution in China in the 1960s.

To the average citizen, who is certainly painfully and impotently aware of the impact that factional disputes have on individual lives, it often seems as if party leaders and the bureaucracy that they direct are more than potentially malignant in their drive to secure power. One Eastern European theoretician, for instance, noted that in the "Stalinist" perversion of Marxist thought the goal was not the humanization of man and society but "the perpetuation of a full control over society's members by means of a powerful state and one-party rule."[92] Djilas too had something like this in mind when he inveighed against the "bureaucratic ruling class." Legitimizing their administration of collective ownership by an elaborate ideology, he claimed, was but a complicated facade for brutal and all-embracing control.[93] For the class of political bureaucrats spawned by Communist victory, the workers, said Djilas, remain a mere instrument by which further organizational power can be consolidated.[94]

When power is sought for its own sake the organizations of society can be used to perform tasks for which they were not nominally established. Prisons become places for both criminal internment and preventative detention, asylums the home of both the mentally ill and the politically deviant, and schools the environment for both learning and indoctrination. It is this type of broadly based disregard of negative rights by the deliberate manipulation of organizations that so raises the hackles of dissidents.

Systemic guardian perversion is often best seen through the eyes of those who oppose it. A particularly striking example surfaced in China in 1979–80. At the start of 1979, official support had been given to the right of people to put up critical wall posters, a practice that had carried over from the Cultural Revolution. As a *People's Daily* (*Renmin ribao*) editorial said, "Let the people say what they wish, the heavens will not fall."[95] On display in both Shanghai and Beijing were posters critical of the Chinese Communist Party. In April of that year, however, Wei Jingshen, the son of a party official and a disillusioned Cultural Revolution activist who had become an editor of the most extreme underground dissident publication, *Exploration* (*Tansuo*), was arrested along with a colleague. In March Wei had described in a wall poster the torture of political prisoners in the largely secret Qin Cheng Prison. Earlier, in December 1978, in another poster, he had advocated a fifth modernization—democracy—to complement the officially sponsored four modernizations (in agriculture, industry, science and technology, and defense). On March 25, 1979, Wei apparently went too far. He wrote in *Exploration*, "Does Deng Xiaoping want democracy? The answer is no."[96]

On trial later that year, Wei was charged with a number of crimes. The most dubious of these was the accusation of giving military information to foreigners. More substantial by far was the charge of writing "reactionary" articles advocating the overthrow of the dictatorship of the proletariat. In the People's High Court the prosecutor stated, "Democracy has a class character. In socialist China, there is extensive democracy . . . [but] . . . the handful of people who tried to sabotage the socialist revolution should be denied democracy." Wei, he said, described the dictatorship of the proletariat as "despotism" and attacked the leaders of the nation as "autocratic careerists." Such statements, the prosecutor said, "were not helping to perfect the social system and were not simply a case of raising criticism." Rather, Wei "wanted to overthrow China's socialist system."[97] It was reported that the judge echoed these sentiments, charging Wei with attacking the leadership of the Communist party, the socialist past, the dictatorship of the proletariat, and Marxism-Leninism-Mao Zedong Thought.[98] Wei was sentenced to fifteen years imprisonment.

In December the wall posters were removed from their downtown location in Beijing to a more secluded wall in a park three miles to the west. In doing this the government did not violate stipulations in the 1978 Constitution (Article 45) permitting expression. The reason for the shift, it was stated, was that "a few persons with ulterior motives had used the wall and the posters illegally to disrupt stability."[99] Henceforth, those wishing to put up posters would first be required to register their names, addresses, and places of employment. People were told that in the future it would be more appropriate to air their grievances through neighborhood committees and at places of employment. Then, early in 1980, Democracy Wall was banned altogether. Eight months later the limits of criticism were spelled out. Party members or citizens could criticize the specific work practices of an organization or one of the organization's leaders, but they were not to criticize the political system itself. Moreover, no institutional mechanisms were established to protect a person who might wish to voice disagreement.

Earlier, at the start of 1979, a *People's Daily* editorial had warned, "The people, under the influence of various kinds of nonproletarian ideology, are prone to anarchy and ultrademocracy once they are divorced from the leadership of the party."[100] Deng Xiaoping had also been worried. According to an associate Deng had stated, "The strength of these people should not be underestimated. . . . Their number is small but . . . they have organizations. Their organizations are secret . . . and in mutual liaison all over the country."[101] The dissidents, however, had an alternate explanation. As Lu Lin, a successor to Wei Jingshen as editor of *Exploration,* put it, "It looks like the bureaucrats are willing to sacrifice one billion people to keep themselves in power."[102]

5. Rights and Political Change

The study of political change has fascinated commentators from Plato and Confucius in the ancient world to modern scholars such as Marx and Max Weber. In the post-World War II era, and especially in the decade of the 1960s when radical protest movements arose worldwide in tandem with terrorism and urban rioting, there was a marked upsurge in the popularity of this subject.[1] As would be expected, criticisms of theories of change have kept pace, charging irreconcilability among theoretical formulations, subjectivity, ambiguity, and self-contradiction.[2] Yet recent scholarship has made significant advances. Descriptive theorists such as Sorokin and Brinton were followed by thinkers such as Davies, Gurr, Johnson, and Smelser, who emphasized structural-functional and frustration-aggression theories. More recent analysts like Eisenstadt and Skocpol have developed theories that stress interest-group conflicts which exceed the conflict-mediation capabilities of political institutions.[3]

Part of the difficulty with theories of political change is the propensity of many thinkers to focus attention on the most dramatic case, that of revolution. The problem here is that although all modern societies are experiencing change few, in fact, have revolutions. Revolutions are the extreme expression of change; they involve the rapid and violent disruption of existing institutions concomitant with the mobilization of new groups into politics and the creation of new political structures.[4] Even when revolutions take place there is a difference between the majority of these and the cataclysmic explosions of the French, Russian, and Chinese examples. Valuable though a focus on revolution is, dramatic resort to violence may obscure motivations that are common both to revolutionary situations and to more mundane, but far more common, occurrences of change. Violence, in fact, may be the response of only a certain type of actor; the seizure by this person of a central role in the drama of change may be possible only under special circumstances. In contrast, the expression of ideological heterodoxy, struggle over the control of political institutions, and opposition to government are characteristics of many types of political movements.[5] If one is to see political change in full perspective, therefore, one must isolate the elements that hold for all categories of change. One must understand the behavior of elites no less than that of those who are in opposition. One must know which general processes bear on the stability of authority structures and which processes lead to extreme instability. By understanding the relationship between them, one can see political disorganization as the reverse of the conditions that facilitate tranquility.[6]

Crane Brinton has noted that "Men may revolt partly or even mainly because they are hindered . . . but to the world—and, save for a very few hypocrites, also to themselves—they must appear *wronged.* Social change cannot do without the word, 'justice.'"[7] In fact, frustration over injustice and a sense that oneself and others have been slighted[8] are basic to theories of motivation regarding change. Sociobiological data suggest that among primates there may be an innate preference not to be subordinate.[9] Freud, from a very different perspective, earlier reached the same conclusion and noted its possible consequences. He said: "It is to be expected that . . . underprivileged classes will envy the favoured ones their privileges and will do all they can to free themselves from their own surplus of privation. Where this is not possible, a permanent measure of discontent will persist within the culture concerned and this can lead to dangerous revolts."[10]

These feelings of discontent can be heightened by social strains. Inflation and depression can intensify feelings of privation and erode confidence; so also can population growth unmatched by economic expansion. Increasing bureaucratism to cope with strain may further aggravate the problem as people come to feel that their lives are increasingly hedged and thwarted by faceless authority. In Western Europe, for instance, where bureaucratic procedures and restrictions are prevalent and becoming more so, there is a related general drift toward alienation.[11] Without doubt, however, the worst of these feelings of estrangement are in those one-third of the world's countries reported by Amnesty International whose governments systematically torture their own citizens.

More common feelings of resentment about inequality, or lack of justice, derive from differential access to privileges, within organizations or as a consequence of a general dominance pattern. Social rewards, symbolic as well as material, are often associated with self-respect and esteem. Differences among individuals and strata in the rewards that are received are translated into different evaluations of social positions and become a component of a person's self-identity. On the one hand the norms that are associated with social differences promote stability and continuity through definitions of acceptable rewards for different roles; on the other hand, they also determine the power of unequal groups and, in a rough sense, how these groups feel about themselves.[12] Social rules become thought of as unjust when their exercise prevents individuals and groups from acquiring the rewards and self-esteem to which they feel entitled.

Regardless of what society one speaks of, and taking full account of the differences among them, not all tasks in any division of labor are equally attractive all of the time. People everywhere recognize this. In attempting to minimize subordination, therefore, they do not seek absolute equality among roles but rather, according to a relatively widely shared set of values, a proportionate and "just" relationship between the contributions that people make and the rewards that are received. If envy and jealousy are not to erupt, the benefits that elites obtain must not reduce the benefits to which subordinates feel entitled. Anger especially occurs when the values that undergird work and status are violated, when, for example, equal work is progressively unequally rewarded, or when elites are thought to be hoarding, speculating, or obtaining unwarranted rewards.[13]

When one is told that one is inferior, and is constantly reminded of the truth of it, it is difficult not to feel inferior.[14] These feelings, of course, may not prompt change if the polity is widely believed to be fixed and immutable. Under these circumstances the classic responses are withdrawal, nonparticipation, ritualistic behavior, or, less frequently, passive resistance. In many modern states, however, neither immutability nor passivity pertains. A striking characteristic of modern people is their belief that they have choices and can and should seek alternatives. This concept of obtainable remedy is what Hannah Arendt described as the most powerful and devastating emotion impelling proponents of change. As a consequence, when elite policies, especially those pursued by government, begin to diverge significantly from people's expectations, discontent and lack of trust rise markedly;[15] as one finds oneself increasingly in a situation of fundamental and threatening value conflict with dominance norms, the appeals of reformist or revolutionary groups take on significance. If, at that point, elites who possess the skills for peaceful politics are lacking or are rejected, then passive dissatisfaction can become active disaffection.[16]

People become angry when changing conditions violate their values or when their values change and are no longer suited to customary activities or circumstances. A demand for rights (i.e., for a different evaluation of obligations) is a response to an increasing awareness of perversion (objective or subjective) of the obligations owed by dominant groups. The search for justice in the face of perversion is fueled by moral outrage. Emler, Renwick, and Malone's study supports strongly the conclusion that active proponents of change do so with a vocabulary and values that are charged with the rhetoric of principled moral reasoning.[17]

Strain need not be synchronous in all areas of society; it can manifest itself with varying intensity in different spheres—the market, political structures, and so forth.[18] Tension, therefore, may remain isolated or can affect many areas of life. Change, when it occurs, may involve sudden, sometimes violent activity or be characterized by a long-term erosion of particular criteria for dominance—economic, political, social, sexual, racial, religious, generational, or other. Whether the focus is wide or narrow, the search for remedy is always centered to some degree on organizations as the units within the community that establish and maintain limits on the rewards that individuals and groups can obtain. As a consequence there is a propensity to perceive organizations—especially those governmental organizations at the apex of the dominance system—in moral terms and to say, as Apter does, that "no government is better than its moral standard."[19]

Reciprocating Change

Historically, demands for rights in predatory dominance systems usually met with no success. When substantial change did finally occur, beginning about five hundred years ago, the result was not moral dominance. Rather, elites in modern organizations have justified their status according to the values of entrepreneurial or guardian dominance with the consequence that there exists today sharp tension between these two systems and their legitimating values.

In entrepreneurial and guardian organizations rights tend to be most fully realized for elites while others suffer variable degrees of deprivation. The widely held aspiration in the modern world for equally shared rights is thwarted by the differential rewards and opportunities for participation that are available to people depending on a society's model of development. Low mobilization, relatively high individual autonomy, and increasing income inequality are associated with entrepreneurial development while high mobilization, low individual autonomy, and relative income equality are associated with guardian dominance.[20] The creation of a combinatory model that has an optimal trade-off of pluses and minuses has so far eluded realization. This, I believe, is largely because organizations, which are essential for development, have not functioned well without an ideology that provides enhanced rewards in income and power for elites concomitant with deprivation for followers.

For most nonelites physical security and well-being, adequate wages, housing, lower rents, and so forth are primary goals. Is the food that is available shared equitably? Are the benefits of industrialization channeled into the hands of only a few? Does government allow people the right to work where they choose, the right to strike and organize, or the right to keep the full rewards that come from what they do? Although these questions are particular and mundane, each can also be rephrased and asserted in terms of a general category of right. Demands for adequate housing and food, for instance, are claims that embody positive rights (i.e., fair shares) while the right to strike or to work where one chooses are claims in the area of negative rights (i.e., freedom from undue interference).

In broad-based political movements it is often difficult to separate cleanly demands for positive and negative rights. The difficulty arises because large-scale movements generally involve many groups, some of whom seek "freedom to" while others seek "freedom from." Indeed, even among individuals, one set of demands on authority may be for positive rights while another is for negative rights. A call, for instance, for both greater equality in income distribution and greater freedom of expression (including, at times, the relaxation of economic restrictions on some group or groups) has been characteristic of many Third World movements. Despite the complexity in particular instances, however, a longer view suggests that one type of demand predominates. In fact, given that organizational elites control societies in distinctive ways, any major challenge will embody demands for the type of right that is deemphasized within the framework of that dominance system.

The demand for positive rights is for a fair share of material resources, for access to the productive output of society, and for a say about what goes on. The demand for negative rights is for free choice, demanded in purely economic terms as in the right to labor where one wishes or, as intellectuals often think of negative rights, as protection for free expression and belief. In movements for change this right frequently has mundane aspects. In early periods of modernization, for instance, entrepreneurs often seek freedom from governmental restrictions on economic activity far in advance of demands for free speech for the general citizenry.

A claim stated as a positive right is justified by the manner in which elites exercise negative rights. It is manifested as accusations against excessive privilege, an unfair distribution of wealth and property, corrupt practices (often including claims of sexual laxity) that enrich a few, and discriminatory practices based on racism, sexism, religion, and so forth. These particular accusations can also be generalized to the dominance system as a whole. Unrestrained capital accumulation that results in inequalities in the overall distribution of rewards, sectoral imbalances, unemployment, and strains on local and regional economies that result in underdevelopment or differentials in the deployment of new technologies can be criticized in arguments against a prevailing ideology that stresses negative rights.[21] The demand for positive rights, therefore, for greater equity in distribution and participation, is asserted when the benefits of negative rights—especially the right to accumulate resources and to have a say over their distribution—seem to be prerogatives only of the elite.

Positive rights are sometimes asserted in terms of an ideology (e.g., Marxism) and at other times are less systematically articulated. In either case resistance against those who benefit from inequality has a moral flavor; opposition is rationalized in the public interest. The expression of concern over the way that social products are distributed and the uses to which these products are put is rarely phrased in a judiciously neutral manner but rather involves fierce and impassioned accusations (e.g., about integration, busing, civil liberties, jobs, pollution, the draft, or funding allocations). As the movement develops, opposition groups that espouse positive rights can fall under the sway of individuals who justify their leadership on the basis of their knowledge of the new morality. Such people come to form a core of ideological authority within the opposition. In some cases, such as Cuba under Castro or Vietnam under Ho Chi Minh, these people may become guardians and builders of a new moral order.

Power based upon ideological authority may include coercion or control of economic resources. The legitimation of dominance, however, is not in terms of these factors but rather in terms of moral criteria. Guardian authorities set forth guidelines that justify a new dominance system. In the turmoil that follows their coming to power, extra effort is expended to insure that people know the new values and behave accordingly. If strongly enforced, however, guardian control violates negative rights that permit an individual—within limits—to explore and establish a life plan determined by that person alone and not by authority.

In societies where elites use ideological authority to enforce positive rights, people who seek alternate values are stigmatized as deviants—antisocial elements who must be dealt with by a variety of means ranging from execution to imprisonment in forced labor camps to exile abroad or internally, to ostracism and the deprivation of normal citizenship rights. Ultimately, although the perception may take a long time to gain momentum, these punitive actions may be seen as a perversion of authority. The first sign is when dissident intellectuals begin to point out how the denial of negative rights deprives society of any mechanism for preventing excessive punishments and dictatorial power. Interestingly, the aggrandizement by authority of special benefits (bigger houses, more income, special stores) may come to be regarded as a violation of the positive rights of ordinary citizens and fuel feelings of alienation and demands for the negative right to speak out against these practices. Since "exit," to use Hirschman's term, plays a small role in guardian societies, "voice" becomes extremely important, not just for making complaints about quality and service in economic life, but as a factor that protects the integrity of citizens in social life generally.[22] When voice is denied tension mounts. Individual citizens seeking negative rights will exit if they can (e.g., from the Soviet Union, Cuba, Vietnam, East Germany); but even whole societies may, with no small amount of danger, exercise an exit option within the bloc (e.g., Yugoslavia and China, although not changing their dominance patterns) if their leaders feel that control from the center is too restrictive. De Tocqueville surely had some sense of this in mind when he presciently noted, "in order to combat the evils which equality may produce, there is only one effectual remedy: namely political freedom."[23]

I believe that there is a continuous alternating relationship between perversions of dominance and the long-term search for either positive or negative rights. When negative rights are excessively emphasized aggrandizement may occur in the form of seizure of economic or social advantage by dominant individuals. Ultimately, these seizures progressively violate the positive right of others to a fair share and fuel moral outrage and movements to establish a new system of greater equity. A puritanical enforcement of the new orthodoxy, however, motivates a demand for negative rights. Which rights are demanded depends on the dominance pattern of a society at a given time, its level of economic development, the groups that are involved, and the degree to which moral maturity infuses the dominance system. What remains constant is that the call for positive rights occurs when some individuals have abused negative rights in order to aggrandize rewards for themselves such that altruistic awareness and empathy in social life are eroded. The demand for negative rights takes place when power based on positive rights is abused—when little independent discussion of goals, values, and elite behavior is allowed so that individual responsibility is denied and empathy declines. The patterns inherent in systems that promote positive rights impel a search for negative rights while systems that grant negative rights have patterns that lead to a search for positive rights. When the goals of movements for change are institutionalized, the cycle begins again. Over time the names of the challengers and challenged change: round heads oppose cavaliers, bourgeois life styles supplant puritanism, communists oppose capitalist entrepreneurs, and dissident intellectuals and workers struggle against the dictates of central committees.

The most important tension in our era is between entrepreneurial dominance with its emphasis on negative rights and guardian dominance which stresses positive rights. The social movements of our time are an oscillating effort to obtain positive and negative rights; as long as the search for justice, for a moral life, is basic to modernity, these movements are endless. The critical factor is the universal belief of modern men that a moral society is possible. Since that belief became enshrined every political system has been subjected to pressure for change.

Reciprocating Change in Historical Perspective: Peasants and Puritans as Agents of Change

There is, prior to the active phase of any political movement, a perception of injustice. These perceptions may be scattered, poorly connected, or unfocused; but even when they are widely and intensely shared nothing may happen. Fear may constrain people, or thought control, however primitive in form, may be sufficient to identify and isolate those with deviant thoughts. Where fear is not too great, however, or where a failure to act may result in even worse conditions and where feelings of injustice are shared by many people, movements that seek change may begin. In traditional times these activities were almost always termed rebellions by those who were dominant. In fact, they were frequently little more than cries of rage and despair in the face of unbearable exactions, often without any concrete guide for further action. Although these movements were not always futile, success, when it occurred, usually never brought about a fundamental change in the prevailing predatory dominance pattern. As a consequence, there was always a strong probability that similar exactions would occur again. In Western Europe these rebellions frequently had a religious millinerian aspect, doomed in the face of martial power. Such outbursts intensified during periods of social and political disruption such as occurred in France and the lowlands during the Hundred Years War.

Peasants or small-town artisans whose way of life has been threatened, especially in terms of subsistence, may initially be hostile toward those who seek change. Much of this is related to the inward nature of peasant orientations. In traditional peasant societies there was often a high degree of give and take with great concern that no family fall below the subsistence level. Within peasant communities and the guilds of small town artisans efforts were made, especially among kinfolk, to protect the livelihood of others. People expected that if they offered help this year they would receive the same in the future if the wheel of fortune turned against them.[24]

New groups with new interests markedly threaten the patterns of reciprocity of traditional peasant and small-town artisan life. Whereas produce may formerly have been traded in barter-type arrangements or given on a face-to-face basis to a landlord (who exacted his share depending on the peasant's ability to give), new-style commercial arrangements introduce forms of market behavior involving cash transactions and impersonal contractual terms that must be met regardless of production levels.[25] Within the growing cities, guild life and handicraft production give way to wage relationships and factory discipline while in the countryside absentee landlords, who themselves deal with new urban-based commercial enterprises, facelessly take the place of the local "big man." In communist systems, the commune or collective farm destroys the old forms of peasant life, eroding village autonomy and changing the nature of the traditional relationship between work and reward. Modern communication facilities make it easier for new-style organizations to impinge upon the peasant. At the same time the civil service and police become increasingly effective as instruments to enforce compliance.

Peasants and artisans feel threatened by new values that treat them and their production as mere objects to be bought and sold. Among them the feeling grows that the social order has become perverted, for as objects they will be little cared for should their ability to obtain a livelihood be eroded. They fear that their opportunity for a share of society's rewards will decline or even be completely denied. As a consequence, the first reaction to threat by peasants, artisans, and also by segments of the traditional dominant class whose power is associated with these groups[26] is to maintain or bring back the patterns of traditional life.

Yet although the shift from older patterns may be deeply threatening to many peasant families, change for some represents an opportunity, and there are always those who are ready to seize it. Some families adjust to new forms of market relations and new patterns of interaction between landlords and peasants and use these to enhance their own well-being.[27] It is these families that become the new sources of credit in the countryside. They may adhere to many traditional customs in their own lives, but they also progressively introduce new economic relationships and often ruthlessly drive from the land those who cannot survive under the new conditions. As a result, it is frequently the middle-income peasants who are most affected, for the richer ones have the resources to absorb the shock while the poor peasants are either driven off the land into the cities or exist as before at a minimum and miserable level of subsistence.[28]

In the countryside those who are threatened and see change as a perversion do not suffer in silence. Their losses to a new way of life are denounced as immoral and as violations of values that stress accommodation, cooperation, family or village autonomy, and mutual aid and help among neighbors. The denunciations are usually accompanied by specific proposals designed to guarantee subsistence. Depending upon circumstances, peasants demand easier credit, lower taxes, less control from the outside, and often more land. To an outsider unfamiliar with the context of these demands, they may seem narrowly self-interested and even self-defeating. This, however, would be misleading. The cry for lower taxes and more readily available credit, for instance, is not so that the peasant may become rich and prosperous, although few peasants would deny the desirability of this condition over its opposite; rather, the effort is to secure the peasant's own welfare and, most especially, that of his family and kin. Indeed, it is the deeply felt threat to family that first elicits the cry of immoral abuse.

The search for a restoration of tradition in the countryside becomes muted only when the old forms of life have been eliminated or when new peasant and farmer organizations, linked effectively with central policy-making bodies, constructively use new organizational patterns for the peasant's own benefit in areas of credit, taxation, education, birth control, rural welfare, and health. Farmers' associations, the Grange, and agricultural-based political parties are all mechanisms whose use transforms those who live on the land from angry respondents to change to active advocates for rights within a new society.

In the twentieth century change in the countryside has assumed epic proportions, involving hundreds of millions of people. Yet until quite recently theories of change took scant notice of the peasantry. In the tradition of Marx, Max Weber, and others, peasants were acted upon rather than having any positive role in social transformation. Instead, the Protestant Reformation and the rise of an urban bourgeoisie and working class were seen as the most significant forces bringing about the great social, economic, and political revolutions that shook Western Europe, and later the world.

Peasant revolutions in the twentieth century have become significant because the peasantry has been mobilized and organized by segments of the urban elite in a countryside that has already been disrupted by change (e.g., loss of traditional elite control, war) and exposed, even if minimally, to change in education, communication, government, and commercial activities. Five hundred years ago these factors were relatively weak or nonexistent. Peasant responses to change, which did occur, were not integrated and organized systematically. Moreover, and more important, powerful segments of both the new and old elites had an interest in thwarting peasant demands. What is ironic is that in the initial phases of the Reformation, perhaps the most significant break-point in the rise of modern man, a major thrust was for protection of the less privileged in the form of positive rights. What did not exist was any unified sense of how to fulfill these demands politically in society as a whole.

Unrest in Europe became noteworthy about two centuries after transition to commercialization. Disturbances reflected the changes in obligations that arose with the growth of trade, urban centers, population, and the use of money. As towns and their leaders (urban nobility, merchants, and artisans) grew strong enough to demand some independence (i.e., negative rights) from a heretofore all-powerful rural aristocracy, the repercussions were felt throughout society.[29] The initial aspirations of many, however, were not for negative rights (freedom from authority being barely conceivable) but for a more equitable sharing of society's rewards and privileges.

Martin Luther, the avatar of the Reformation, approached life with the spirit of a mystic and the heart of a lusty peasant. Although he unleashed the idea of the supremacy of the individual conscience, he hated commerce and capitalism and sought instead a vanished age of peasant prosperity—and of strict peasant obedience to authority.[30] Even Calvin, who acknowledged the main forms and institutions of a commercialized society and who supplied a creed that allowed money-making groups the same respectability in their earnings as belonged to the laborer and rural landlord, saw the new church as a community whose members harmonized their own gifts with others for the good of all. The "restored society," according to Calvin, was to be bound together by economic interdependence and mutuality in which, within the church, there would be a just redistribution of goods. When it came to independence and voluntarism versus theocratic control for the "benefit" of all, Calvin weighed toward the latter.[31]

In England the Puritan leaders also stressed mutuality and were adamant against any purely democratic polity (i.e., allowance for individual volition) within the church. But in the late sixteenth and early seventeenth centuries there was a decline of direct government regulation in economic matters that ultimately affected ideas about governance generally. Puritan tradesmen opposed monopolies granted to needy courtiers and detested the interference of royal commissioners in their business activities. The Puritan money-lender opposed the interference of bishops—who carried on the tradition of the medieval church in proscribing certain economic practices—in temporal affairs. The Puritan country gentleman was angered by the actions of the depopulation commissions with respect to enclosures.[32] Sir Edward Coke, the famous attorney-general, had much support in his rulings that monopolies were opposed to the common good and common right and against "the freedom and liberty of the subject."[33] By degrees the question of who is to control economic life became one of what kind of control, with the answer increasingly emphasizing unhampered activity by individuals acting, it was presumed, with self-restraint guided by religious concern within a framework of reconstituted contract law. The calling of God could be expressed, it was thought, in economic terms. Some, however, began to suggest that if liberty in economic matters progressed, then liberty in the church should also; and, by extension, so also should liberty in political matters. So, at least, argued the Independents in the New Model Army.

Cromwell and other Puritan leaders wanted their followers to be pious and respectful of property, a theory which helped the more successful of these leaders in their land-grabbing activities. Respect for property was a common interest linking the gentry on both sides of the civil war. King James I, who lost his head in an act of regicide that was a precedent for others elsewhere in later times, had been deprived of natural allies among the rural gentry by their fear that a restoration of Catholicism would mean a return to the Church of monastic lands that had been previously seized and sold to them. Charles II, James's grandson, regained these allies after the revolution had spawned radicals who called private property into question. It was the desire to protect property, albeit an increasingly commercialized rather than "feudal" property, that was ultimately the basis for restoring the king, the House of Lords, and bishops in 1660.

Prior to the civil war there was a battle of ideas in which one major strand was the factually flawed (but nonetheless powerful) notion that the Norman Conquest had resulted in the theft of property that belonged to all the people and the suppression of ancient Anglo Saxon rights and institutions. This theory of the "Norman Yoke," which survived down to the days of Gladstone, became a rallying cry in the English Revolution against Royalist theories of absolutism; it worked to focus moral outrage on the presumed perversions of traditional authority. The notion of property belonging to all the people, however, looks forward to theories of socialism and thus was also used as an argument about the perversions of those, both new and old in origin, who defended the rights of property.[34]

The Independents in the New Model Army abhorred ecclesiastical discipline and compulsory conformity and through democratic agitation sought an end to traditional institutions of authority. When applied to property these arguments worked against the idea of a moral code favoring mutuality enforced by the Church, a characteristic of early Calvinism, and instead favored economic individualism. In that sense they were, ironically, strongly endorsed by the new elites; they also, however, became a weapon in the hands of the poor against the rising importance of wealth as a criterion for differentiating people. The Levellers, the radicals of the revolution, wanted self-governing congregations in which all were equal in opportunity. They appealed to the Anglo Saxon past but moved past a concept of recovery of rights to a conception of natural rights, the rights of man, in which positive rights or fair shares were a major strand. As might be expected, such ideas held no interest for those who owned property. These men wanted property safeguarded by law and a predominant role in society reserved for gentlemen and merchants. If the royal party, on suffrance, could strengthen their position then it should be restored. In the confrontation between the Puritans of the left and those of the right the left—the Levellers and others—were defeated. Fearing social revolution the old elite was recalled; in the words of Hill, "the deceased feudal order still sat coroneted at Westminster."[35]

An entrepreneurial society dressed in the trappings of a previous age was now in the making. Its ultimate ascendancy was not foreordained; nor did it go unchallenged. Residues of a previous concern for positive rights continued to be manifested, perhaps most clearly on May 6, 1795, when the justices of Berkshire, worried about the lot of the poor, met at the Pelikan Inn in Speenhamland, near Newbury, and decided that "subsidies in aid of wages should be granted in accordance with a scale dependent upon the price of bread, so that a minimum income should be assured to the poor *irrespective of their earnings*."[36] These regulations were anathema to those who believed that the national need was for a supply of free laborers, put under the threat of starvation if they failed to comply with the rules of wage labor. After several decades, following increasing pressure, a competitive labor market was fully established in England with the passage of the Poor Law Reform Act of 1834, inaugurating the modern era of industrial capitalism. The repeal of the Speenhamland regulations which the act represented was the work of the triumphant leaders of the new industrial organizations; almost immediately counterpressures arose.[37] Karl Marx, with Frederick Engels, published *The Communist Manifesto* in January 1848 and went on to mount the most successful and well-known theoretical attack on the entrepreneurial society. Marx, who vigorously repudiated moral norms as the trappings of dominance, was nevertheless an explicit supporter of positive rights in all his work and became the foremost champion of those who sought justice in a society where negative rights had become supreme. A century later societies formed to enshrine positive rights are themselves the target of attack by angry workers, farmers, and intellectuals demanding freedom from ideological restraint and stultifying bureaucratic practices. East Germany, Hungary, Czechoslovakia, China, Poland, and even the Soviet Union have shared these tendencies in varying degrees. They have been made visibly known to others by agitation and reformist, sometimes even revolutionary, activity. Most recently and dramatically, spurred by difficulties in stimulating growth and by increasing popular cynicism, negative rights have become, in limited fashion, the goal of party and government policies.

Activists and Allegiants in Reciprocating Change

New elites frequently shift away from activism once their own success is assured. In the formation of entrepreneurial societies these elites initially pressed for their right to participate in the political process and for access to greater rewards as well as for the right of assembly, free speech, and relief from burdensome taxes and regulations. In later phases, however, their descendants became allegiant; having legitimized their own dominance, they had no interest in further change. Thus, for example, many who prosper under entrepreneurial dominance oppose steps toward income distribution that might alter the nature of the system that favors them. Some who are descended from the nineteenth-century entrepreneurs in the United States, who successfully challenged an older dominance pattern based largely on landholding, now resist further change; they and their ideological allies look with suspicion on the aspirations of nondominant groups. Such conservatism also occurs in guardian societies. In the early years of communism in the Soviet Union there was much hope for a new era of free intellectual creativity as well as a more equitable social and political order. Yet in Communist countries many leaders of the party and the government have also slipped into the allegiant role. They are the ones who respond most negatively to pressures by workers for positive rights and by intellectuals for negative rights, for an end to the rigid conformity enforced by the party.

The shift by any group from being activist to allegiant is an indication of continuing change as other powerfully organized groups continue to press for rights. A new aspiring leadership frequently stresses the immoral qualities of previous leaders who no longer desire change. In American society, for example, blacks emerged in the last two decades with strong demands for an extension of positive rights. In many cases they felt that the old liberal white leadership was inadequate to head their movement, being basically satisfied with the status quo. Although the most powerful voices of black leadership sought peaceful change within the entrepreneurial dominance system of American society, some went further and called for radical alterations in social, political, and economic life through an extension of positive rights. These leaders justified their demands on the basis that white American elites were immoral in failing to heed the claims of nondominant groups. A similar pattern was evident in Poland from 1980 to 1982. Workers and intellectuals challenged an inflexible Communist leadership to extend negative rights. The old leadership was taunted as both ineffectual and moribund. The party, which there as elsewhere had trumpeted itself as the vanguard of change, found itself in the uncommon position of being labeled as immorally unwilling to grant these rights to the workers, farmers, and others.

As tension increases there is a continual tendency for nondominant groups to be organized by those who appeal to the virtues of a new pattern of authority. In France, for instance, in the late eighteenth century the bourgeois leaders of the third estate threw over the monarchy and the old nobility and called for the creation of a republic of virtue. In Russia in the early twentieth century the tension that existed between an old nobility and autocracy allied with some members of an emerging bourgeoisie and the largely bourgeois leadership of the reformist and revolutionary parties was ultimately resolved in favor of the latter. In China ideologically fervent Communist forces fought for three decades against traditional landlords, warlords, and a Nationalist party dominated by a modernizing military and a newly emerged commercial class.

If established elites exert influence with the government to suppress the demands of nondominant groups, the resulting violence may squeeze out those who are unaligned and force people to become allegiant or activist. Clearly this is the situation today in Central America and many other parts of the world. Events in a number of countries show how continued pressure for change by some groups has been mirrored by an increasing stress on allegiance by others. At earlier stages some leaders attempt to moderate the increasing hostility, but as violence escalates they lose their ability to influence events. Challenge by nondominant groups can be discerned in every society although rigorous control at all levels in guardian and predatory systems makes organization there by dissident groups difficult. As events in China in the Cultural Revolution of the 1960s showed, however, students, workers, and peasants can organize to attack their erstwhile leaders and accuse them with the same moral invective that these leaders had used earlier in asserting their own authority.

The unending war between activism and allegiance is fought over the overall configuration of rights within a dominance system. Out of the ensuing clash a lesson emerges that is a difficult one for dominant groups. In all of the history of the modern world there is no example of a dominant group that survived when it ceased to lead others toward the attainment of rights. A levee against change can be erected, but it has never held indefinitely. Rights can be suppressed, but they cannot be forever denied.

Accommodative Change

Movements for change vary according to the type of dominance system and the perversions that people seek to eliminate.[38] Generally speaking, movements do not occur when people are at or below the subsistence level or when they live isolated in a local culture with little conception of how to attain a different way of life. When change does occur it is often so gradual as to be unnoticed. Since most change is accommodative in nature (i.e., within the framework of the existing dominance system), less attention is provoked than when a wholesale transformation of values and social structures takes place.

Unlike in the past, the rate of change in our time has no precedent. Yet it is still difficult to perceive dramatic shifts in our daily lives. One reason for this is the generally nonviolent nature of change and the long period of time required for any new custom to be completely established. A transformation in the role of the father, for instance, from being a sacrosanct authority figure to adult partner, is a shift that takes several generations. It involves changes in attitudes about the role of the father, the roles of children, and most especially the place of women in society. A whole set of complex transformations occurs. Women enter work organizations and the nature of these organizations changes; they are less tied to the home by childbearing, and attitudes regarding maternal rearing thus alter. Children become increasingly expected to make their own decisions regarding occupations and marriage. All of these changes affect the role of the father. Many small "revolutions" take place in many homes but in a manner where the attainment of rights by women and children does not involve a sudden violent upheaval for society as a whole.

Although change is often slow and incremental its pace can be quickened by deliberate policy. The Meiji reformers of Japan instituted policies that radically altered Japanese society within a few decades. The same has been true for China under Communist rule. Although these are particularly striking examples, the fact is that deliberate policy to bring about change is true for virtually all modern governments in the allocations of their budgets and in their directives to their agencies. Establishing a universal educational system, for instance, produces educational ambitions in people who previously had no access to such opportunities. Yet while the decision to apply to a college or university is an individual one, the cumulative result of a policy that encourages new groups to obtain an education leads to a decisive alteration in traditional social patterns and an erosion of the values that previously granted privilege and status to some at the expense of others.

Change can also occur rapidly and sometimes violently, with a strong component of anarchic passion. Groups become aroused by excessively repressive actions, by the erosion of marginal economic surpluses, or by the defeat of the nation in war. This is the time for street politics and rural vendettas, for demonstrations, and for acts of violence against public institutions and prominent individuals. In many societies change has all of the qualities noted above. While usually slow and relatively peaceful it can, at other times, be swift and anarchic.

No society responds to change in exactly the same way as another. Certain aspects of change are universally shared but take on a unique coloration depending upon social and cultural circumstances. European societies differ from non-European, but even within the European area countries in Southern Europe differ from those in Eastern Europe and so on. Peasant societies have ways of life that are markedly different from those of free farmers. Because peasantry is prevalent in most present-day developing societies, it is difficult to utilize the lessons learned from societies that underwent change with free farmers. Analysis of nineteenth-century rural America, for example, may not provide information that is relevant for an understanding of twentieth-century rural India. In like manner a study of change in traditional, monolithic, bureaucratic empires may give few useful clues for understanding social transformation in more fragmented societies. Despite these wide disparities, however, there are uniformities along certain dimensions that permit a general overview. Change has universal characteristics in spite of the clear differences that exist from one society to another.

Most people wish for increased social status and material well-being without the bother and the threat that may be involved in political activity. They become involved when privileged groups are seen as violating their obligations under the protection of an existing political system.[39] Rather than remain as passive victims they initiate a debate concerning the ground rules of social interaction[40]; frustration is expressed by demands on those in dominant positions for rights. The motives of those who make demands, of course, are varied. Many advocates of change have a genuine commitment to rights and are morally mature. But that is not always the case. By undermining the prevailing system of beliefs that confers legitimacy on existing elites some hope to reap personal gain or status in a new type of dominance structure; still others seek to enhance rights for their followers, though it might involve the ruthless subjugation of others. Whatever their motives (and these have an important bearing on the nature of political change), all who advocate change are initially usually considered to be deviants.

In most societies those with higher status are more politically involved, using participation to get and keep power and to achieve other social, economic, and political goals.[41] As a consequence, pressing claims for rights, especially in predatory societies where there is a ready use of coercion by elites, can involve personal risk. The original advocates of change are not a large group relative to the population as a whole. Speaking out when it would be safer not to involves a calculation, an assessment of net benefits and costs mediated by psychological variables. Before starting debate those who wish change undoubtedly first weigh the probability of change occurring, the incidence of previous failure, the benefits they personally can expect, their feelings about the enterprise, the likelihood of group or organizational support, the sanctions that might be experienced by doing nothing, and the costs that might be incurred by doing something.[42] Action may be constrained if strong feelings of frustration are absent, if the issues are not thought to be highly relevant, or, although relevant, if they can be solved by normal political processes. When such feelings and beliefs do not act as restraints, an activist emerges.

Debate about change shifts from an individual to a collective phenomenon as large numbers of intellectuals cease to support the values that legitimize dominance and as sharp conflicts of interest develop within the elite. These conditions, of course, occur with varying degrees of intensity and effect (e.g., unsuccessful calls in East Germany for democratization of the party, a restoration of autonomy for universities, and abolition of the political police and secret trials[43]). Only when the elite loses control over the army and the police (or is effectively challenged by an alternative coercive force) is the situation aggravated to the point of revolutionary change. In more normal circumstances, when the values that undergird dominance are widely accepted as appropriate, a shift from a natural acceptance of a dominance system to vigorous opposition is subtle, widely diffused in the population, and often years in occurring. The alterations in underlying conditions that bring about this change take place over long periods of time. In addition, the transcendence of limits, which some members of dominant groups are prone to, such as shifting from defense of the community to internal oppression, is not a universal phenomenon within the dominant strata, nor does it occur with any traumatic suddenness. Rather, it usually takes many years before significant numbers of the dominant class are clearly violating the values that justify their position in a manner that has systemic implications. Moreover, even when the underlying rationale for dominance has changed and when significant numbers of dominant people are acting contrary to currently held values, nondominant groups may still uphold the prevailing system. They do this because they may not be able to perceive an alternative, because they still believe in some of the values that legitimize dominance and hope for changes in the dominant class, because they are extremely fearful of the consequences should they question the legitimacy of the prevailing system, or because elites, through their control of important resources, are able to mobilize support for their own dominance. Indeed, those with moderate status may be the most fearful of change. They dread that if the current system is overthrown and the values behind it repudiated they will lose all that they have in a subsequent general reorganization. The opposition of large numbers of lower middle class people to social change is well known; they have formed the bulk of conservative alignments from the most benign types in democratic societies to the more virulent and oppressive forms that are associated with military authoritarianism or fascism. In Third World countries, the difficulties encountered by radical parties in their attempts to mobilize peasants or urban workers are also well known. Workers and peasants do not automatically flock to the banner of change but rather do so only after extreme social disorder, intensive indoctrination, or as a by-product of an appeal to other values such as nationalism.

The first challenge to a dominance system is often made by people who seek reform rather than revolution. Often, but not always, the reformers are morally mature people who are perceptive of the way that dominance patterns no longer correspond to social goals. In discussing the relationship of dominance to values the critics often move subtly and without particular self-knowledge from a position where dominance is criticized in terms of current values (the infringement of existing rights and obligations) to one where new values are espoused as more viable for present circumstances, more just on general principle, and more appropriate for the legitimation of a new dominance system. Moral and political opinions merge; there tends to be discussion about rights and the relationship of these to existing conventions or institutions.[44]

Regardless of which route discussion takes, the critics tend to perceive their arguments as nondestructive. What they do is to initiate debate. Subsequently these issues may become matters of speculation in the salons of the elite as well as in the dwellings of common citizens. Such periods of debate occurred prior to the great political upheavals of the modern world. In the decades before the French Revolution, for instance, discussions about the nature of French society were popular among plebians and patricians alike. The same was also a notable feature of the years before the October

Revolution in Russia although greatly restrained by the czarist police. The important point is that movements for change never start without extensive groundwork. Debate politicizes a population, makes people aware of the appropriateness of dominance values, and serves as the soil from which new visions grow and around which social action coalesces.

At this stage the debate about rights is most intense and widespread within the elite and the strata just below the apex of dominance. It is no accident that the most famous protesters in history, men like Martin Luther, Gandhi, Thomas Jefferson, Lenin, or Mao Zedong, were not from the lowest levels of society but from the elite or closely allied strata. Those who first demand rights are, in one sense, the cousins of those who uphold the existing order. Their proximity to those who are dominant sharply focuses their claims about perversions of obligations and increases the probability that some elites in the military, business, and government will identify with the cause they espouse. Such people have access to resources that can help them to resist frightening pressures, and they possess the intellectual training that is necessary both to recognize perversion and to conceive of ways to end it. As a consequence, the crucial initial disjunction takes place within and between dominant and closely associated groups. This homogeneity makes invalid any analysis of change that views these groups as solid blocs or classes. Rather, elements of the dominant strata oppose each other, often enough within the government itself.[45]

In the first instances of cleavage the lowest levels of society may be barely involved. Fragmented in their associations (sometimes as a consequence of deliberate policy) and frequently viewing any political involvement as risky, they stand initially on the sidelines, often even unaware of the debate about deprivation that may include reference to themselves. As dominance progressively loses its aura of inherent justness and as its influence is challenged, however, the implications of change become increasingly evident to everyone. Subordinate groups, with a new sense of consciousness, may then organize and begin to press demands, sometimes of the same type as those made by disaffected members of the dominant strata (and in alliance with them) and sometimes uniquely their own.[46] Along with others in society who are drawn to agitation, they too may begin to use legal or illegal techniques of mobilization—assemblies, strikes, appeals to public opinion, petitions, and so forth.

Activists and dominant individuals often have different perceptions of the implications of shifts in underlying economic or social conditions. Despite allegations to the contrary, not every conservative defense of an existing system is deliberately evil. The moral question arises when new needs and problems reveal the inadequacy of traditional practices and bring into question the legitimacy of prevailing patterns of dominance. Many elites may not realize that their defense of existing norms and structures is questionable on the basis of the fullest possible rights for others. Indeed, they may perceive this defense as necessary in order to protect all in society. Some few may be aware of other motives—of a desire to maintain an advantageous access to scarce resources. Many, however, truly perceive the norms and values that legitimize a particular form of dominance as beneficial for society. The defense of these values and the social and political structures related to them is seen as appropriate and good, and as justifying whatever actions are required to maintain them. Although elites are usually the most important segment of this allegiant group, their power can be augmented by others who gain from the maintenance of the status quo. The strength of conservatism in present-day Japan, for example, is based on an alliance between urban organizational elites and a peasantry that benefited from land reform following the Second World War.

Debate about the merits of a dominance system may stretch over decades or last only a few years. It may end in gradual and peaceful change, in violent confrontation, or in the reassertion and reinvigoration of the prevailing form of dominance. A crucial determinant of the outcome is the moral maturity of influential members of the dominant group. When such people are active participants in the debate there is a strong likelihood that discussions will focus on reform and that change will take place gradually and peacefully. The probability of this being the case, however, is by no means unrelated to existing social and political structures. Societies where debate is not restricted, where severe punishments are not meted out to those who initiate discussion, where concessions are not viewed as humiliating defeat, and where a widely accepted legal order places limits on the behavior of both challengers and challenged are those where participation is most likely to include morally mature people from all levels of society. In these circumstances altruistic awareness and empathy infuse the debate, reducing the feelings of threat and anxiety that people feel in discussions about change.

Accommodative change appears to be correlated with an under-

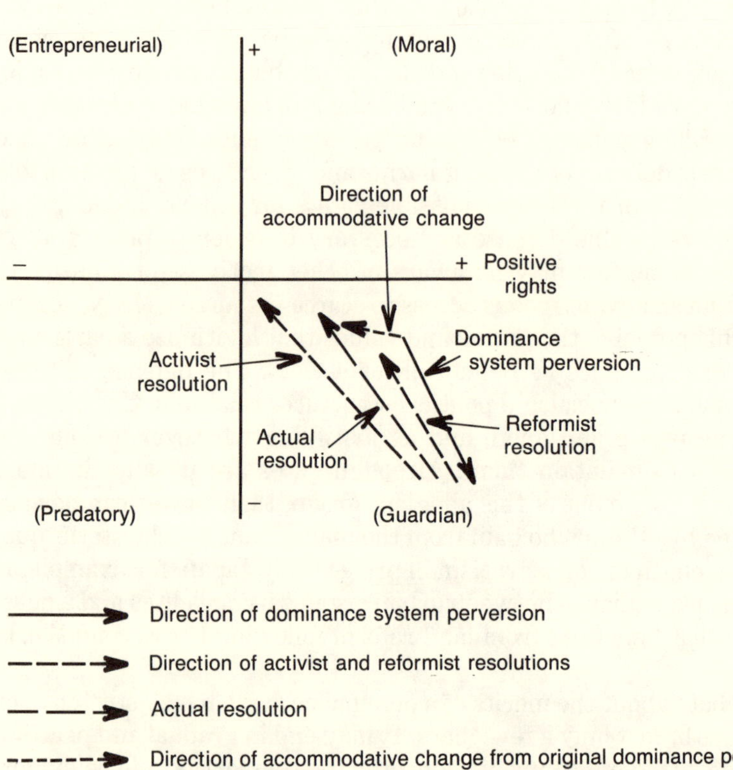

Figure 4. Outcome of Interaction Between Activists and Reformers to a Perception of Perversion Within a Guardian Dominance System

Note: Measurements along the axes are indeterminate. Vector values are also thus indeterminate and are meant to be descriptive only.

standing between the activists and sympathetic reform-minded members of the dominant class who are able to sponsor compromise policies. Even when institutional forms and procedures favor compromise, however, the outcome is often not without strain. Nor is it always nonviolent. Relatively peaceful accommodative change is fostered when those who are involved are morally mature, when the perversion of dominance that has aroused the activist is limited in extent, when reformist forces retain a capability for action, when dominance values are considered to be relatively legitimate by broad segments of the population, and when the reformist and activist responses are relatively congruent. The absence of any of these conditions does not foreclose accommodative change but does increase the likelihood of violence and undermines the probability of a reduction in tension. Figure 4 shows one way that accommodative change proceeds. For the sake of simplicity I have given an example within the guardian dominance quadrant, modeled roughly after the events in China following the end of the Cultural Revolution, the death of Mao Zedong, and the fall of the Gang of Four. As is noted, the actual change that takes place is always some form of continuous vector resolution of the forces involved.

If perversion is thought of as passive, the consequence of unintended social changes, malaise and alienation may develop regarding the entire system of dominance accompanied by an anxious hope for a new direction under fresh leadership. If perversion is thought of as intentional, where obligations are being consciously avoided, then tension and hostility may result. When the understanding between activists and reform-minded members of the dominant class is relatively strong the resolution is likely to be peaceful (e.g., events in Spain since the death of Franco in 1975). Where conservative forces are overwhelmingly in control, reform, when it occurs, is largely supportive of prevailing dominance values and is often accompanied by riots, strikes, and demonstrations by still disaffected persons (e.g., the pattern in South Korea). Where the allegiant group is split by different evaluations of the claims of activists and reformers, the result may be conspiracy, coup d'etat, sudden but legal change of government, or palace revolution depending upon the various assessments of the likelihood of displacing or eliminating rivals within the dominant class (e.g., Poland in 1981).

Violence and Transformative Change

A Chinese scholar, discussing the extraordinary events that shook his country during the Spring and Autumn and the Warring States periods more than two millennia ago, described that time of change as follows: "In a whirlpool, objects tend to change position much faster and more suddenly than in still water; waterweed may be drawn to the surface while flotsam is pulled to the bottom."[47] Truly, in times of social transformation, roles shift dramatically and traditional statuses crumble; the insistent awareness of the need for reform escalates from peaceful public demands to the clash of arms and the judicial murder of elites. In the last five hundred years, with increasing fury and scope, ancient predatory societies have been transformed into entrepreneurial or guardian dominance systems. These momentous changes are a modern phenomenon that make our age unique. Although not always characterized by violence (i.e., accommodative change can continue "relatively" peacefully until a transformative change of rights and obligations occurs, as in the Industrial Revolution), the process everywhere has usually involved blood and pain. Why? What is it about a claim for rights, for greater morality in social life, that is so agonizing for so many people? Why, in the search to bring society closer to an ideal of justice, should so much hatred and cruelty be unleashed—often by those who proclaim their own selflessness most loudly?

As Merelman has pointed out, the stiffening of resistance to change is most apparent when those who head the current dominant strata assert the overriding validity of prevailing norms.[48] Many dominant individuals respond collectively to a perception of threat by intensifying their adherence to regnant dominance values.[49] This defense centers on specific laws, regulations, and the customs that are said to embody current values. People who appeal to the morality of rules are, in Kohlberg's scheme, at a midrange in development.[50] The rigidly allegiant individual is a person whose level of moral competence is rule maintaining (or who, from fear or other causes, has regressed to this level). Such a person perceives the rightness of rules per se as more important than any reflective notion of what is morally correct.

In the defense of a dominance system highly allegiant people tend to come to the fore. This occurs not only because of the feelings of threat that potential change arouses in some members of society but also because of the relative clarity and forcefulness that often go with defense of an already clearly articulated value position. Allegiant elites perceive pressures for a radical shift in the balance of rights and obligations as a pronounced type of deviance, abetted by some of their own kind, that erodes the values that bolster their dominance and leaves them vulnerable to victimization. As the Anglican Archbishop Whitgift put it regarding the objectives of the Puritans, "[they] all tend to one end, which is liberty of doing what men list, contrary to the lawes established, and to the practice of all well-ordered states and churches."[51]

Because dominance values are part of the group-solidarity values of social systems, some elites may perceive attacks against the dominance system as impugning their moral worth. The strong response thus invoked makes less likely a more tolerant view of opposition that could permit an early accommodative resolution of social tension. Against the assertions of activists and reformers, these elites set forth a countervailing interpretation of justice that stresses respect for authority, tradition, and law. There is frequently a concomitant effort on their part to take over social control organizations and to establish procedures that will bolster the dominance system, even in cases where that system has become grossly perverted. Finally, when dominant people feel that the threat to their status involves physical violence, a heightened willingness to use force is enhanced. At this point the leadership of the dominant group may fall into the hands of people who deny any obligation to protect the rights of those who challenge them.

When individuals who raise questions are morally mature and when debate is permitted to proceed openly there is a high probability that discussion will be marked by compassion, tolerance, respect, and a willingness to compromise. When openness does not occur, however, and when "exit" is impossible, there is an equally strong probability that the moral competence of those who espouse change will shift to lower levels. As was true for dominant groups, the proponents of change may begin to include people who are rule maintaining, but in their case in terms of a new set of values. As the goals of those who seek change assume paramount importance, individuals who can define these ends in terms of new values decisively enter the scene. Lenin, bursting like a shock wave on a society in stress, was such a figure when he appeared at the Finland Station in Petrograd in 1917.

As activists increase their dedication to new values and goals, their ability to relate to the feelings and goals of elite opponents is sharply reduced. If, at the same time, threat and intimidation are experienced, then activists become increasingly hostile and fixated on their own principles to the exclusion of feelings of altruistic awareness and empathy toward elites and their followers, who come to embody all that is unvirtuous. The guilt that might arise from such behavior is avoided by self-identification with the now completely virtuous in-group, and by attributing all wrong to opponents.[52] As Mao Zedong put it, "There must be a revolutionary party because the world contains enemies who oppress the people and the people want to throw off enemy oppression."[53] At this point accommodative change or a peaceful maintenance of the status quo may still occur if dominant forces are powerful and widely supported. The stage is set, however, for violent confrontation.

There is, it has been suggested, a powerful relationship between economic backwardness and violence.[54] Violence has a negative effect on effective policy making and, when severe, a negative effect on social equality.[55] Most brutality, of course, is first exercised by the government, which uses the police and the military to repress activist activities.[56] Strike breaking, mob dispersal, undercover police activity, use of the militia or national guard to quell disturbances, and outright military action are all measures that governments have at their disposal, the use of which is often successful, particularly in the face of largely unorganized groups whose coalescence around protest issues is episodic.

When groups that advocate change reflect broad popular sentiment, however, then violent suppression may lead only to a superficial aura of security while the opposition, defeated on the open field, recoups its strength from underground. Eventually, mobilized opposition will arise again. This is especially likely if some socioeconomic development has taken place (because mobilized participation in politics has an inverted U-shaped relationship with socioeconomic development) and to the degree that protest issues (rents, education, etc.) are preempted by one well-organized umbrella group (e.g., the Communists).[57]

Initially, militant idealists are in alliance with morally mature activists. As the intensity of violent confrontation mounts, however, the latter give way to those with better fighting ability who are more ideologically extreme and willing to mobilize others to violence. Increasingly the challengers are motivated by hostility and fixated on their own principles to the exclusion of feelings of altruistic awareness and empathy toward members of the dominant class and their adherents.[58] Such people have been termed "revolutionary ascetics,"[59] men and women who claim morality in the name of their own social goals and who, in the pursuit of their beliefs, are capable of the ruthless destruction of their fellow men.

The likelihood of social disruption increases as the morally mature activists are replaced by those who seek change for personal reasons and who work to bring new groups into the movement as a means of increasing their own power. These amoral individuals justify their behavior in terms of the ideals articulated by the morally mature activists but direct their actions as much toward the fulfillment of their personal needs and the expression of hostile impulses as toward the attainment of rights for others. An example of this process is revealed in studies of the 1964 Free Speech Movement at the University of California at Berkeley. Initially the movement was fueled by students at the principled moral reasoning stage: 59 percent of the participants who were tested scored at that level.[60] (As Emler has shown, left-wing students do obtain higher scores on postconventional moral reasoning than do students who describe themselves as right wing or moderate.[61]) But as student activity across the United States mounted in the 1960s, other individuals joined who used the movement as a vehicle for the expression of repressed anger. Police intervention and violence mounted. Within a few years the movement shifted from the Port Huron Statement of 1960, which stated that men are "infinitely precious and possessed of unfilled capacities for reason, freedom, and love,"[62] to the Weatherman slogan of "Death to the pigs." In the end the moderate leaders were completely replaced by amoral individuals who justified their violent behavior in terms of the goals articulated by the morally mature activists but who directed their actions as much toward the expression of hostility as toward the achievement of social goals.

Lower levels of moral development include an inability to empathize and to be sensitive to the needs of others and a tendency to assert one's own position and to be unwilling to deal with the views of opponents. Cognitive ability may be highly developed but it is used to justify hostility, persuasively indoctrinate followers, and develop the tactics and strategy of confrontation. The values of one's own group or organization are seen as transcendent to the point where those who disagree—regardless of their motives—are perceived as guilty of deliberate malfeasance. It is under these conditions that the most violent forms of political change occur, with the ascent to power, both in revolutionary organizations and in the forces of social control, of amoral individuals who might otherwise have occupied more peaceful stations in life. Toward opponents individual responsibility is suspended, and with it those "stirrings of decency" that might have inhibited cruelty and ruthlessness.[63] As behavior on both sides becomes increasingly predatory, ascetic militant revolutionaries confront hanging judges in an explosion of violence and terror in which each side attempts to discredit and eliminate its adversary.

Tension escalates as the revolutionary forces strive to achieve parity with the forces of social control. At this point prolonged internal war can occur as both sides attempt to gain control. In the 1980s this is the situation in Afganistan as an unpopular Communist government (with the aid of the Soviet military) attempts to suppress a hostile countryside. In Peru a similar but more isolated confrontation exists. There the Sendero Luminoso, or Shining Path, attempt to mobilize the Ayacucho peasants against the government under the leadership of an extremist Maoist organization.[64]

Where elite cohesion remains strong, however, and where there is substantial popular support, there may be an intensification or reimposition of the prevailing form of dominance. Throughout the world governments have used their military authority to suppress the demands of nondominant challengers. Events in Turkey, South Korea, Thailand, Pakistan, Argentina, Brazil, Spain, Greece, and Chile have reflected this pattern. In these countries some elites have become dissatisfied with the efforts of the government in the face of radical demands and have imposed military control as a solution. Similar events take place in guardian systems. In the 1950s and 1960s in Hungary and Czechoslovakia governments that appeared to be acceding to demands for negative rights were overthrown with the aid of the Soviet military which, in conjunction with local forces, reimposed control by allegiant party leaders.

Against a government that has firm control over the military, revolutionary forces have scant chance for ascendancy. When aided by outside forces, however, as in South Vietnam, the probability of success improves markedly. The defection of the military and the overthrow of the government becomes more likely when there is a further crisis, sometimes engineered by outside forces, affecting the dominance system. The French, Russian, and Chinese revolutions, for example, all took place in an environment of systemic crisis. Such an event could be an economic collapse, a depression for instance, but the most obvious and usual one is defeat in war, which brings about a rapid loss of support for the existing system. When dominance is thus brought into question a politico-military crisis results in which the new people of society, having developed like a chrysalis within the old order, move to fill the power vacuum created by the loss of legitimacy of the old system. As the revolutionary forces increase their capability relative to social control organizations, the violent resolution may tend toward a transformation of the existing dominance system (e.g., China in the late 1940s). Clearly, such transformations, although not common, have been a marked feature in our own endlessly conflicted and bloody century. Whatever the outcome, whether the revolution succeeds or there is a shift back toward the prevailing form of dominance (e.g., Argentina in the 1970s), rights will have fallen victim to desires for dominance for its own sake.

6. Organizations and Political Change

Many revolutionary movements in this century, in Europe, East Asia, Southeast Asia, the Middle East, Africa, and Latin America, have had a strong affinity for guardian rather than entrepreneurial dominance. Why should this be so? Let me begin by analyzing further the actors and groups who participate in the drama of change.

Class Theory

The modern nation, as we know it, has a history that stretches back about two hundred years; indeed, states have been created more rapidly in the last four decades than at any other time. In earlier days there were, of course, political structures with fiscal, judicial, and control mechanisms that approximated modern systems. But few people then had a loyalty to political organizations that equaled or transcended their loyalty to group life in the village or region. Concerns were highly parochial, focused on guild, clan, and family. In such circumstances nationalism and other forms of large group consciousness involving a comprehension of commonality uniting many people hardly existed. With the exception of religious affiliation, awareness of others only marginally transcended the local arena of acquaintances. Because societies were largely agricultural—80 percent or more of the population working on the land—with power concentrated in the hands of a tiny "aristocratic" elite, the divisions of interest within the local area were relatively clearly demarcated, often legally so, and were commonly and appropriately referred to as class divisions. As far as daily life was concerned this meant for most people a separation between the largest landowners and virtually all the rest of the people.

As traditional patterns changed with commercialization, new modes of interaction and interdependency developed that brought into question the legitimacy of prevailing regulative structures and principles. Inequality in the distribution of goods and authority became increasingly noticeable (inequality in societies is most apparent after they have begun the process of change[1]), giving empirical credence to notions of distinct class entities. Intellectuals, large numbers of whom were in religious orders and were not from the aristocratic formations of the traditional social order, progressively developed a perception of social relations as sharply divided, especially in terms of access to material goods. As states slowly changed their political and economic forms, and as intellectuals as a group increased in number both absolutely and relatively, questions about distribution grew apace. As has been noted, the Puritan Revolution, spearheaded by articulate preachers, aimed specifically at a solution to social tensions, although phrasing questions about distribution in theological terminology.

The tensions that surround redistributive issues appear as class conflict because structurally societies are divided in terms of haves and have-nots.[2] Groups are defined by their relationship to the means of production and by the criteria that govern the distribution of the rewards that flow from production. Production relations, then, determine the dominant (i.e., have) and subordinate (i.e., have-not) roles in given historical periods. Surplus value to one group versus another correlates with status differences in a differentiated division of labor. Unfortunately, although this formulation appears empirically straightforward, not the least of the problems in class analysis is in defining class composition. This is especially true for modern, urbanized polities, which are far more complex than traditional agricultural societies.

The work of current class analysts reflects the new complexity and the ambiguity that has arisen. One theorist, for example, noting that a requirement for a theory of socialist revolution is to differentiate the various classes in the revolutionary process, states opaquely that "class consciousness has its basis in the class struggle, and the class struggle is rooted in class consciousness."[3] But what does this mean? Apparently it is related to the further thought (expressed by the same author) that there is nothing less useful for understanding the emergence and actions of intellectuals in revolutionary activities than class background. Participation in struggle, it is averred, is more important than social origin as a definition of class membership, presumably because many "revolutionary" intellectuals cannot muster impeccable proletarian class credentials.[4] More tightly reasoned efforts do not dispel these difficulties. Perhaps the currently most influential class theoretician is Nicos Poulantzas, who approaches the problem from three dimensions: economic, political, and ideological. Class, according to Poulantzas, does not designate a reality. Since there is in class struggle a coexistence of several classes or fractions of classes, class itself is said to be merely a concept that demonstrates the effect of the admixture of economic, political, and ideological structures; these are derived from the mode of production, which is supported, in turn, by the form of social relations.[5]

Modern class theoreticians recognize the complications that inhere in class analysis when they seek to conceptualize revolutionary classes as "effects" or as entities that include, for theoretical consistency, those who are engaged in revolutionary activity. In fact, although class as a concept is a useful heuristic device, defining precisely who is and who is not a member of a class is not only empirically impossible, it is also irrelevant. No one-dimensional factor separates groups in societies: not income, nor occupation, and certainly not any homogeneity of interest.[6] Political participation in movements for change is rooted in different group bases: patron-client relations, neighborhood, party, faction, and communal group.[7] Some issues such as anticolonialism cut across and appeal to many different sections of a society. Cleavages of language, race, ethnicity, or region may be far more significant than putative differences of class.

Definitional difficulties are compounded when class is linked theoretically with social change. Revolutionary classes, it is said, are the products of, and respond to, economic transformation; they are the human motor for change, acting to realize collective needs for an end to deprivation, the deprivation itself being the consequence of unequal production relationships. There is here, although almost never fully recognized or articulated, a psychological theory that is wrongly formulated. Needs, which psychologically vary among individuals, are for theoretical reasons treated as an aggregate phenomenon in order to derive a central theoretical construct called class consciousness. The problem is that need is simply attributed on the basis of social (i.e., class) categories; those who don't manifest these needs are then said to be people who don't know what their "real" needs are; they have false needs or false consciousness. In contrast, those who uphold class theory accredit themselves (as guardians) with the power to state what the real needs of groups are (e.g., the needs of the proletariat or the needs of the masses).[8]

The error here, of course, is psychological reductionism. Yet the reductionism is unrecognized for needs are denied the independent status that they in fact have in the analysis of change. Instead, they are deductively aggregated and subsequently conceived of as an intermediate variable in the sense that they are said merely to reflect the exploitation that is inherent in production relationships. This, of course, is the reason why they can be ascribed, for needs, in this formulation, are a *knowable product* of deprivation. The line of causation in class analysis thus runs in one direction from production relations to needs to change.

The problems inherent in class theory have never been adequately solved, theoretically or empirically. Alienation, which is said to be the major underlying emotion of those who are deprived and which presumably triggers a "need" for change, has never been found to be linked in any direct, linear way with social background characteristics. Survey data indicate, moreover, that in explaining political behavior it is not just what attitude a person has about a situation that is important; more significant by far are attitudes about behavior, the appropriate means for resolving the issues that inhere in a particular situation. These dispositions are not the property of any one group, as class analysts are constantly made aware of when they try to fit intellectuals into class categories. Two people from the same group can share the same attitude about a situation yet behave differently because they have different behavioral orientations. Two people from different groups can share the same attitude about a situation and behave similarly because they share a common behavioral orientation.[9] But if this is so, and the data are relatively conclusive, then the lines of causation that relate need to class membership per se are, from a strict scientific perspective, incorrectly conceived.

The situations in class theory that presumably trigger a need for change have also proven to have empirical and logical legs of sand. The impulse toward change is said to be heightened by a crisis in production relations. Originally, as Marx formulated these ideas, a crisis was expected to arise from anarchical economic competition and a related (due to the drive for profit) impoverishment of the general population. This did not occur. As a consequence it was then predicted that the crisis would flow from imperialism (competition for overseas markets) and related wars, war expenditures, and the eventual rise of garrison states. To some degree crises related to these events have occurred, but they have not led to major transformations in the areas (the most industrialized states) where class analysis originally predicted change would take place. Instead, crisis in our century is most apparent and severe in societies that still have large peasant populations. Currently a popular interpretation of crisis in advanced societies states that it will occur as a consequence of social welfare expenditures unmatched by revenue income, especially as revenues are reduced by demands for exemptions by powerful special interests. To date, this crisis has also not occurred although dire warnings abound from many sources.[10] Peculiarly, however, these warnings do not come from any particular social group, nor are calls for tax reform, which is widely seen as the solution to the problem, from any well-defined social formation. These multiple difficulties, in sum, add up to an inescapable conclusion: the theory is flawed. Clearly some alternate formulation is required. For one must not suppose that no groups are important for understanding political change.

Organizations Versus Class

In communist theory organization or bureaucracy belongs to the state level of development. That is to say, the bureaucratic phenomenon is seen as preeminently a characteristic of the capitalist state, an aspect of the hierarchical organization of the state "apparatus" (involving rules/laws, separation of functions, salaries, impersonality) with class-conscious capitalists operating at the highest level to coordinate policies for the state as a whole. Within this overarching state framework other capitalists at a slightly lower level have responsibilities for a particular range of organizations while those with the lowest degree of class consciousness manage individual organizations or firms. As Poulantzas says, "Bureaucratism is due *both to the structures of the capitalist state and to the impact of the dominant capitalist ideology on the normative rules of organization of the state apparatus.*"[11] As capitalism changes to advanced forms of socialism bureaucratism will presumably give way, since it exists as a reflection of a capitalist economic and political order.

Marx and Engels, as is well known, said almost nothing about the communist society that they envisioned for the future. Instead, in a tradition that has been followed by subsequent Marxist theoreticians, they concentrated their attention on the factors that affect transition. For this, ironically, they viewed modern organizations as critical, recognizing for practical purposes their power and efficiency but refusing theoretically to grant them centrality either in the hoped for communist future or as the major, dynamic social structure of the modern world (this is less surprising when one remembers that large-scale organizations, as we know them, had not yet come into existence).

In 1850, in his "Address of the Reconstituted Central Committee to the Communist League," Marx noted that the revolutionary workers' party, after it had helped the petty bourgeoisie to win the revolution, must move to establish revolutionary workers' governments in the form of municipal committees or councils or as workers' clubs. After the petty bourgeois government was, in its turn, overthrown, Marx foresaw, under the aegis of the workers, "the most determined centralization of power in the hands of the state authority."[12] Here, certainly, is a recipe for organization and change for loyal disciples. And indeed, Lenin was an avid organizer and centralizer, developing the concept of the revolutionary organization to its highest form. Like Marx, however, Lenin had no understanding of the central role of organizations in modern life. Only after the revolution in 1917, when early attempts at dismantling prerevolutionary bureaucracies had had disastrous economic consequences, did bureaucratic organization become a pronounced feature of Soviet life. Whatever theory may say, these socialist organizations have grown in scope and complexity beyond even those known in capitalist societies. As Poulantzas could not bring himself to realize, bureaucratism is a worldwide phenomenon, as pertinent for the communist as the capitalist world. These bureaucracies share a common form in all modern states but have different status rules depending on the dominant ideology. And it is here, precisely, not in the ways that "classes" distribute material awards but more crucially in the way that rights are distributed according to status rules as an aspect of organizational life, that one comes to the true source of change in the modern world.

A focus on organization shifts attention from owners and nonowners of the means of production to factual control. The term bureaucrat then assumes its true meaning, designating a functionary in the process of control. Deprivation in terms of prestige, material rewards, the right to make normative pronouncements, and so forth, is an aspect of this control, exercised at times with regard to particular issues and at other times more generally in support of overarching regulative principles. The leaders of organizations attempt to channel the feelings of subordinates toward support and away from demands for rights that will weaken the prevailing dominance pattern. This is sometimes achieved by force (use of police, etc.) or by various forms of semicoercive control (manipulating wages, requiring travel and work permits, enforcing attendance at political study sessions), but the primary method is administrative discipline within organizations combined with heavy emphasis on organizational loyalty. The patterns range from diffuse encouragement of feelings of obligation to demands for overt displays of loyalty such as occur in Japanese enterprises.

The demand for allegiance, however, never entirely displaces feelings of slight and deprivation. No matter what corner of the globe, there is a pressure for rights within and among organizations. It is noted in entrepreneurial societies by the activities of unions, women's organizations, tenant associations, civil rights groups, and others. In guardian societies, where autonomous organizing is less possible due to restrictions on negative rights, demands for rights can nevertheless be seen in the Solidarity movement in Poland and in the demands of Chinese workers in the Cultural Revolution. The goals of activist organizations differ; their activity does not.

Rights are asserted vis-à-vis organized control as claims for distributive or commutative justice. Since control can be manifested coercively, remuneratively, administratively, and normatively (and often in combination), no group defined by unidimensional status or income criteria (e.g., nonowners) has a central or crucial role in the demand for rights. Nobles may unite with bourgeoisie in the Tennis Court Oath at the start of the French Revolution. Women from all socioeconomic levels may join forces against male dominance. Even bourgeois intellectuals may become members of revolutionary organizations. The line of causation is thus not from social background characteristics to needs to change, but from needs and behavioral dispositions (determined, in part only, by social influences as described in chapter 1) to organization to activism or allegiance.

Neither those who demand rights nor those who oppose them have homogeneous social backgrounds. At any given time significant numbers of dominant individuals may be in opposition to the government. One need only think of women's rights movements (e.g., women in prominent families may wholeheartedly oppose government regulations that they believe are sexist), but the same is also true for religious organizations, business groups, and others. It is also possible for the government, under the control of a section of the dominant stratum, to turn repressively on other members of that stratum; this may be particularly the case when a threat to the prevailing system is seen as overwhelming such that dissenting elites are perceived as traitors rather than as mere opponents.[13]

Political activity, as Lenin well knew, is organized activity. Organizations that provide structure for allegiant and activist activities typically are composed of people with a variety of backgrounds who are united by shared dispositions and goals. The army, professional associations, political clubs, and revolutionary parties, among others, are organizations composed of diverse members that work to maintain or overthrow a particular dominance pattern. Depending on circumstances these organizations may, variously, be allied or competitive. Their common attribute, however, is activity aimed at the furtherance of their members' shared interests in terms of agreed upon means (e.g., accommodative or violent), with the success or failure of the group related to its degree of organization. High-status individuals, by definition, are involved in organizations because they head those organizations of a society that are ideologically sanctioned. This gives allegiant elites a pronounced advantage against unorganized opponents. Groups that organize for change, however, can be effective even when they face the possibility of violence. Labor unions, student clubs, religious organizations, large corporations, farm associations, women's rights groups, military cabals, secret party cells, and insurrectionary guerrillas all have a greater probability of success from the fact of organization itself.

Change in Modernizing Nations

Dislocation as a consequence of conflict among organizations would be difficult enough to analyze even if every society was changing simultaneously at the same rate. But this is manifestly not so. Among Third World nations, for example, the poorest have the lowest economic growth rates in the world while the richest have growth rates higher even than the industrialized West.[14] In fact, around the globe enormous differences exist. In isolated pockets in Africa, Latin America, and Southeast Asia a few tiny remnants of nomadic hunter-gatherer people still survive. In far broader areas, especially in the southern hemisphere, hundreds of millions of people live in agricultural societies; their way of life is hauntingly similar to that of their great-great-grandfathers. These are the people who belong to the 42 percent of the world's 4.2 billion people who share only 3.6 percent of the world's gross national product. In some countries, such as China, the cities are well advanced into industrial life while overall the society has not yet approached transition to the most advanced state. And in some relatively industrialized countries, such as Italy, certain sectors have entered the latest stage of development while others have not. The differences among people, in fact, are so great that it is difficult for those who live in the most modernized societies to visualize or understand the problems of those who live in agricultural communities. The latter, in their turn, often have only a hazy and distorted view of life in advanced nations such as Japan or the United States.

Change from predatory dominance was *sui generis* five hundred years ago in Western Europe; it is no longer. In a broad sense modern peasant societies confront technologically advanced nations relatively directly. Modernization is no longer "within," beginning, as it did in Europe, with gradual commercialization and evolving from the unique concatenation of antiquity and feudalism. At that time there was no countermodel and no idea of the structural changes that flow from the rationalization of agriculture, the spread of trade, the growth of industry, and the uprooting of rural laborers. Partly as a consequence, European townspeople interacted for many centuries with the rural aristocracy in an oscillating pattern of conflict and accommodation. These townsmen, who were often tapped as sources of wealth by aristocrats and princes, represented the forward edge of rationalism, civil liberty, and meritocracy as against the patterns of the old predatory order. They were on occasion used by the crown to enhance absolute royal power; at other times, as with the conflict over enclosures in Britain, they were vigorously opposed by the monarch. It took many hundreds of years for elites in new, urban-based organizations to develop fully and for their power decisively to supersede that of the old nobility.

Change in the modern world is different from the past in the sense that there is now an interconnectedness between internal events and external influences. Within societies commercial and industrial leaders still promote growth in a manner that favors, especially for themselves, autonomous mobility and freedom from restrictions on individual volition and reward; in many areas priority is also given to urban over rural interests. But today these interests are often effectively opposed by those who see collective mobility for the least privileged as the most pressing issue. When urban migration for peasants is possible, the subsequent organization of squatters into political parties and the organization of recently arrived workers into unions is likely. If urban migration is blocked then peasants may begin to participate in oppositional political activity in the countryside. These moves, although they may clearly antagonize the new commercial and industrial elites and may be blocked by police or military activity,[15] are very different from the fragmentation that characterized the organization of the less privileged in the past.

Economic development can occur equally in entrepreneurial or guardian societies. Within the organizations of these societies this development sets the stage for modernization by the provision of material surpluses. Modernization itself, however, only truly begins with solutions to questions about the regulative structures and principles that govern the distribution of resources. By revealing deficiencies in the rights that people possess, economic development acts as an independent but neutral variable in the process of change, exposing the obligations people hold regarding how the benefits of development (material, political, etc.) should be distributed. This is why China and Taiwan, poles apart ideologically, can be equally associated with dramatic economic development but differ in terms of rights and obligations; employing different regulative structures and principles both societies sponsor poverty reduction involving land reform, institutional renovation in the countryside, and an integrated linking of policies connected with agrarian and industrial production and of issues regarding health, education, population planning and rural welfare.[16] Viewing economic development as possible in different dominance structures helps explain why organizations that seek "modernization" can direct their activities variously at breaking down traditional structures (seeking negative rights), at taming capitalism (seeking positive rights), or at championing autonomy from imposed collectivist policies (seeking negative rights).

Core and Peripheral Organizations

Although change characterizes all societies, its increasing rapidity for those at the most advanced stage of development has led to a widening gap between them and societies that are still predominantly agricultural or early industrial. Yet despite this disparity there has been an inexorable movement toward increasing interdependence among the world's nations. It is this factor that makes change in the modern world so different from the relatively self-contained development process that occurred historically in Western Europe.

The interaction among nations does not consist of equal reciprocal flows. All advanced nations have more complex and economically powerful organizations than do agricultural or early industrial societies. Consequently, the impact of advanced countries on others is far greater than in return, since the organizations that stimulate interdependence are largely based in these societies. Not all of these organizations have as their objective the production of goods. Many are oriented toward service (e.g., health) or defense (e.g., military advisory groups). Although the goals of an organization (commerce, communication, etc.) determine the particular area of its influence, a basic shared characteristic is the attempt to acquire resources that are useful for the organization and augment its capabilities (diplomatic support, military alliance, intellectual expertise, etc.). For entrepreneurial economic organizations, such as multinational corporations, this may involve a transfer of wealth and natural resources from what are sometimes called peripheral countries to an organization that is located in an advanced core nation. But the pull of resources occurs regardless of whether the advanced society is entrepreneurial or guardian. In the Soviet bloc, for instance, where only certain sectors are now entering the highest stages of development, there is a pull toward centers in the Soviet Union and East Germany through the activities of the at least fifty socialist transnational organizations.[17] In entrepreneurial societies the major pull is toward organizations in the United States, with lesser, but increasing, flows toward Japan and Western Europe. A common complaint in Third World countries is that organizations in societies such as the United States take resources in a manner that creates a dependency of the weaker area on the stronger. Whatever the truth of this allegation, and there would appear to be much to it, the basic pattern is for resources to flow toward the most advanced sectors regardless of their political and economic complexion.

All modern societies have a mix of international interests that are at least semi-interrelated. Clearly U.S. and Soviet military establishments do serve worldwide to protect the political and economic activities of their respective countries. To say, however, as one theorist has, that U.S. economic, political, and cultural hegemony is the consequence of the operations of a military-industrial complex in the context of world capitalist development is to place a premium on conspiratorial collusion that is not warranted (e.g., both the U.S. and Soviet military organizations face great restraints on what they can do internationally to protect other interests).[18] Or to say that organized labor and monopoly capital have a common interest in foreign economic expansion and the control of overseas markets that will open up job opportunities at home is to be, seemingly, unaware of the cross-purposes to which organizations work depending on their own interests (e.g., transnational corporations seeking overseas labor markets that damage domestic labor interests and labor unions seeking protectionist import legislation that damages transnational corporate marketing efforts).[19] This does not mean, of course, that there is no interaction among the organizations of a particular dominance system that serves to integrate normative, economic, organizational, and individual goals. What is not the case is that this interaction is systematic, subject to some sort of overall control based on a conscious, ideological perspective, and binding regardless of the particular interests of the organization.

The extent of overseas involvement by core nation organizations is enormous. Between 1945 and 1977 U.S. foreign investment grew from 7 billion to 148 billion dollars. From 1967 to 1976 the value of the sales by majority-owned foreign affiliates of U.S. companies increased from 108.5 billion to 514.7 billion dollars. Bank assets abroad in 1976 were 181 billion dollars serviced by more than 100 banks and overseas branches.[20] In the noncommunist world at least 10,000 transnational corporations of all countries had affiliates overseas. Of 382 firms with annual sales over 1 billion dollars, 242, or 63 percent, had 25 percent or more foreign content in terms of sales, assets, exports, earnings, or employment. In 1971 on any given day these organizations held short-term liquid assets that were more than twice the total of all international monetary institutions on the same day.[21] Approximately three thousand American parent companies employ about five million foreigners, a number higher than the entire labor force of many developing countries.[22] Hundreds of international professional associations have also developed which socialize their members to common values and generate organizational and occupational loyalties. Of the estimated three to four thousand international congresses of intergovernment organizations held annually and involving at least one million people, at least half are convened by international professional associations.[23]

The pulling of resources from periphery to core takes place under the aegis of this general type of international organization. These organizations, however, do not directly plunder a peripheral country but rather work through subsidiary or allied organizations in joint ventures that facilitate the acquisition process. The development of these satellite organizations (trading companies, research organizations, local political parties, etc.) occurs as a consequence of the core organization's activities but sometimes independent of any direct initiative, control, or prompting from the core. Whatever the initial impetus the consequence is that the peripheral organizations exist in a degree of junior partnership with the external core organizations, being emulative of them and structured so as to facilitate interaction between the two.

Change in peripheral societies results from the activities of core and satellite organizations which serve as conduits and seedbeds for new skills and attitudes.[24] A whole series of changes occur. The development of new techniques of organization calls for different educational goals and practices. In the settlement of disputes, new organizations press for compatible judicial structures and procedures. Travel by core organization personnel to peripheral areas stimulates the development of medical, entertainment, and other facilities similar to those found in the core areas. Increasingly, core organizations and their satellites come to have a stake in the political orientation of the peripheral society. This interest ultimately stimulates direct or indirect activity for the creation of supportive forms of government.

Another major outcome of core organization penetration is the introduction of new occupations that have no place within the traditional society. The existence of industrial workers, air force pilots, political activists, surgeons, accountants, and information specialists, to name but a few, severely disrupts long-established social rankings. As such these "new men" are a threat to that society's traditional dominance system.

New occupations mean new values, related not only to the desirability of a specific job but to the legitimacy of that job in terms of a particular dominance pattern. Tension develops between the more personal, diffuse, and often religious values that characterize most older systems and the attitudes shared by those who have acquired new outlooks and responsibilities. Regardless of whether new organizations in the peripheral societies are emulative of entrepreneurial or guardian core organizations, their members always stress secularization and impersonal rationality, the legitimacy and desirability of change, and the necessity for the organization's members to support a new way of life. These become the creed and manifesto of the new men of society as they seek to create a new social order.

People who make demands for greater recognition do not always see themselves as revolutionaries and, in fact, often consciously reject that label. Yet what they seek is nothing less than the overthrow of existing political, social, and economic structures for they want rights that will legitimize their role in society, allowing them to function in peace and security. They demand these rights in the name of a new consciousness about social obligations that undercuts traditional dominance patterns. Prevailing justifications of leadership come to be viewed as perversions, setting in motion a debate about the old society. Specific instances of elite misconduct may be singled out for opprobrium or traditional organizations and their members in general criticized. Ultimately these criticisms merge into an overall accusation of systemic perversion.

Once started, the pressure for rights is continuous. As people come to value new techniques that provide benefits (e.g., medical skills), this valuation erodes the legitimacy of denying rights and recognition to those who have mastered these techniques. A successful assertion of rights, for a greater share of rewards or for less interference by traditional authority, heightens the prestige of the new men and the organizations that they belong to and increases awareness of their contributions to society. As rights are gained, fresh energy is released and demands arise for additional people who can provide services. Structural changes occur with the development of new organizations that move societies away from purely traditional forms and procedures. In this continuous process new skills are constantly needed and new occupations in new organizations are created. Concomitantly, fresh demands by ever newer groups for more equitable reward or greater autonomy are generated.

Responses to Core Organization Penetration

Ironically, core organizations, whose dominance patterns are themselves the result of an historical demand for rights, are the cause of the introduction of a debate about obligations throughout the peripheral world in a manner that sometimes acts against the interests of the core organization itself.

There is an implicit contract between organizations and society in the sense that patterns of obligation within organizations reflect dominance values and are acceptable or unacceptable according to the degree of adherence to those values in society generally. This leads to exceptional problems when an organization from a core area intrudes into a foreign society in order to strengthen its capability. The impact causes disruptions precisely because the organization's dominance system may not be compatible—in either values or procedures—with dominance as it is exercised in the peripheral society. The points of friction are most evident in the case of satellite organizations whose members owe allegiance both to the organization and to the peripheral society. Satellite organizations that are allied with core entrepreneurial organizations have internal patterns that justify entrepreneurial dominance; guardian-style organizations in peripheral areas stress learning an alien ideology as a prerequisite for authority; neither may have very much in common with the forms of dominance that currently prevail. The degree of impact of an external dominance system is a function of the efficacy of the core organization in inculcating its values within satellite organizations and the peripheral society generally.

It is often the case that there are no organized groups in a peripheral society—similar to those in the core society—that can act as a countervailing force against tendencies generated by the core organization's particular form of dominance to overstress one type of right and obligation. Thus, a peripheral society may have no organized labor movement to contest the exploitative labor practices of a multinational corporation or widely based political parties that can contest the hegemonic ideological claims of a revolutionary organization. Moreover, new and old elites may work at cross-purposes in dealing with core organizations as when new domestic commercial organizations are crippled in competition with organizations from the outside by traditional tax practices.[25] The ability of state elites to extract taxes, obtain credit, and deploy resources may be severely hampered by long-standing domestic institutional arrangements as well as by concessions—sometimes extracted unwillingly—made to external core organizations.[26] At the same time, as education levels improve and as media penetration increases, those who are the best trained and have the most initiative often opt for association with the core organizations (i.e., in professional associations, the military, commercial enterprises, political groups), further depriving faltering local organizations of help in maintaining their viability. Ultimately there develops a widespread recognition that the sole force that can cope with destabilizing influences is the government itself, with the consequence that control of government becomes an overriding concern of the intruding organizations and their local allies as well as of those people and groups who resist them. In earlier centuries this often resulted in old-fashioned imperialism (e.g., when an organization like the British East India Company secured control in its own name of portions of India). In the twentieth century the drive to insure core organization survival is no less critical and often no less forceful. The activities of U.S. corporations in Chile in engineering the violent overthrow of the Allende government or the support provided by the Soviet military in Afghanistan for a beleaguered Communist government are recent examples. The inevitable result of these activities, of course, was and is to polarize groups in society around the issue of control of the "nation."

In the modern world, rather than direct intervention, the more common way that core organizations seek stability and viability is by strengthening ties between the organization and those internal groups whose own interests are furthered by the organization's operations. Historically, the outstanding model for this type of activity was the pattern of Western penetration into China. Intrusion involved not merely the securing of treaty ports and forcing the Chinese government to accede to trade agreements. There also developed a new group of Chinese known as compradors who acted as liaison between the Western organizations and the Chinese populace and who ultimately built sizable organizations of their own which sometimes competed successfully with their Western mentors.

The viability of core organizations generally depends upon some local support, for without it interaction with the target population is virtually impossible. Although the relationship between particular core and peripheral societies may be exploitative overall, the local groups that support the core organization must be sustained by appropriate rewards. The benefits that supporters obtain, of course, need not be material and can include intangibles such as a belief that one is building a better society. Importers, military officers, industrialists, and members of revolutionary cells, among others, have different motivations for supporting external core organizations and different expectations regarding the benefits that can be derived from such support.

The activities of a core organization can ultimately break down traditional forms of dominance and lead to a paralysis of government. When the core organization's local networks become so intrusive that their activities influence local policy priorities then the peripheral government will either defend itself against the threat or begin to identify with the core organization and its internal supporters. Whether the peripheral government allies itself with the intruding core organization or opposes it depends on the congruence between the core organization's dominance patterns and the goals and values of local dominant groups.[27] For instance, in the nineteenth century, Chinese elites perceived the methods and aims of Western core organizations (missionary organizations, commercial enterprises, etc.) as exemplifying values that threatened the dominance patterns of their society; these elites and the government of China subsequently made strong efforts to resist Western penetration. Although repeatedly unsuccessful, this resistance frequently took the form of military action or mob violence instigated by local gentry. In like manner, in twentieth-century South Vietnam, large segments of the local dominant classes opposed the insurrectionary revolutionary activities of Communist military and party units that were supplied and supported from North Vietnam (and the Soviet Union and China). In South America, on the other hand, dominant groups have allied themselves with multinational corporations and other organizations (frequently the military) from capitalist core societies. In this case a correspondence of interest is perceived between the predatory goals of the traditional dominance system and the entrepreneurial objectives of the core organizations.

In social conflict the most common pattern is contention among a variety of small groups with different interests vying for rather specific objectives. This pattern may change, however, when local elites ally themselves with a core organization such that political and economic policies within the peripheral area are intimately influenced by the organization. At that point the nature of further opposition to the organization may be radically altered. Since local elites have abdicated the role of a countervailing force, diverse groups may unite to denounce the moral worth of those in local dominant positions, raising the costs of control and even wresting concessions for themselves. Peasants may be mobilized into insurrectionary organizations founded by students, intellectuals, and disaffected members of middle-income groups.[28] Nationalists, claiming rights in the name of a people, come forth to unite different groups under the banner of opposition and change. These nationalists come in many forms—as Communist revolutionaries who assert the importance of a particular national road to socialism, as military officers or religious leaders, or even as advocates of gradual directed change such as the reformers in nineteenth-century Meiji Japan who broke down the old feudal forms of their society, revoked the privileges of traditional dominant groups, and gave great opportunities to previously excluded people within a context of intense loyalty to the new state.

The activities of oppositional organizations may elicit repression and violence by the local government leading to the dissolution of the opposition. When the government has ceased to be widely supported, however, repression may merely solidify opposition and cause the dissenting forces progressively to restructure themselves into revolutionary organizations. Ironically, this may be highly antithetical to the interests of the core organization and end with the ouster of both the local elite and the core organization. The fate of American corporations in Cuba followed this pattern. Less well known perhaps was the fate of the Communists in Indonesia at the time of the fall of Sukarno when the party, which supported him, was destroyed and the government taken over by a moralistic military regime.

There is no predetermined outcome from the tensions and polarization that occur in the conflict for rights. Often a movement favoring new directions succeeds. At other times traditional appeals can be effectively asserted and used to mobilize those segments of a population who feel threatened by change yet have no ready way to express their emotions. When these feelings are forged into broadly based organizations that oppose change, they can be an exceptionally powerful force. Led by leaders who invoke nativistic moral standards, the drive to protect selected aspects of tradition may assume explosive proportions. Iran, for example, had undergone more rapid change in the thirty years following the Second World War than most societies. Its urban population had expanded greatly, and many new occupations associated with an entrepreneurial style of life had become privileged. Women, especially in the cities, had cast aside the subservience that was their lot in traditional Islamic society. A modern military had been created, and people spoke of Iran as the new great power of the Persian Gulf. Yet in the space of a few short months a political system friendly to the West collapsed and the influence of multinational corporations was curtailed with losses totaling approximately eighty billion dollars.[29] Although many elements of a new way of life are well established, the Islamic revolution is strikingly traditional in form. Clearly, many people felt highly threatened by the rapid changes that had taken place and were affronted by the new values held by people with Western-style occupations. Led by leaders invoking traditional moral standards, they spasmodically rejected the entrepreneurial-style dominance system of the West and the values associated with it and took steps to curb the activities of leftist groups as well. Women were told to reassume their traditional place in society. Legal proceedings returned to a traditional religious format. There has been, in general, a reassertion of the validity of the traditional system and its patterns of dominance. That this assertion is almost surely doomed to failure does not minimize the potency of this type of allegiant response when people feel threatened by change.

In the last century traditional allegiant opposition to entrepreneurial intrusion has been widespread. These responses have not, however, had long-term success. More common by far has been the rise of movements for change directed against both the predatory past and the influence of change-inducing but highly destabilizing entrepreneurial core organizations. Since these organizations vastly outnumber those from guardian dominance systems, much of the drive for change in the modern world involves the assertion of positive rights against the dominance pattern of the entrepreneurial system. Where the influence of outside guardian organizations is very large, however, as was the case in Egypt in the 1960s, then those who seek change champion autonomy vis à vis these organizations.

Organizations are a critical stimulus to change. But their own internal patterns of dominance make them incapable of handling demands for rights that are not congruent with the obligations they sanction. Perceived as perversions by local populations, these patterns of obligation generate issues about rights that lead to movements for change. How that change proceeds is determined by the strength of the various contending organizations, allegiant and activist, shaped by the existing and the intruding dominance systems. The pressure for change itself is unending.

Conclusion: Autonomy and Community

Who will take the first decisive steps toward the creation of a society that honors both positive and negative rights? Will it be the United States or the Soviet Union, today's superpowers, or is their path to a moral social order blocked by the intensity of their bitter ideological dispute and the unwillingness of their elites to concede the prerogatives of their dominance? Perhaps it will be smaller countries like Sweden, New Zealand, or Yugoslavia, all of whom have already taken steps in this direction. From their experiments it may be possible for larger societies to perceive the advantages of a newer way of life. Or perhaps, and this seems quite possible, it will be a large, populous nation like China, whose experiments in change may lead it to become the economic and moral superpower of the twenty-first century.

No one who knows of the horrors of Nazism or of the repressions by political leaders in Latin America, Africa, Eastern Europe, or elsewhere needs to be reminded that cruelty and savagery are still rampant in the world. These horrors, in fact, have been so intense that they have made us pause and have undermined any self-assured confidence in the inevitability of the triumph of good over evil. Nevertheless, the barbarism of our own age notwithstanding, we are not Romans or Aztecs and it does our spirits no harm to recollect our triumphs over Leviathan. Unevenly to be sure, and with painful difficulty, the path has been away from the use of private armies for personal advantage, human sacrifice, slavery, cannibalism, blood feuds, savage economic exploitation, brutal and sadistic public performances, and other forms of cruel mistreatment. In many places physical abuse of children has declined, and in some countries it is even legally prohibited. Ridicule in front of others with the object of fostering uncritical acceptance of the group and its leaders has been scrutinized for its effect. Racism, nationalism, and sexism are increasingly perceived in terms of the damage they do to the development of moral competence. Slowly, often haltingly, and with many lapses, older patterns are eradicated. Unfortunately, not all evils have been everywhere eliminated, and the greatest scourges of all, war, genocide, and judicial torture, are alive and well.

For most people throughout history, life consisted of intense hard work accompanied by a gnawing anxiety about food and shelter. Indeed, except for the citizens of a few privileged nations, this condition still holds for many in the world, making understandable the great attraction of dominant status with its assurance of rewards and its promise of a life of greater security. Some men, of course, seek dominance because the power that it gives satisfies deep personal needs. For others, however, dominance insures and secures the resources that protect life. Were there a solution to scarcity, the corroding effect that dominance has upon moral behavior would be lessened. For although movements for rights can mitigate the harshest aspects of dominance, a final solution is difficult in environments of want where competition is intense and fear of others is widespread. The paradox, of course, is that when the obligations that are paired with rights are widely shared, men are freed from anxieties about their fellows and their energies can be channeled toward producing benefits for all. Greater abundance, in its turn, makes more possible the furtherance of rights.

The pace of change in the modern world is explosive. New inventions, discoveries that vastly improve the life of everyone, occur at an accelerating rate. At the same time intractable problems remain. Population growth threatens food supplies and political boundaries senselessly fragment cooperative endeavor. In one society after another and in many differing contexts efforts to protect the old clash with movements for a new way of life. At times, slowly, new values are institutionalized that provide protection from abuse and allow participation in social life for many whose ancestors could not even dream of such privileges. Yet the process is by no means continuous or unidirectional. The question that therefore haunts the minds of modernizing men is what social forms and processes influence people to behave morally.

The Dilemma

Justice, as Michael Walzer says, begins with persons in the social world.[1] But over the millennia this very fact has been a major quandary—how to balance the rights of the individual and those of the community. Social control to solve community problems imposes hierarchical values, but the discarding or rejecting of these values can lead to anarchical self-seeking with harmful effects for the group.[2] How then can both individual and community needs be met and moral competence fostered?

Robert Dahl, from a structural perspective, has placed his finger on the nub of the problem: although there are a large number of variations in the way that people can be controlled, there are no cases where centralized direction and socially owned property coexists with decentralized autonomous organizations that function in a market environment that recognizes private control.[3] How, Dahl asks, can the rational direction of decision making by a centralized authority be at the same time subject to democratic controls by autonomous subunits? Concomitantly, how can autonomus units, which often stabilize inequality, deform civic consciousness, and alienate the control of the public agenda by citizens, remain autonomous yet at the same time be subject to community control?[4] As he says, "no satisfactory way has been discovered, either in theory or in practice, for eliminating markets and at the same time allowing enterprises a substantial degree of autonomy. Theory and historical experiences argue strongly that a system of enterprises governed *neither* by the market *nor* by central planners would run headlong into chaos."[5]

The First Step—Changing Attitudes

Societies become increasingly moral as more and more people possess higher levels of moral competence and as social processes and forms increasingly reflect this competence. When this happens the scope of action for the amoral person is progressively narrowed; the moloch, robber baron, and ideologue are all constrained even though never eliminated. Those who manipulate dominance because of a lack of empathy and altruistic awareness have less opportunity to exploit others in their search for an answer to their personal needs. Social values no longer support and glorify dominant behavior that denies worth to others.

All social systems have beliefs and preferences that influence the way people act. During socialization differences in hierarchy are learned and the reasons for the differences (age, sex, wealth, power, learning) are also acquired. These reasons gain widespread acceptance. The predators, entrepreneurs, or guardians are justified in their high rank because their behavior exemplifies the values that people feel have worth. Learning about hierarchy and about the values that bolster it supports status systems. In traditional societies this learning accustomed people to accept a predetermined place in society. A low-caste Indian, for instance, learns that the Brahmin, not he, is one who in his various incarnations has most closely lived according to the values that are honored in Indian religious thought. In the same manner people in information-stage societies learn that academic skill is essential in order to enjoy high status.

In modern societies generally most people develop no further than a conventional level of moral reasoning (i.e., securing the approval of authority and living by the rules). Obedience to norms is a common, indeed expected, consequence of socialization. The virtue of this is that rights, once enshrined as and protected by rules, become defended as part of a conservative bias. Conversely, since existing systems predominantly enshrine only one form of right, the same conservative bias acts to perpetuate dominance forms that deny the full range of obligations associated with both positive and negative rights. How then can people's attitudes and the rules by which they justify their behavior be changed?

Every society has some members who have high moral competence. Moreover, the qualities of mature moral competence prompt a desire for moral values to be shared by others, above and beyond those values sanctioned by group authority.[6] Morally competent people goad social consciousness, although as individuals they are often unlikely to generate widespread change; for this they need support and connection with like-minded others. Chilton suggests that a decalage of moral development occurs from the use of new socialization techniques and from exposure to higher-stage reasoners or the practices of institutions that encourage morally competent behavior.[7] The most important factor encouraging decalage, however, is social crises (e.g., foreign conflict, economic decline, internal war) which require people to deal with moral issues. The outcome, of course, can be moral decline as well as advance. But in the debate concerning the crisis people are exposed to solutions arrived at on the basis of several types of moral reasoning with a probability that the moral competence of some will advance as a consequence.[8]

In the modern world one major and continuing crisis, unequal and uneven in intensity, is associated with a deprivation of rights. Over time there are periods of marked upsurge in the debate about rights (e.g., the 1960s throughout much of the world). Among those who experience the upsurge there may be sufficient decalage that the extension of rights becomes a permanent part of social values. When that happens these values become important in the learning of the next generation. The enlargement of negative rights, for instance, then leads to an emphasis on the development of autonomous capabilities; as this happens individual responsibility becomes more valued. The extension of positive rights underlines the importance of altruistic awareness and empathy toward people who previously did not have a fair share of the benefits of society; as a consequence, the content of explicit morals training changes. Books or movies with prejudicial content become unacceptable; remarks with sexist or racist overtones, for example, become more noticeable and less permissible. At the same time groups that were previously denied rights are referred to in literature or television in a positive or flattering manner in order to make people aware that rights have been extended.

As younger generations attain maturity their own experience is the basis from which they observe life. What appeared as an advance in rights for their elders may seem to them, from their new perspective, a failure to extend rights far enough. Such perceptions fuel the moral indignation of the young who, in their turn, once again raise a call for rights. With each such occurrence or upsurge the number of people with higher moral competence grows.

The Second Step—Changing Organizational Dominance

The fact that hierarchy and dominance are characteristics of all societies does not mean that their form is immutable. Adult-child relationships, for instance, may be highly rigid with older people granted authority and prestige solely on the basis of age; or, they may be more egalitarian where children are encouraged to question and seek justification for the authoritative statements of adults. If some industrial or commercial organizations are highly authoritative and hierarchical, it does not follow that other organizations need be equally so. In fact, present-day experiments with worker-management committees and with communal forms of decision making suggest that organizational dominance can vary considerably from the traditional mold. Serious impediments to such changes, however, do exist.

In advanced societies spectacular economic growth, the amelioration of harsh conditions, and the spread of middle-class values and consumption patterns have not led to a uniform sense of purpose about social life. Indeed, there is considerable disgust with materialism, inefficiency, and related cases of corruption.[9] Polls in many countries indicate the deep concern of people about material values and their worry about their lack of control over economic matters.[10] More than half of respondents in a survey of American and Norwegian workers voiced a desire for greater participation in decisions affecting jobs, indicating their sense of exclusion from any significant say about one of the major areas of their lives.[11] At the same time, other findings show how little the public as a whole supports the right of workers for more say at work and, indeed, how little freedom of speech itself is prized in comparison to law and order or economic values. A survey of six Western European countries, for example, asked respondents to choose among selected values; freedom of speech held last place with 13.8 percent.[12]

Although economic matters may be paramount in people's thoughts, it is clear that policies designed to address redistributive issues have not been overly successful. Nationalization of industry, for example, has not created a more equal society or a greater sense of justice in relationships generally. Nor have groups like labor unions been notably successful in achieving greater redistribution. These failures are at least partly explained by the fact that in entrepreneurial societies resources, including political power, are unequally shared. Giant corporations are de facto public enterprises with enormous impact upon societies as a whole; they differ from governments, however, in being beyond public control and in having power that can be exercised with little regard for the views of ordinary people.[13] Because the most important arena in modern societies for moral behavior is in organizations, theories and policies that do not account for the concentration of power in these structures (internally and within society as a whole) run a serious risk of error.

Those who find defects in modern entrepreneurial societies criticize the "market," economic expansion overseas, the collaboration of big business and organized labor against groups like unorganized labor, migrant workers, and immigrants, and the skewing of tax policies and budgetary priorities in favor of the advantaged.[14] None of these should be minimized as sources of perversion of entrepreneurial dominance, but they tend, I think, to focus attention unduly on the macro level. Less examined are the working structure of the enterprise, the content of jobs, and the degree of worker participation in organizational life.[15] In fact, the transformation of social relations and of authority patterns at the micro level is perhaps as urgent as macrolevel considerations. Certainly isolating the two makes no sense, if only because the oligarchical and hierarchical authority patterns within organizations are different from those that hold in public life. Social experience is thus bifurcated, suggesting, at the least, that macrolevel solutions can have only a cosmetic rather than a fundamental effect on dominance values. To permit authoritarian decision making in organizations at the same time that democratic controls pertain elsewhere is to make equality forever only a conditional commodity.[16] Clearly what is required is a new set of microlevel relationship patterns, embodying equality, that will decisively affect macrolevel interactions.

Internal changes in organizations are in fact occurring. On the one hand these are built into the very dynamism and success of modern organizations. To paraphrase Schumpeter and broaden his point of reference to contemporary societies generally, success creates for everyone a new standard of living that undermines previous justifications for power differences; rational habits of mind associated with increasing bureaucratism destroy unreflective habits of superordination and subordination in organizational life; a concentration on growth allows the development of critical views that espouse different goals; and dominance values in general lose their hold as lifestyles change.[17] These shifts can lead to questions about the whole relationship between work, ownership, and governance. For instance, in entrepreneurial societies who hires what or whom in what contractual time period is a question that, if taken far enough, leads to an analysis of the way that organizational relationships are legitimized. Must the capital-owning party and the party undertaking the capital-using production process be the same? Does the relatively autonomous and unaccountable power of managers really flow from the essentially money-lending function of shareholders, the owners of capital? Can workers hire capital and become the firm, and if so, what kinds of title should they hold (e.g., direct title, title held by a supporting corporation)?[18]

In the United States there has been a radical shift in the style of entrepreneurship fueled by the generation that came of age amid the idealism of the 1960s. Often operating small businesses—which have been the sole provider of new jobs in the United States since the 1970s—they have eschewed the bureaucratic forms of governance of large organizations whose patterns since the turn of the century have cast such doubt on the possibility of creating a genuine moral society.[19] Without completely dismissing the prevalent pyramidal design of authority, there has nevertheless been an effort to infuse organizations with humanistic values. Most new entrepreneurs, however, are owners of capital—or are responsible to risk venture capitalists—and are also managers of capital-using production processes. As a consequence, although the changes that many of them have instituted in their organizations cannot be minimized, their innovations are not as important for change to moral dominance as are those in self-governed or worker-owned enterprises. These latter organizations encourage more people to be part of the decision-making process and allow entrepreneurship (i.e., the exercise of negative rights in economic matters) to be shared by everyone, to everyone's advantage, rather than by only one or a few people. In the United States there are more than seven thousand employee-owned companies representing about 8 percent of the work force (a figure that will, it is estimated, be in the range of 20 percent by the year 2000[20]). Characterized generally by rapid growth, improved efficiency, and broadened ownership of wealth, employee-owned companies tap loyalty and creativity in a way that no conventional organization can.[21] They include among their number some truly notable successes such as the Parsons Corporation of Los Angeles and Rochester Products, a division of General Motors, at Tuscaloosa, Alabama.

Many experiments in job enlargement, job rotation, and job enrichment are imposed by management with no worker participation. To the degree that high control from above continues to exist, these plans may, in fact, reduce the effectiveness of work groups. In contrast, participative management is a major characteristic of high-achieving groups.[22] In employee-owned companies this participation allows workers to have a say about things that matter to them most: security of tenure, staffing, job design, opportunities for self-improvement, the duration and intensity of work, sanitary conditions, and, significantly, the highest possible income for everyone. Although income maximization and equalization are not the only objectives of participation (in China and Yugoslavia an avowed goal is also to create a new type of person), a recent study of American experiments in employee-owned organizations shows these to have been a widespread result.[23]

With regard to productivity some findings suggest that it is changes in pay (income maximization) rather than participation in decision making that most encourages increased output; other data suggest that when workers have high choice (i.e., the option to refuse working on a project), even with low pay their productivity will be as great as that of workers who have high pay and high choice.[24] Attention to employees, not work conditions, seems to have the most effect on productivity. But what kind of attention? Such things as comfort, challenge, job security, and cooperative relations with coworkers are important, but the most significant factors are a combination of reward and autonomy.[25] Not surprisingly, these two factors, involving as they do consideration for a person's well-being and allowance for personal responsibility, are related to high moral competence. Although the data are far from conclusive, it seems that organizations that support the obligations of moral dominance also stimulate productivity.

The Third Step—Participation in Organizations

Apathy was and is a basic fact of life in traditional organizations. Workers accepted their wage status as a customary part of the job and provided loyalty in exchange for the rewards that were received. Few opportunities for participation existed, and virtually no scope for the development of self-evaluative capabilities regarding work performance. Information-stage organizations, on the other hand, have internal dynamics that break down these patterns. Task complexity, which has risen markedly, means an increase in personal specialization, which in turn increases the volume of communication as a greater need evolves to coordinate diverse occupational specialists. One consequence of this trend is less reliance on programmed pyramidal interactions to achieve the necessary linkages between parts of the organization. There is more emphasis on reciprocal information flows. This horizontal differentiation has been consistently and positively associated (to the level of middle management) with decentralization of decision making.[26] The result, at least at some levels of the organization, is to reduce distinctions, improve feedback, foster role enlargement and group responsibility, and, above all, increase participation. As these patterns become more characteristic for all levels, apathy and an unwillingness to be self-evaluative decline generally.

Fostering participation lessens the possibility of authoritarianism by organizational leaders. But this is not a rapid or wholesale process. Workers' desires to participate begin with demands for a say in lower-level rather than higher-level decisions. It takes time for workers to overcome feelings that they have no relevant knowledge and information and that they genuinely can use their own initiative to make decisions regarding their jobs. As efficiency and organizational capability are spurred by greater participation (consequences that are frequently, although not invariably, realized), and as policies regarding income distribution and occupational opportunities become more the result of public decisions, workers gain confidence in their ability to manage, control, and exploit their common endeavor.[27] These possibilities reach their ultimate point in self-managed, employee-owned concerns where the principles of equal voting and of elected leadership accountable to the led, which are part of public life, become aspects of organizational life.

The causal influence is stronger from participation to socioeconomic equality than the reverse.[28] Equally, participation in the workplace has a positive effect on the ability of people to take responsibility and to reflect on other people's needs when goals are formulated, decisions made, and objectives achieved. Not leisure but active participation affects the development of moral competence. Participation is educative, broadening outlooks and developing capacities; by extending the scope of participation, conformity and blind loyalty are reduced while critical evaluation increases. The evidence indicates that participation diminishes tendencies toward nondemocratic attitudes and instead develops feelings of political efficacy.[29] The conclusion is relatively clear and straightforward and equally valid for guardian as well as entrepreneurial societies: a necessary condition for establishing a society that balances autonomy and community is the development of organizational patterns that provide opportunities to participate in decision making. How far organizations can move in this direction is one of the crucial questions of modernization.

The Fourth Step—The Transition to Autonomy and Community

Socialization to greater moral competence for a large number of people is likely only over a very long period of time. Even with massive indoctrination a wholesale transformation of values is not a genuine short-term possibility, as modern guardian leaders are well aware of from experience (e.g., the failure of China's Great Leap Forward). Greater participation at the workplace has, perhaps, the most potential for stimulating moral maturity, but democratization of industry is a direct threat to property ownership and ideological control. What then can be done when changes that improve the lot of subordinates threaten the values of dominant groups?

A strategy for achieving autonomy and community requires a recognition that the benefits associated with both positive and negative rights are everyone's due. Police protection and protection from police are two such. So also are ameliorative policies in the area of poverty reduction, medical care, education, economic growth, and limitations on elite power. Attaining those needs that are related to positive rights by large-scale asset transfers or by strengthening judicial powers is a political matter requiring collective decision making; at the same time there must also be guarantees of autonomy and protection from abuse. The main issue then becomes how public-sector activity can solve fair-share needs without creating a guardian dominance system that crushes the ability of individuals to make a life plan free from undue restriction.

In the present day, large-scale organizations play a critical role in the process of transition from predatory dominance. Needs, especially economic ones, depend for their realization on authoritative decisions regarding tapping unused natural resources, developing appropriate skills and technology, allocating labor to exploit resources, finding and directing capital, developing structures that can organize and distribute production, and training people to norms and beliefs that support large-scale cooperative ventures. These activities can be carried out by autonomous organizations functioning within a market structure or by governments. But it is clearly the case that with the former model, one group, the entrepreneurs, tends to have its needs overfulfilled while others are distinctly less favored. Although government intervention can ameliorate the worst possibilities that might occur, inequality of reward and opportunity is generally common and widespread.

The way that assets are initially distributed sets the pattern of future growth. Large initial inequalities usually mean that additions to income from growth will be distributed unequally.[30] In most developing entrepreneurial societies movement from low to medium levels of economic development does result in greater equality, but this must be placed in the context of large initial inequality. Moreover, continuing development—after achieving medium levels—brings only marginal further increases in equality.[31] Aggrandizement of resources by one group, therefore, tends to become institutionalized. The inequality, however, as was pointed out in chapters 5 and 6, may be sharply challenged, leading to political instability and an undermining of negative rights as private ownership is questioned. The problem here is that in achieving political stability and social equality (and the evidence shows a long-term positive relationship between them[32]), negative rights may be sacrificed as electorates or influential actors such as military officers move to end confrontation by making government more powerful and stabilizing. The result frequently is policies that favor greater equalization in the distribution of income but at the expense of negative rights, higher rates of inflation, and an increase in the costs and controls associated with the development of a public economy.[33]

Problems associated with government control can be lessened, of course, by reliance on market structures. It seems clear, however, that although the market can be used as a device for coordinating economic activity, sponsoring growth, and disciplining inefficient producers, its adverse qualities must be hedged by public policy if any redistribution of income that will have the least hope of satisfying the basic needs of the poor is to be effected. Seventy percent of the rural population of nonsocialist Third World countries show a tendency toward absolute impoverishment. As a consequence redistributive tax laws, full-employment measures, limited rationing for the poor and price controls on rationed supplies, and the development of government-chartered and financed development banks for financing cooperative ventures are all measures that governments must take—but often don't—to help the worst-off segments of the population.[34] It must be recognized, of course, that on the negative side these activities can result in declining overall growth rates, inflation, and increased frustration as upper-income sectors reduce support for the government and slow investment.[35] These are costs, however, that must be measured against the severe political instability that will occur if positive rights are ignored.

If development is to be successful, involving the extension of both positive and negative rights, a particular kind of government role is therefore crucial. Decentralization of decision making and planning at the organizational level (i.e., enhanced participation, as in the self-managed firms of industrialized societies) must go hand in hand with strong government-supported organizational linkages at the village level and between the villages and higher levels. Governments, in this sense, do become larger and more intrusive, more coordinating and controlling, regardless of the type of dominance system. More and more people have their needs met through a system of interlocked governmental and nongovernmental organizations. This fact makes clear why throughout the world it is no longer possible to talk of genuinely autonomous markets, organizations, or individuals. On the other hand, it is also not possible to speak of a centralized system that by itself can perfectly meet the various needs of citizens in complex modern societies. Although Dahl notes accurately enough the potential for chaos in a system of organizations governed neither by the market nor by central planners,[36] there is now an equal potential for chaos in systems that are governed solely by central planners or by the market. A devolved administration with local organizations accountable to the local people and involved with local development must coexist with state policies that support reform. The poor cannot be passive recipients of help nor helpless pawns of market mechanisms. Rather, as in South Korea or the People's Republic of China, they must become active participants in administering and implementing reform. Only then will both their income and their political power increase.[37]

Why should elites support such policies? They will do so, I think, only if they have a strong commitment to change, if the element of personal threat in change is absent, and if overall growth provides benefits for elites as well as the impoverished. All of these imply organizational processes that on the one hand provide inducements (prestige, fulfillment, and, variably, market benefits) and on the other hand safeguard personal security. Prestige and fulfillment are increasingly likely to be satisfactory rewards to the degree that an effective socialization process inculcates a belief in their value; they are also more likely to be sufficient when material rewards are progressively equalized and responsibilities progressively shared in organizations that promote worker or peasant participation in decision making.

The danger with emphasizing fulfillment and prestige as rewards is that a socialization process that touts these goals as desirable can become the route for guardian control even in well-meant efforts to correct the perversions of entrepreneurial dominance. Despite the belief of some scholars that socialization is the route to a more just social system, this can only be partly true.[38] There is every reason to believe that some members of every society will fail to become morally mature, and to the extent that such people become elites some form of deprivation of rights for others is likely. A well-designed socialization process may minimize this possibility, but it cannot eliminate it. Those who are morally mature and who seek to move beyond guardian and entrepreneurial dominance need support in laws and organizational forms and processes that are independent of socialization although linked to it in a feedback loop. The most effective way that legal norms, organizational patterns, and socialization practices can become mutually reinforcing is when people in organizations, rather than elites, set the limits on material and moral incentives in a way that is legally binding and has implications for general value structures. That requires devolution of authority within a framework of authority. In the end the possibility of both positive and negative rights coexisting is where the people themselves, under a framework of law that prompts government activity and sets limits on its interference, participate in the unending process of adjusting the claims of "freedom to" and "freedom from." Equitable rewards from the community and protection and immunity against arbitrary demands then both become possible.

Changing attitudes without changing organizational structures—or vice versa—is a prescription for disaster. If societies are genuinely to give people a greater sense of control through enhanced rights then the giant corporation or socialist mass organization must give way to a form of shared minority power. It is not enough to say that moral incentives must substitute for income incentives in order to induce people to respond and that elites, who must play a significant leadership role, must give greater importance to social duty satisfactions.[39] How is this to happen? Changes in ideology, especially changes that are not self-defeating from being wrought by a centralized, tightly controlled bureaucracy, cannot come about solely from socialization in schools, families, or workplaces. If sponsored change is to occur and, at the same time, public authority to remain limited, then ideas about who owns and controls production and who has mangerial rights must change through practices that are rooted in individual participation.

Organizational structures that support labor for rent, with all its associated concepts of hierarchical division of labor income, or the inherent merit of education must give way to organizational structures that stress labor as a participant in the entrepreneurial process and the guide for community needs and individual rewards. To say that education and technical knowledge should increasingly be the dominant criteria of worth in the organizations of the future is to open the door to the possibility of endless guardian control. It is true that when organizations reward education and punish the lack of it they emphasize competence rather than factors like class, sex, or age. But a new organizational elite that uses educational criteria to bolster status is very dangerous and may become impervious to challenge. Unless, that is, more people, with better-informed expectations and diversified skills, work to end the separation of the political and economic spheres by allowing the individual to function as a voter in organizations. A responsible citizen has as much place within an organization as outside. Indeed, guaranteeing citizen rights within organizations is the only way to end that state of affairs where those who command organizations use their unanswerable power to negate the concept of a society composed of equal citizens.

Concluding Remarks

Allowing workers to have a say about work hours, the general conditions of labor, the tasks that will be done, the methods for handling disputes, the mechanisms for tapping creativity, and, in some cases, the levels of pay has proven no easier in guardian Chinese factories than in entrepreneurial American ones. Why? The answer is that such powers in the hands of subordinates are a threat to elites and the ideologies that justify their status in modern societies generally. In entrepreneurial organizations allowing workers to make crucial work- or pay-related decisions is said to encroach upon the freedom of owners and managers that is derived from ownership. In guardian organizations allowing workers the right to make decisions may lead to questions about why decisions cannot be made in other areas; subordinates may begin to feel that it is not enough to have access to community goods, one must also be allowed to question the ideological dictates that require this access.

Fortunately, the pattern in our world of cyclical movements for positive and negative rights is a sign of growth and creativity rather than of decline and decay. These movements are an indication that rigidity has not occurred, that dominance within organizations is not beyond challenge. It is, in fact, in the alteration in the search for rights that our civilization in all its diverse, even antagonistic, forms affirms its commitment to change and its belief in the possibility of a more moral social order.

But if there is a commitment to change in our world there is still a considerable failure on the part of social scientists to construct a theory of democracy that is appropriate for the coming age. Without such a theory to guide social action the opportunity that strategically placed elites have to exploit important social goods for their own advantage will remain. Bureaucratic processes, rather than liberating and giving people greater access to opportunities, will become the vehicle for power and privilege. There will be no exit from the oscillation between entrepreneurial and guardian dominance; central authority will strive to check private privilege while individuals will seek scope for their aspirations against the conformity enforced by bureaucratic power.

There is no good reason for pessimism, however. Entrepreneurial and guardian dominance are rooted in the conditions of this time and are the necessary first steps toward ending the cruel conditions of predatory dominance that for so long were the lot of mankind. People do not want a return to predatory dominance; in like manner, if they have negative rights, they do not wish to surrender these for positive rights, or vice versa. Rather, they seek to add to the rights they have. In pursuing these goals they turn to governments and to autonomous organizations to fulfill, respectively, their potential for simultaneously restraining the aggrandizing impulses of the few and releasing the possibilities for a new social life for the many.

In the Third World many people, still struggling to free themselves from predatory forms of dominance, want first a fair share in a new social order. They wish the positive right to participate in decisions that affect their lives and to be free of the fear of unchecked exploitation. Mobilized to obtain these goals, many have become members of guardian societies and staunch believers in the inherent perversion of negative rights. Yet, in fact, the transformation to a social order that honors both autonomy and community may be easier from entrepreneurial societies. Justice has more scope where authority can be challenged, and guardian societies are not noteworthy for their ability to tolerate criticism. Quick to change when leaders are committed to change, these societies are equally prone to obdurate conservatism and an inability to sanction messy but innovative individualism. Challenges are not handled well psychologically or institutionally whereas in entrepreneurial societies such competitive, questioning stances are common and expected.

Notwithstanding, whatever disadvantages guardian dominance systems may have in the process of change, entrepreneurial systems have not been especially effective in devising institutions that guarantee positive as well as negative rights. The drive for advantage has more often than not taken precedence over cries for protection. Unless entrepreneurial systems genuinely transform themselves quickly, the advantages they possess may be forever unrealized.

The starting point for the transformation of entrepreneurial dominance is the recognition that the laws and guarantees that pertain to the strictly political realm, the checks and balances that prevent one set of elites from becoming all powerful, and the mechanisms (voting especially) for competition for leadership are regulatory procedures that must pertain to organizational life as a whole. The essence of government according to James Madison is to "first enable the government to control the governed; and in the next place oblige it to control itself."[40] This dictum is no less pertinent for the great organizations of modern society. Indeed, only when elites check elites throughout a social order, when law sanctions rights regardless of place, and when authority is required to submit to tests of competence by those who are governed is it possible to have the advantages both of centrally directed innovation and protection and of autonomous subunit control, to have both autonomy and community.

If moral dominance can never fully be achieved it can at least be partially realized. Its root lies in the ceaseless actions of citizens to seek their rights and defend them. Beyond that it lies in a society with a strong commitment to the total welfare of all its citizens, to a market constrained by community needs, to local participation in political and administrative affairs, to laws that protect belief, security, and public meetings and debate, and to governance by people of the organizations in which they work as well as in society as a whole.

Notes

Introduction

1. David O. Sears, *Political Attitudes Through the Life Cycle* (San Francisco: W.H. Freeman, forthcoming).

2. The seminal psychohistorical study was Erik H. Erikson's *Young Man Luther: A Study in Psychoanalysis and History* (New York: Norton, 1958). See also E. Victor Wolfenstein, *The Revolutionary Personality: Lenin, Trotsky, Gandhi* (Princeton: Princeton University Press, 1967).

3. As an example see Geoffrey Gorer, *The American People: A Study in National Character* (New York: Norton, 1948). Also David Riesman (with Reuel Denney and Nathan Glazer), *The Lonely Crowd: A Study of the Changing American Character* (New Haven: Yale University Press, 1950).

4. As an example see David C. Schwartz, *Political Alienation and Political Behavior* (Chicago: Aldine, 1973).

5. David C. McClelland et al., *The Achievement Motive* (New York: Appleton-Century-Crofts, 1953).

6. Theodor W. Adorno, E. Frenkel-Brunswik, D. J. Levinson, and R. N. Sanford, *The Authoritarian Personality* (New York: Harper, 1950).

7. The International Society of Political Psychology, recently founded, has as one of its objectives making more widely known the usefulness of work in political psychology with, of course, a focus on motivation.

8. Howard Margolis, *Selfishness, Altruism, and Rationality: A Theory of Social Choice* (Cambridge: Cambridge University Press, 1982), 15.

9. Shawn W. Rosenberg, "The Study of Ideology: The Validity, Power and Utility of the Theories We Construct," paper presented at the annual meeting of the International Society of Political Psychology, Oxford University, Oxford, England, July 1983, 45.

Chapter 1

1. John Rawls, *A Theory of Justice* (Cambridge: Harvard University Press, 1971).

2. B. F. Skinner, *Beyond Freedom and Dignity* (New York: Knopf, 1971), 109, 112–13.

3. Edward O. Wilson, *On Human Nature* (Cambridge: Harvard University Press, 1978), 167.

4. Jean Piaget, *The Moral Judgment of the Child* (New York: Collier Books, 1962).

5. Lawrence Kohlberg, "Stage and Sequence: The Developmental Approach to Socialization," in *Handbook of Socialization Theory and Research*, ed. David A. Goslin (Chicago: Rand McNally, 1969).

6. Helen Weinreich-Haste, "Kohlberg's Theory of Moral Development," in *Morality in the Making: Thought, Action, and the Social Context*, ed. Helen Weinreich-Haste and Don Locke (Chichester: John Wiley & Sons, 1983), 12.

7. Lawrence Kohlberg, *The Philosophy of Moral Development: Moral Stages and the Idea of Justice*, vol. 1, Essays on Moral Development (San Francisco: Harper & Row, 1981), 409–12.

8. Ibid., 24–25.

9. Robert R. Holt, "Freud's Impact on Modern Morality and Our World View," in *Darwin, Marx, and Freud: Their Influence on Moral Theory*, ed. Arthur L. Caplan and Bruce Jennings (New York: Plenum Press, 1984), 175.

10. Cheryl Armon, "Ideals of the Good Life and Moral Judgment: Evaluative Reasoning in Children and Adults," *Moral Education Forum* 9, 2 (Summer 1984), 21.

11. Robert Hogan, "Moral Conduct and Moral Character: A Psychological Perspective," *Psychological Bulletin* 79 (April 1973), 223. See also Martin L. Hoffman, "Empathy, Role Taking, Guilt and the Development of Altruistic Motives," in *Moral Development and Behavior: Theory, Research, and Social Issues*, ed. Thomas Lickona (New York: Holt, Rinehart & Winston, 1976), 124–43.

12. Carol Gilligan, *In a Different Voice: Psychological Theory and Women's Development* (Cambridge: Harvard University Press, 1982), 160.

13. Ibid., 164.

14. James Chowning Davies, "The Proper Biological Study of Politics," *Political Psychology* 4, 4 (December 1983), 735.

15. Robert Kegan, *The Evolving Self: Problem and Process in Human Development* (Cambridge: Harvard University Press, 1982), 107–108, 144, 207–209.

16. James R. Rest, "New Approaches in the Assessment of Moral Judgment," in *Moral Development*, ed. Lickona, 198–218.

17. Nicholas Emler, "Morality and Politics: The Ideological Dimension in the Theory of Moral Development," in *Morality in the Making*, ed. Weinreich-Haste and Locke, 59.

18. Ibid., p. 68; Weinreich-Haste, "Kohlberg's Theory," 16.

19. James Garbarino and Urie Bronfenbrenner, "The Socialization of Moral Judgment and Behavior in Cross-Cultural Perspective," in *Moral Development*, ed. Lickona, 70–83.

20. Augusto Blasi, "Bridging Moral Cognition and Moral Action: A Critical Review of the Literature," *Psychological Bulletin* 88, 1 (July 1980), 37.

21. Kohlberg, *The Philosophy of Moral Development* 1:167.

22. Ibid., 175.

23. Herbert D. Saltzstein, "Social Influence and Moral Development: A Perspective on the Role of Parents and Peers," in *Moral Development*, ed. Lickona, 253–65.

24. Ian Vine, "Moral and Political Ideals in the Light of Sociobiological Theory," paper presented at the annual meeting of the International Society of Political Psychology, Oxford University, Oxford, England, July 1983, 7.

25. Michael Walzer, *Spheres of Justice* (New York: Basic Books, 1983), 29.

26. Margolis, *Selfishness*, 97; Holt, "Freud's Impact," 170; Vine, "Moral and Political Ideals," 7.

27. Piaget, *Moral Judgment.*

28. Jean Piaget, assisted by Anne-Marie Weil, "The Development in Children of the Idea of the Homeland and of Relations with Other Countries," *International Social Science Bulletin* 3 (Autumn 1951), 562.

29. Kegan, *The Evolving Self*, 70.

30. Lawrence Kohlberg, "Development of Children's Orientations Toward a Moral Order," in *Educational Psychology*, ed. Richard C. Sprinthall and Norman A. Sprinthall (New York: Van Nostrand-Reinhold, 1969).

Chapter 2

1. Kohlberg, *The Philosophy of Moral Development* 1:24–25.

2. Justin Aronfreed, "Moral Development from the Standpoint of a General Psychological Theory," in *Moral Development*, ed. Lickona (New York: Holt, Rinehart and Winston, 1976), 67.

3. Stephen Chilton, *Defining Political Development*, Monograph Series in World Affairs, Graduate School of International Studies, University of Denver (Boulder: L. Rienner, 1988), chap. 5.

4. Aronfreed, "Moral Development," 67.

5. James Hay, "A Study of Principled Moral Reasoning Within a Sample of Conscientious Objectors," *Moral Education Forum* 7, 3 (Fall 1982), 8.

6. Garbarino and Bronfenbrenner, "The Socialization of Moral Judgment," 70–83.

7. Denis G. Sullivan, Robert T. Nakamura, and Richard F. Winters, *How America Is Ruled* (New York: John Wiley & Sons, 1980), 24. See also John L. Sullivan, James Pierson, and George E. Marcus, *Political Tolerance and American Democracy* (Chicago: University of Chicago Press, 1982); and Herbert McClosky and Alida Brill, *Dimensions of Tolerance: What Americans Believe about Civil Liberties* (New York: Russell Sage Foundation, 1983).

8. Nicholas Emler, Stanley Renwick, and Bernadette Malone, "The Relationship Between Moral Reasoning and Political Orientation," *Journal of Personality and Social Psychology* 45, 5 (1983), 1079.

9. G. G. Coulton, *The Medieval Village* (Cambridge: Cambridge Uni-

versity Press, 1925), 393, cited in John H. Kautsky, *The Politics of Aristocratic Empires* (Chapel Hill: University of North Carolina Press, 1982), 316.

10. S. N. Eisenstadt and Louis Roniger, "Patron-Client Relations as a Model of Structuring Social Exchange," *Comparative Studies in Society and History* 22, 1 (January 1980), 65.

11. John U. Nef, *War and Human Progress: An Essay on the Rise of Industrial Civilization* (New York: Russell and Russell, 1968), 5, 27. Also Carlo M. Cipolla, *Before the Industrial Revolution: European Society and Economy, 1000–1700* (New York: W. W. Norton, 1976), 182–83.

12. Nef, *War and Human Progress*, 14, 81.

13. David Little, *Religion, Order, and Law: A Study in Pre- Revolutionary England* (New York: Harper & Row, 1969), 141–42. Also Michael Walzer, *The Revolution of the Saints: A Study in the Origins of Radical Politics* (London: Weidenfeld and Nicolson, 1965), 307.

14. Walzer, *The Revolution of Saints*, 260–61.

15. James Turner Johnson, *A Society Ordained by God: English Puritan Marriage Doctrine in the First Half of the Seventeenth Century* (Nashville: Abington Press, 1970), 31, 33, 93, 97.

16. Edmund S. Morgan, *The Puritan Family: Religion and Domestic Relations in Seventeenth-Century New England* (New York: Harper & Row, 1966), 45.

17. Ibid., 103.

18. R. H. Tawney, *Religion and the Rise of Capitalism* (New York: Harcourt, Brace, Mentor Books, 1926), 104, 183, 185.

19. Nef, *War and Human Progress*, 100.

20. Reuben Fine, "The Protestant Ethic and the Analytic Ideal," *Political Psychology* 4, 2 (June 1983), 249.

21. Jay Hall and Susan M. Donnell, "Managerial Achievement: The Personal Side of Behavior Theory," in *The Study of Organizations*, ed. David Katz, Robert L. Kahn, and J. Stacy Adams (San Francisco: Jossey-Bass Publishers, 1980), 366–83.

22. Tawney, *Religion*, 111–12.

23. Nef, *War and Human Progress*, 72, 78.

24. Ibid., 107, 219.

25. Ibid., 116, 175.

26. Ibid., 282, 291.

27. Karl Polanyi, *The Great Transformation* (Boston: Beacon Press, 1944), 180.

28. Ibid., 41, 57, 74–75.

29. Michel Foucault, *Discipline and Punish: The Birth of the Prison*, trans. Alan Sheridan (New York: Pantheon Books, 1977), 11–12.

30. Francis X. Sutton et al., *The American Business Creed* (Cambridge: Harvard University Press, 1956), 277.

31. Robert Presthus, *The Organizational Society* (New York: St. Martin's Press, 1978), 44, 51, 54, 84.

32. Max Weber, "Bureaucracy," in *From Max Weber: Essays in Sociology*, ed. H. H. Gerth and C. Wright Mills (New York: Oxford University Press, 1946).

33. Charles E. Lindblom, *Politics and Markets: The World's Political-Economic System* (New York: Basic Books, 1977), 197.

34. Harry Eckstein, "The Idea of Political Development: From Dignity to Efficiency," *World Politics* 34, 4 (July 1982), 482, 484–85.

35. Margaret Mead, *Soviet Attitudes Toward Authority* (New York: McGraw-Hill, 1951), 35–36.

36. Robert A. Dahl, *Dilemmas of Pluralist Democracy: Autonomy vs. Control* (New Haven: Yale University Press, 1982), 67.

37. Alvin Toffler, *The Third Wave* (Toronto: Bantam Books, 1981), 55.

38. Sidney L. Greenblatt, "Organizational Behavior in Chinese Society: A Theoretical Overview," in *Organizational Behavior in Chinese Society*, ed. Sidney L. Greenblatt, Richard W. Wilson, and Amy A. Wilson (New York: Praeger, 1981), 14. Also Harry Harding, *Organizing China: The Problem of Bureaucracy 1949–1976* (Stanford: Stanford University Press, 1981), 357.

39. Walzer, *Spheres of Justice*, 28, 309–11, 316–21.

40. Lawrence Kohlberg and Dan Candee, "Relationships Between Moral Judgment and Moral Action," Cambridge, Mass., 1979, ms., pp. 10, 13, 33, 58–59.

41. Foucault, *Discipline and Punish*, 178.

42. Quoted in Kurt Glaser and Stefan T. Possony, *Victims of Politics: The State of Human Rights* (New York: Columbia University Press, 1979), 59.

43. Thomas J. Peters and Robert H. Waterman, Jr., *In Search of Excellence: Lessons from America's Best Run Companies* (New York: Harper & Row, 1982), 259, 280.

44. Richard L. Rubenstein, *The Cunning of History; The Holocaust and the American Future* (New York: Harper & Row, 1975), 6, 36–47.

45. Daniel Katz and Robert L. Kahn, *The Social Psychology of Organizations* (New York: John Wiley & Sons, 1966), 201, 204, 209, 334. Also Jerald Hage, Michael Aiken, and Cora B. Marrett, "Organization Structure and Communications," in *The Study of Organizations*, ed. Katz, Kahn, and Adams, 304.

46. Chris Argyris, *Integrating the Individual and the Organization* (New York: John Wiley & Sons, 1964), 47–49, 294.

47. Herbert Kaufman, *The Limits of Organizational Change* (University: University of Alabama Press, 1971), 11–13, 31, 96; also Katz and Kahn, *The Social Psychology of Organizations*, 246.

48. Claus Offe, *Industry and Inequality: The Achievement Principle in Work and Social Status*, trans. James Wickham (London: Edward Arnold, 1976), 24, 28–31, 38.

49. Bertil Gardel, "Autonomy and Participation at Work," in *The Study of Organizations*, ed. Katz, Kahn, and Adams, 284.

50. Argyris, *Individual and Organization*, 306.

51. Cornell Self-Management Working Group, "Toward a Fully Self-Managed Industrial Sector in the United States," in *Organizational Democracy: Participation and Self-Management*, ed. G. David Garson and Michael P. Smith (Beverly Hills: Sage Publications, 1976), 96.

52. Rodney Clark, *The Japanese Company* (New Haven: Yale Universi-

ty Press, 1979), 41, 129, 136, 201, 216–17, 222.

53. Michael Brower, "Experience with Self-Management and Participation in United States Industry," in *Organizational Democracy*, ed. Garson and Smith, 73–92.

Chapter 3

1. Reported in Argyris, *Individual and Organization*, 277.
2. Lindblom, *Politics and Markets*, 246, 291.
3. James O'Connor, *The Fiscal Crisis of the State* (New York: St. Martin's Press, 1973), 66, 83, 86.
4. Ralf Dahrendorf, *Class and Class Conflict in Industrial Society* (Stanford: Stanford University Press, 1959), 254.
5. Barrington Moore, Jr., *Injustice: The Social Bases of Obedience and Revolt* (White Plains, N.Y.: M. E. Sharpe, 1978), 77-78.
6. Kegan, *The Evolving Self*, 107–108, 144, 207-209.
7. Gilligan, *In a Different Voice*.
8. Ibid., 100.
9. Kohlberg, *The Philosophy of Moral Development* 1:24–25.
10. Richard W. Wilson, *Learning to Be Chinese: The Political Socialization of Children in Taiwan* (Cambridge: M.I.T. Press, 1970). See also Richard W. Wilson, "Some Comments on Stage Theories of Moral Development," *Journal of Moral Education* 5, 3 (June 1976), 241–48.
11. Eckstein, "The Idea of Political Development," 457.
12. Earl Warren, "The Law and the Future," *Fortune* (November 1955), 124.
13. Maurice Cranston, "Are There Any Human Rights," *Daedalus* 112, 4 (Fall 1983), 10.
14. Iradell Jenkins, *Social Order and the Limits of Law: A Theoretical Essay* (Princeton: Princeton University Press, 1980), 241, 243.
15. Ian Brownlie, ed., *Basic Documents on Human Rights* (Oxford: Clarendon Press, 1981), 21-27.
16. Ibid.
17. Shen Baoxiang, Wang Chengquan, and Li Zerui, "On the Question of Human Rights in the International Realm," *Beijing Review* 25, 30 (July 26, 1982), 13, 16, 17.
18. Isaiah Berlin, *Two Concepts of Liberty* (London: Oxford University Press, 1958), 11, 15.
19. Jenkins, *Social Order*, 246–49, 252–53. Also Walzer, *Spheres of Justice*, xv.
20. Charles R. Beitz, "Economic Rights and Distributive Justice in Developing Societies," *World Politics* 33 (April 1981), 321.
21. Berlin, *Two Concepts of Liberty*, 50-51.
22. Ibid., 50, 56.
23. Charles Fried, *Right and Wrong* (Cambridge: Harvard University Press, 1978), 150, 157.
24. Richard Sennett, *Authority* (New York: Alfred A. Knopf, 1980), 25.
25. Walzer, *Spheres of Justice*, 10.
26. Dahl, *Dilemmas of Pluralist Democracy*, 16, 19–20.

27. Seymour Martin Lipset and William Schneider, *The Confidence Gap: Business, Labor, and Government in the Public Mind* (New York: The Free Press, 1983), 165.

28. Milton Rokeach, "A Theory of Organization and Change Within Value-Attitude Systems," in *Political Leadership: Readings for an Emerging Field*, ed. Glenn D. Paige (New York: The Free Press, 1972), 176–77.

29. Takie Sugiyama Lebra, *Japanese Patterns of Behavior* (Honolulu: University Press of Hawaii, 1976), 38, 106, 133.

30. Lindblom, *Politics and Markets*, 105–106.

31. Ibid., 248–51.

32. Ibid., 269–71.

33. Shirley Jackson, *The Lottery* (New York: Farrar, Straus, 1949), 291–302.

34. Moore, *Injustice*, 11, 438–39.

35. Norman Frohlich, Joe A. Oppenheimer, and Oran R. Young, *Political Leadership and Collective Goods* (Princeton: Princeton University Press, 1971), 7, 115–16.

36. Moore, *Injustice*, 445.

37. Daniel B. Fusfeld, "Economic Theory Misplaced: Livelihood in Primitive Society," in *Trade and Market in the Early Empires: Economies in History and Theory*, eds. Karl Polanyi, Conrad M. Arensberg, and Harry W. Pearson (Glencoe, Ill.: The Free Press, 1957), 342–56.

38. John H. Kautsky, *The Politics of Aristocratic Empires* (Chapel Hill: University of North Carolina Press, 1982), 23–24, 34, 119, 250.

39. Carlo M. Cipolla, *Before the Industrial Revolution: European Society and Economy, 1000–1700* (New York: W. W. Norton, 1976), 28, 29.

40. Kautsky, *Aristocratic Empires*, 172 (citing T. H. Hollingsworth, "A Demographic Study of the British Ducal Families," *Populations Studies* 11 [July 1957], 8–9).

41. Walzer, *Spheres of Justice*, 68.

42. Thorstein Veblen, *The Theory of the Leisure Class* (New York: Penguin Books, 1979), 7–8, 38.

43. William H. McNeill, *The Pursuit of Power: Technology, Armed Force, and Society since A.D. 1000* (Chicago: University of Chicago Press, 1982), 299.

44. Cipolla, *Industrial Revolution*, 142–44. Also Perry Anderson, *Lineages of the Absolutist State* (London: NLB, 1974), 20, 422–23.

45. Anderson, *Absolutist State*, 414–15.

46. Ibid., 31, 403.

47. Ibid., 527.

48. Mark Elvin, *The Pattern of the Chinese Past: A Social and Economic Interpretation* (Stanford: Stanford University Press, 1973), 19.

49. Tawney, *Religion*, 62.

50. Cipolla, *Industrial Revolution*, 55.

51. Christopher Hill, *Puritanism and Revolution: Studies in Interpretation of the English Revolution of the 17th Century* (London: Secker & Warburg, 1958), 37–39.

52. Tawney, *Religion*, 119, 126.

53. Hill, *Puritanism*, 155–56, 167.

54. Anderson, *Absolutist State*, 125–26, 129.
55. Ibid., 138–39.
56. Tawney, *Religion*, 193.
57. Ibid., 152.
58. Ibid.
59. Nicos Poulantzas, *Political Power and Social Classes* (London: NLB and Sheed and Ward, 1973), 114.
60. Sutton et al., *The American Business Creed*, 251, 256, 352.
61. Little, *Religion*, 121.
62. Michael Walzer, *The Revolution of the Saints: A Study in the Origins of Radical Politics* (London: Weidenfeld and Nicolson, 1965), 209.
63. Ibid., 53, 87, 304.
64. Parks M. Coble, Jr., *The Shanghai Capitalists and the Nationalist Government, 1927–1937*, Harvard East Asian Monographs #94 (Cambridge: Council on East Asian Studies, Harvard University, 1980), 3, 10–12.
65. Robert C. Tucker, *The Marxian Revolutionary Idea* (New York: W. W. Norton, 1969), 49.
66. Harding, *Organizing China*, 17.
67. Deng Xiaoping, "On the Reform of the System of Party and State Leadership," *Beijing Review* 26, 40 (October 3, 1983), 15, 22.
68. Zhang Nan, "How Chinese Workers Exercise Their Democratic Rights," *Beijing Review* 25, 40 (October 4, 1982), 19–22.
69. Articles 2, 3, 4, and 35 of the Constitution of the Communist Party of China listed as reference (pp. i-xii) for the following document: The Decision of the Central Committee of the Communist Party of China on Party Consolidation—Adopted by the Second Plenary Session of the Twelfth Party Central Committee on October 11, 1983. Reported in *Beijing Review* 26, 42 (October 17, 1983).
70. An Zhiguo, "Implementing the New Constitution," *Beijing Review* 26, 2 (January 10, 1983), 4.
71. Moore, *Injustice*, 503.
72. Noted in Nancy Rosenblum's review article, "Moral Membership in a Postliberal State," *World Politics* 36 (July 1984), 582.

Chapter 4

1. Aristotle, *Politica*, book 3, chap. 6, in *Introduction to Aristotle*, ed. Richard McKeon (New York: Random House, Modern Library, 1947), 590.
2. Dahl, *Dilemmas of Pluralist Democracy*, 148, 153.
3. Joseph H. Carens, *Equality, Moral Incentives and the Market: An Essay in Utopian Politico-Economic Theory* (Chicago: University of Chicago Press, 1981), 199.
4. Douglas La Bier, "Bureaucracy and Psychopathology," *Political Psychology* 4, 2 (June 1983), 229.
5. Andrew Carnegie, "The Gospel of Wealth," in *The Gospel of Wealth and Other Timely Essays*, ed. Edward C. Kirkland (Cambridge: Harvard University Press, 1962), 19.
6. From Lenin's *One Step Forward, Two Steps Back*. Quoted in Sennett, *Authority*, 174.

7. Geoffrey Barraclough, *An Introduction to Contemporary History* (New York: Basic Books, 1964), 207.

8. Presthus, *The Organizational Society*, 110–11, 163.

9. Matthias Schmidt, *Albert Speer: The End of a Myth*, trans. Joachim Neugroschel (New York: St. Martin's Press, 1984).

10. S. N. Eisenstadt, *Revolution and the Transformation of Societies: A Comparative Study of Civilizations* (New York: The Free Press, 1978), 28–29, 37–38.

11. Offe, *Industry and Inequality*, 52.

12. Foucault, *Discipline and Punish*, 181.

13. Sutton et al., *The American Business Creed*, 103, 106–107, 366.

14. J. Patrick Wright, *On a Clear Day You Can See General Motors: John Z. De Lorean's Look Inside the Automotive Giant* (Grosse Point, Mich.: Wright Enterprises, 1979), 51.

15. Eisenstadt and Roniger, "Patron-Client Relations," 50.

16. Anderson, *Absolutist State*, 540.

17. From Richard Sennett and Jonathan Cobb, *The Hidden Injuries of Class* (New York: Alfred A. Knopf, 1972), 246–47.

18. Mancur Olson, *The Rise and Decline of Nations: Economic Growth, Stagflation, and Social Rigidities* (New Haven: Yale University Press, 1982), 174–75.

19. Samuel P. Huntington and Joan M. Nelson, *No Easy Choice: Political Participation in Developing Countries* (Cambridge: Harvard University Press, 1976), 71. (Data from Irma Adelman, Cynthia Taft Morris, and Michael Brower.)

20. Dahl, *Dilemmas of Pluralist Democracy*, 174.

21. Cipolla, *Industrial Revolution*, 22–23.

22. Noted in Little, *Religion, Order, and Law*, 12.

23. Seymour Martin Lipset and William Schneider, *The Confidence Gap: Business, Labor and Government in the Public Mind* (New York: The Free Press, 1983), 170, 174, 183, 378.

24. Roger Ricklefs, "Public Gives Executives Low Marks for Honesty and Ethical Standards," *The Wall Street Journal*, November 2, 1983, 33.

25. Joseph Lelyveld, "When the Boss Gets a Raise," *The New York Times Magazine*, July 24, 1977, 47.

26. Ann Crittenden, "The Age of 'Me-First' Management," *The New York Times*, August 19, 1984, section 3, 12.

27. John A. Byrne, "Executive Pay: Who Got What In '86," *International Business Week*, no. 2995-325, May 14, 1987, 51.

28. Mark Green and Bonnie Tenneriello, "Executive Merit Pay," *The New York Times*, April 25, 1984, A23.

29. Byrne, "Executive Pay," 50.

30. Robert B. Reich, "Expropriations," *The New York Times*, November 29, 1982, A19.

31. Byrne, "Executive Pay," 50–51.

32. Green and Tenneriello, "Executive Merit Pay."

33. Deng Xiaoping, "Reform," 18.

34. Argyris, *Individual and Organization*, 89. Based on a 1962 survey of 407 auto workers by Arthur Kornhauser.

35. Ibid., 117.

36. Albert O. Hirschman, *Exit, Voice, and Loyalty: Responses to Decline in Firms, Organizations, and States* (Cambridge: Harvard University Press, 1970), 93.

37. Offe, *Industry and Inequality*, 66.

38. Argyris, *Individual and Organization*, 81.

39. Roger D. Masters, "The Biological Nature of the State," *World Politics* 35, 2 (January 1983), 187.

40. Gil Eliot, *Twentieth Century Book of the Dead* (New York: Scribner, 1972), 41, 94, 124. Cited in Rubenstein, *The Cunning of History*, 6.

41. For an excellent summary of these experiments see Larry D. Spence, "Moral Judgment and Bureaucracy," in *Moral Development and Politics*, ed. Richard W. Wilson and Gordon J. Schochet (New York: Praeger, 1980), 137–71.

42. Alan L. Lockwood, "Moral Reasoning and Public Policy Debate," in *Moral Development*, ed. Lickona, 322 (citing Lawrence Kohlberg, "Education for Justice: A Modern Statement of the Platonic View," in *Moral Education: Five Lectures*, eds. N. F. Sizer and T. R. Sizer [Cambridge: Harvard University Press, 1970], 57–83).

43. Kermit Vandivier, "Why Should My Conscience Bother Me?" in *Corporate and Governmental Deviance: Problems of Organizational Behavior in Contemporary Society*, ed. M. David Ermann and Richard J. Lundman (New York: Oxford University Press, 1978), 90–92.

44. Jeb Stuart Magruder, *An American Life: One Man's Road to Watergate* (New York: Atheneum, 1974), 317.

45. G. M. Gilbert, *Nuremberg Diary* (New York: Signet Books, 1947), 238–39.

46. Richard Hammer, *Court Martial of Lieutenant Calley* (New York: Coward, McGann and Gehegan, 1971), 105.

47. Jeb Stuart Magruder, *From Power to Peace* (Waco: World Books, 1978), 57.

48. Wright, *General Motors*, 216.

49. Ibid., 33–34, 53–56.

50. Gilbert Geis, "Deterring Corporate Crime," in *Corporate Power in America*, ed. Ralph Nader and Mark J. Green (New York: Grossman, 1973), 197.

51. Veblen, *Leisure Class*.

52. Magruder, *From Power to Peace*, 82, 30.

53. Quoted in Kohlberg and Candee, "Relationships," 48–49.

54. Wright, *General Motors*, 69.

55. Helene Ann Cooper Jackson, "The Impact of Combat Stress on Adolescent Moral Development in Vietnam Veterans," Ph.D. dissertation, Smith College School for Social Work, 1982.

56. Kohlberg and Candee, "Relationships," 45.

57. Mark Green, "The Corporation and the Community," in *Corporate Power in America*, ed. Nader and Green, 53.

58. La Bier, "Bureaucracy," 45.

59. Gitta Sereny, *Into that Darkness: From Mercy Killing to Mass Murder* (New York: McGraw-Hill, 1974), 202.

60. Ibid., 178.
61. Ibid., 201.
62. Ibid.
63. Eisenstadt and Roniger, "Patron-Client Relations," 73.
64. Terrence G. Carroll, "Secularization and States of Modernity," *World Politics* 36, 3 (April 1984), 371.
65. Olson, *Rise and Decline of Nations*, 18, 48.
66. Ibid., 32, 34, 44.
67. Ibid., 124–25.
68. Ibid., 67, 69, 72, 86.
69. Jan De Vries, "The Rise and Decline of Nations in Historical Perspective," *International Studies Quarterly* 27, 1 (March 1983), 12–14.
70. Olson, *Rise amd Decline of Nations*, 74–75.
71. Edward R. Tufte, *Political Control of the Economy* (Princeton: Princeton University Press, 1978), 141.
72. Anderson, *Absolutist State*, 544.
73. Cipolla, *Industrial Revolution*, 10–11, 18.
74. Moore, *Injustice*, 29.
75. Foucault, *Discipline and Punish*, 82.
76. McNeill, *The Pursuit of Power*, 185.
77. Foucault, *Discipline and Punish*, 156, 222.
78. Polanyi, *The Great Transformation*, 102, 133, 224, 226.
79. Robert W. Jackman, *Politics and Markets: The World's Political-Economic Systems* (New York: Basic Books, 1977), 174–75, 189.
80. Charles E. Lindblom, *Politics and Markets: The World's Political-Economic Systems* (New York: Basic Books, 1977), 175, 189.
81. Cited in Walzer, *Spheres of Justice*, 293.
82. Keith Griffin and Jeffrey James, *The Transition to Egalitarian Development: Economic Policies for Structural Change in the Third World* (New York: St. Martin's Press, 1981), 9.
83. O'Connor, *The Fiscal Crisis of the State*, 14, 21, 203–205.
84. Robert A. Bennett, "Chilling Specter at Continental," *The New York Times*, May 20, 1984, section 3, 1.
85. Lipset and Schneider, *The Confidence Gap*, 199, 220, 289, 380.
86. Noted in Tufte, *Political Control*, 87. See also Fernand Braudel, *The Perspective of the World*, trans. Sian Reynolds, vol. 3 of *Civilization and Capitalism: 15–18th Century* (New York: Harper & Row, 1984).
87. Dahl, *Dilemmas of Pluralist Democracy*, 33, 40.
88. Green, "Corporation and Community," 53.
89. Michel Korzec and Martin King Whyte, "Reading Notes: The Chinese Wage System," *The China Quarterly* 86 (June 1981), 248–73.
90. Shen Baoxiang, Wang Chengquan, and Li Zerui, "On the Question of Human Rights in the International Realm," *Beijing Review* 25, 30 (July 26, 1982), 17, 22.
91. Lucian Pye, *The Dynamics of Chinese Politics* (Cambridge: Oelgeschlager, Gunn and Hain, 1981), 1–37.
92. Zagorka Golubovic, "Marx's Concept of Man vs. a Stalinist Ideology of the 'New-Man,'" paper presented at the sixth annual meeting of the International Society of Political Psychology, Oxford Uni-

versity, England, July 1983, 16.

93. Noted in Dahrendorf, *Class and Class Conflict in Industrial Society*, 82–83.

94. Milovan Djilas, *Memoir of a Revolutionary* (New York: Harcourt Brace Jovanovich, 1973), 97.

95. "China Backs Poster As Citizens' Forum," *The New York Times*, January 4, 1979, 1.

96. Ta-ling Lee and Miriam London, "A Dissenter's Odyssey Through Mao's China," *The New York Times Magazine*, section 6, November 16, 1980.

97. "4 Arrested in China at Democracy Wall," *The New York Times*, November 12, 1979, A7.

98. "Leading Peking Dissident Loses Appeal in Higher Court," *The New York Times*, November 8, 1979, A3.

99. "Peking Closes Democracy Wall, Banishes Posters to Remote Park," *The New York Times*, December 7, 1979, 1.

100. "Freer Expression in China Part of a Search for New Path After Chaotic Years," *The New York Times*, January 14, 1979, 12.

101. Lee and London, "A Dissenter's Odyssey," 136.

102. "Leading Chinese Dissident Gets 15-Year Prison Term," *The New York Times*, October 17, 1979, A3.

Chapter 5

1. Gabriel A. Almond, Scott C. Flannigan, and Robert J. Mundt, eds., *Crisis, Choice, and Change: Historical Studies of Political Development* (Boston: Little, Brown, 1973); David E. Apter and Louis Wolf Goodman, eds., *The Multinational Corporation and Social Change* (New York: Praeger, 1976); Henry Bienen, *Violence and Social Change: A Review of Current Literature* (Chicago: University of Chicago Press, 1968); Fernando Henrique Cardoso and Enzo Faletto, *Dependency and Development in Latin America*, trans. Marjory Mattingly Urquidi (Berkeley: University of California Press, 1979); Robert A. Dahl, *Polyarchy: Participation and Opposition* (New Haven: Yale University Press, 1971); Everett Hagen, *On the Theory of Social Change: How Economic Growth Begins* (Homewood, Ill.: Dorsey Press, 1962); Lindblom, *Politics and Markets*; Joel S. Migdal, *Peasants, Politics, and Revolution: Pressures Toward Political and Social Change in the Third World* (Princeton: Princeton University Press, 1974); Barrington Moore, Jr., *Social Origins of Dictatorship and Democracy: Lord and Peasant in the Making of the Modern World* (Boston: Beacon Press, 1966); Mancur Olson, Jr., *The Logic of Collective Action*, rev. ed. (New York: Schocken, 1971); Jeffrey M. Paige, *Agrarian Revolution: Social Movements and Export Agriculture in the Underdeveloped World* (New York: The Free Press, 1975); Barbara Salert, *Revolutions and Revolutionaries: Four Theories* (New York: Elsevier, 1976); Kay Ellen Trimberger, *Revolution from Above: Military Bureaucrats and Development in Japan, Turkey, Egypt, and Peru* (New Brunswick: Transaction Books, 1978); and Immanuel Wallerstein, *The Modern World-System: Capitalist Agriculture and the Origins of the European World-Economy in the Sixteenth Century*

(New York: Academic Press, 1974).

2. Harry Eckstein, "On the Etiology of Internal Wars," *History and Theory* 4, 2 (1965); Lawrence Stone, "Theories of Revolution," *World Politics* 18 (January 1966); Eisenstadt, *Revolution*, 7.

3. Pitirim A. Sorokin, *The Crisis of Our Age: The Social and Cultural Outlook* (New York: Dutton, 1941); Crane Brinton, *The Anatomy of Revolution* (Englewood Cliffs, N.J.: Prentice-Hall, 1952); James C. Davies, *Human Nature in Politics: The Dynamics of Political Behavior* (New York: John Wiley & Sons, 1963); Ted Gurr, *Why Men Rebel* (Princeton: Princeton University Press, 1970); Chalmers Johnson, *Revolutionary Change* (Boston: Little, Brown, 1966); Neil J. Smelser, *Theory of Collective Behavior* (New York: The Free Press, 1962); Eisenstadt, *Revolution*; Theda Skocpol, *States and Social Revolutions: A Comparative Analysis of France, Russia and China* (New York: Cambridge University Press, 1979). See also Jack A. Goldstone, "Theories of Revolution: The Third Generation," *World Politics* 32 (April 1980), 425–29, 448–49.

4. Samuel P. Huntington, *Political Order in Changing Societies* (New York: Yale University Press, 1968), 266–67; also Harry Eckstein, "Introduction: Toward the Theoretical Study of Internal War," in *Internal War: Problems and Approaches*, ed. Harry Eckstein (New York: The Free Press, 1964), 12.

5. Eisenstadt, *Revolution*, 202, 218–19.

6. Eckstein, "On the Etiology of Internal Wars," 153.

7. Brinton, *The Anatomy of Revolution*, reproduced in part in *Comparative Politics: A Reader*, ed. Harry Eckstein and David E. Apter (Glencoe, Ill.: The Free Press, 1963), 558–59.

8. Rod Aya, "Theories of Revolution Reconsidered: Contrasting Models of Collective Violence," *Theory and Society* 8 (June-December 1979), 41.

9. Davies, "The Proper Biological Study of Politics," 738 (based on a study by J. M. R. Delgado, *Physical Control of the Mind* [New York: Harper & Row, 1969], 166).

10. Sigmund Freud, *The Future of an Illusion*, in *The Standard Edition of the Complete Psychological Works of Sigmund Freud*, vol. 9, ed., James Strachey (London, 1953–1974), 9. Cited in Louise E. Hoffman, "Psychoanalytic Interpretations of Political Movements, 1900–1950," *The Psychohistory Review* 13, 1 (Fall 1984), 19.

11. Michael Crozier, Samuel P. Huntington, and Joji Watanuki, *The Crisis of Democracy* (New York: New York University Press, 1975), 14–19.

12. Eisenstadt, *Revolution*, 41–42.

13. Moore, *Injustice*, 31, 38, 43, 45.

14. Ibid., 462.

15. James D. Wright, "Political Disaffection," in *The Handbook of Political Behavior*, vol. 4, ed. Samuel L. Long (New York: Plenum Press, 1981), 50–55.

16. Schwartz, *Political Alienation*, 87, 156, 158, 196, 239.

17. Emler, Renwick, and Malone, "Moral Reasoning and Political Orientation."

18. Arnold S. Feldman, "Violence and Volatility: The Likelihood of Revolution," in *Internal War*, ed. Eckstein, 125.

19. David E. Apter, *The Politics of Modernization* (Chicago: University of Chicago Press, 1965), 14.

20. For examples of various models of development see Huntington and Nelson, *No Easy Choice*, 23.

21. O'Connor, *The Fiscal Crisis of the State*, 159–60.

22. Albert O. Hirschman, *Exit, Voice, and Loyalty: Responses to Decline in Firms, Organizations, and States* (Cambridge: Harvard University Press, 1970), 34.

23. Alex De Tocqueville, *Democracy in America*, vol. 2 (New York: Alfred A. Knopf, 1956), 105.

24. James C. Scott, *The Moral Economy of the Peasant: Rebellion and Subsistence in Southeast Asia* (New Haven: Yale University Press, 1976), 167; Samuel L. Popkin, *The Rational Peasant: The Political Economy of Rural Society in Vietnam* (Berkeley: University of California Press, 1979), 31.

25. Eric R. Wolf, *Peasant Wars of the Twentieth Century* (New York: Harper & Row, 1969), 280.

26. Scott, *Moral Economy of the Peasant*, 180.

27. Migdal, *Peasants, Politics, and Revolution*, 141.

28. Wolf, *Peasant Wars*, 292.

29. John H. Kautsky, *The Politics of Aristocratic Empires* (Chapel Hill: University of North Carolina Press, 1982), 289, 291.

30. Tawney, *Religion*, 82, 92.

31. Little, *Religion, Order, and Law*, 200.

32. Tawney, *Religion*, 197.

33. Little, *Religion, Order, and Law*, 200.

34. Hill, *Puritanism*, 55, 65–66, 107, 121–22.

35. Ibid., 194.

36. Polanyi, *The Great Transformation*, 78 (italics in original).

37. Ibid., 83, 101.

38. Johnson, *Revolutionary Change*, 129–30.

39. Harry Eckstein, "The Idea of Political Development: From Dignity to Efficiency," *World Politics* 34, 4 (July 1982), 482.

40. Brinton *The Anatomy of Revolution*, 557.

41. Huntington and Nelson, *No Easy Choice*, 29, 43.

42. Salert, *Revolutions and Revolutionaries*, 30–37 (from the work of Olson, *Logic of Collective Action*).

43. Pedro Ramet, "Disaffection and Dissent in East Germany," *World Politics* 37, 1 (October 1984), 101–103.

44. Nicholas Emler, "Morality and Politics: The Ideological Dimension in the Theory of Moral Development," in *Morality in the Making*, ed. H. Weinreich-Haste and D. Locke (Chichester: John Wiley & Sons, 1983), 62–63.

45. Skocpol, *States and Social Revolutions*, 27.

46. Charles Tilly, Louise Tilly, and Richard Tilly, *The Rebellious Century: 1830–1930* (Cambridge: Harvard University Press, 1975).

47. Cho-Yun Hsu, *Ancient China in Transition: An Analysis of Social Mobility, 722–222 B.C.* (Stanford: Stanford University Press, 1965), 77.

48. Richard M. Merelman, "The Development of Political Ideology: A

Framework for the Analysis of Political Socialization," *American Political Science Review* 63 (September 1969), 750–67.

49. Harvey Waterman, "Insecure 'Ins' and Opportune 'Outs': Sources of Collective Political Activity," *Journal of Political and Military Sociology* 8 (Spring 1980), 111.

50. Lawrence Kohlberg, "Stage and Sequence: The Cognitive Developmental Approach to Socialization," in *Handbook of Socialization Theory and Research*, ed. David A. Goslin (Chicago: Rand McNally, 1969).

51. Little, *Religion, Order, and Law*, 27–28.

52. Davies, *Human Nature in Politics*, 45.

53. Mao Zedong, "Rectify the Party's Style of Work," in *Selected Works of Mao Tse-Tung*, vol. 3 (Peking: Foreign Language Press, 1965), 35.

54. Huntington and Nelson, *No Easy Choice*, 19 (citing a summarization of statistics by Robert McNamara).

55. Robert W. Jackman, *Politics and Social Equality: A Comparative Analysis* (New York: John Wiley & Sons, 1975), 101, 106, 109–10.

56. Johnson, *Revolutionary Change*.

57. Huntington and Nelson, *No Easy Choice*, 54, 93.

58. S. Robert Lichter and Stanley Rothman, "The Radical Personality: Social Psychological Correlates of New Left Ideology," *Political Behavior* 4, 3 (1982), 223.

59. Bruce Mazlish, *The Revolutionary Aescetic: Evolution of a Political Type* (New York: McGraw-Hill, 1976).

60. N. Haan, M. B. Smith, and J. Block, "The Moral Reasoning of Young Adults: Political-Social Behavior, Family Background and Personality Correlates," *Journal of Personality and Social Psychology* 10 (1968), 198.

61. Emler, "Morality in Politics," 67.

62. "Port Huron Statement," in *The New Student Left*, ed. Mitchell Cohen and Dennis Hale (Boston: Beacon Press, 1966), 16.

63. Eric Hoffer, *The True Believer: Thoughts on the Nature of Mass Movements* (New York: Harper & Row, 1951), 98.

64. Cynthia McClintock, "Why Peasants Rebel: The Case of Peru's Sendero Luminoso," *World Politics* 37, 1 (October 1984), 48–84.

Chapter 6

1. Huntington and Nelson, *No Easy Choice*, 75.

2. Theodore J. Lowi, "American Business, Public Policy, Case Studies and Political Theory," *World Politics* 16 (July 1964), 677–715.

3. James F. Petras with Morris H. Morley, Peter De Witt, and A. Eugene Havens, *Class, State, and Power in the Third World* (Montclair, N.J.: Allanheld, Osmun, 1981), 156, 166.

4. Ibid., 159. See also Mostafa Rejai and Kay Phillips, World *Revolutionary Leaders* (New Brunswick: Rutgers University Press, 1983), 70.

5. Poulantzas, *Political Power*, 229. I am indebted to Sigmund Krancberg for explaining these aspects of Poulantzas's work to me.

6. Charles F. Sabel, *Work and Politics: The Division of Labor in Industry* (New York: Cambridge University Press, 1982).

7. Huntington and Nelson, *No Easy Choice*, 15.

8. Ross Fitzgerald, "Human Needs and Politics: The Ideas of Christian Bay and Herbert Marcuse," *Political Psychology* 6, 1 (1985), 106.

9. Schwartz, *Political Alienation*, 70, 154.

10. Crozier, Huntington, Watanuki, *The Crisis of Democracy*, 73.

11. Poulantzas, *Political Power*, 347 (italics in original).

12. Robert C. Tucker, ed., *The Marx-Engels Reader* (New York: W. W. Norton, 1972), 369–71.

13. Skocpol, *States and Social Revolutions*.

14. Robert W. Jackman, "Dependence on Foreign Investment and Economic Growth in the Third World," *World Politics* 34, 2 (January 1982), 185.

15. Huntington and Nelson, *No Easy Choice*, 22, 99, 113, 163–64.

16. Jyotirindra DasGupta, "Development and Poverty Reduction in South Asia—A Review Article," *Journal of Asian Studies* 42, 1 (November 1982), 107–108.

17. Alvin Toffler, *The Third Wave* (Toronto: Bantam Books, 1981), 320.

18. O'Connor *The Fiscal Crisis of the State*, 28, 153.

19. William M. Evan, "Multinational Corporations and International Professional Associations," in *The Study of Organizations*, ed. Daniel Katz, Robert L. Kahn, and J. Stacy Adams (San Francisco: Jossey-Bass Publishers, 1980), 97.

20. Petras, *Class, State, and Power*, 85, 96–97.

21. Toffler, *The Third Wave*, 319.

22. Evan, "Multinational Corporations," 98–99.

23. Ibid., 102, 105.

24. Cardoso and Faletto, *Dependency and Development*, 102.

25. As an example see Sherman Cochran, *Big Business in China: Sino-Foreign Rivalry in the Cigarette Industry* (Cambridge: Harvard University Press, 1980).

26. Theda Skocpol, "Bringing the State Back In: A Report on Current Comparative Research on the Relationship Between States and Social Structures," *Items*, Social Science Research Council, 36, 1/2 (June 1982), 5.

27. Cardoso and Faletto, *Dependency and Development*, xvi.

28. Migdal, *Peasants, Politics, and Revolution*, 232.

29. Petras, *Class, State, and Power*, 43 (citing the *Manchester Guardian Weekly*, August 26, 1979, 11).

Conclusion

1. Walzer, *Spheres of Justice*, 261.

2. Crozier, Huntington, and Watanuki, *The Crisis of Democracy*, 21.

3. Dahl, *Dilemmas of Pluralist Democracy*, 112–13, 115.

4. Ibid., 166, 169.

5. Ibid., 128 (italics in original).

6. Kegan, *The Evolving Self*, 67–68.

7. Chilton, *Defining Political Development*, 87.

8. Ibid., 81–83, 97.

9. Crozier, Huntington, and Watanuki, *The Crisis of Democracy*, 6, 157, 159.

10. Gurr, *Why Men Rebel*, 69–70, 130; also Crozier, Huntington, and

Watanuki, *The Crisis of Democracy*, 141.

11. Carole Pateman, *Participation and Democratic Theory* (London: Cambridge University Press, 1970), 56.

12. Crozier, Huntington, and Watanuki, *The Crisis of Democracy*, 141.

13. Dahl, *Deilemmas of Pluralist Democracy*, 110, 183–85, 189.

14. O'Connor, *The Fiscal Crisis of the State*, 44, 46.

15. Dahrendorf, *Class and Class Conflict*, 257.

16. Pateman, *Participation*, 43, 45.

17. Joseph A. Schumpeter, *Capitalism, Socialism, and Democracy*, 3d ed. (New York: Harper & Brothers, 1950), 417–18.

18. David Ellerman, "The 'Ownership of the Firm' Myth," in *Organizational Democracy: Participation and Self-Management*, ed. G. David Garson and Michael P. Smith (Beverly Hills: Sage Publications, 1976), 31–46; also Cornell Self-Management Working Group, "Toward a Fully Self-Managed Industrial Sector in the United States," in ibid., 109.

19. Leslie Wayne, "A Pioneer Spirit Sweeps Business," *The New York Times*, March 25, 1984, section 3, p. 12.

20. William Serrin, "Employee-Owned Companies and Their Fates," *The New York Times*, December 30, 1984, E3.

21. Robert Dahl, "Democracy in the Workplace: Is It a Right or a Privilege?" *Dissent* 31 (Winter 1984), 60.

22. Jay Hall and Susan M. Donnell, "Managerial Achievement: The Personal Side of Behavioral Theory," in *The Study of Organizations*, ed. Katz, Kahn, and Adams, 376.

23. Walzer, *Spheres of Justice*, 117–18 (citing Martin Carnoy and Derek Shearer, *Economic Democracy: The Challenge of the 1980s* [White Plains, N.Y.: M. E. Sharpe, 1980], 175).

24. Robert Folger, David Rosenfield, and Robert P. Hays, Jr., "Equity and Intrinsic Motivation: The Role of Choice," in *The Study of Organizations*, ed. Katz, Kahn, and Adams, 266, 272.

25. David J. Cherrington, H. Joseph Reitz, and William E. Scott, Jr., "Effects of Contingent and Noncontingent Reward on the Relationship Between Satisfaction and Task Performance," in ibid., 257–64; also Bertil Gardel, "Autonomy and Participation at Work," in ibid., 296–97.

26. Andrew Zimbalist, "The Dynamic of Worker Participation: An Interpretive Essay on the Chilean and Other Experiences," in *Organizational Democracy*, ed. Garson and Smith, 51.

27. Pateman, *Participation*, 70, 105.

28. Huntington and Nelson, *No Easy Choice*, 78.

29. Pateman, *Participation*, 105.

30. Keith Griffin and Jeffrey James, *The Transition to Egalitarian Development: Economic Policies for Structural Change in the Third World* (New York: St. Martin's Press, 1981), 7.

31. Jackman, *Politics and Social Equality*, 198.

32. Ibid., 117.

33. Tufte, *Political Control*, 92–93, 99, 104.

34. Griffin and James, *Egalitarian Development*, 6.

35. Ibid., 23, 106.

36. Dahl, *Dilemmas of Pluralist Democracy*, 128.

37. Griffin and James, *Egalitarian Development*, 60–61, 64–66.

38. Joseph H. Carens, *Equality, Moral Incentives, and the Market: An Essay in Utopian Politico-Economic Theory* (Chicago: University of Chicago Press, 1981), 96, 185.

39. Ibid., 14–15, 150.

40. Crozier, Huntington, and Watanuki, *The Crisis of Democracy*, 63 (citing James Madison in the *Federalist*, no. 51).

Selected Bibliography

The books and articles listed below represent only a portion of the relevant literature. I have not included here all of the footnote citations and have deliberately excluded chapters in edited volumes, citing instead the complete work.

Acarian, Gilbert, and John W. Soule, eds. *Social Psychology and Political Behavior: Problems and Prospects*. Columbus: Charles E. Merrill, 1971.

Adorno, Theodor W., E. Frenkel-Brunswik, D. J. Levinson, and R. N. Sanford. *The Authoritarian Personality*. New York: Harper, 1950.

Allport, Floyd Henry. *Institutional Behavior: Essays Toward a Reinterpreting of Contemporary Social Organization*. New York: Greenwood Press, 1969. Originally published in 1933 by the University of North Carolina Press.

Almond, Gabriel A., Scott C. Flanagan, and Robert J. Mundt, eds. *Crisis, Choice, and Change: Historical Studies of Political Development*. Boston: Little, Brown, 1973.

Amdur, Robert. "Rawls' Theory of Justice: Domestic and International Perspectives." *World Politics* 29, 3 (April 1977), 438–61.

Anderson, Perry. *Lineages of the Absolutist State*. London: NLB, 1974.

Apter, David E. *Choice and the Politics of Allocation: A Developmental Theory*. New Haven: Yale University Press, 1971.

———. *The Politics of Modernization*. Chicago: University of Chicago Press, 1965.

Apter, David E., and Louis Wolf Goodman, eds. *The Multinational Corporation and Social Change*. New York: Praeger, 1976.

Arendt, Hannah. *On Revolution*. New York: Viking Press, 1963.

Argyris, Chris. *Integrating the Individual and the Organization*. New York: John Wiley & Sons, 1964.

———. *Personality and Organization: The Conflict Between System and the Individual*. New York: Harper & Brothers, 1957.

Armon, Cheryl. "Ideals of the Good Life and Moral Judgment: Evaluative Reasoning in Children and Adults." *Moral Education Forum* 9, 2 (Summer 1984), 1–27.

Aya, Rod. "Theories of Revolution Reconsidered: Contrasting Models of Collective Violence." *Theory and Society* 8 (June-December 1979), 39–99.

Barber, Benjamin R. *Superman and Common Men: Freedom, Anarchy, and the Revolution*. New York: Praeger, 1971.

Bay, Christian. *The Structure of Freedom*. Stanford: Stanford University Press, 1958, 1970.

Beauchamp, T. L., and N. E. Bowie. *Ethical Theory and Business*. Englewood Cliffs, N.J.: Prentice-Hall, 1983.

Beitz, Charles R. "Economic Rights and Distributive Justice in Developing Societies." *World Politics* 33, 3 (April 1981), 321–46.

Bergeson, Alfred, ed. *Studies of the Modern World-System*. New York: Academic Press, 1980.

Berle, Adolf A., and Gardiner C. Means. *The Modern Corporation and Private Property*. Rev. ed. New York: Harcourt, Brace and World, 1968.

Berlin, Isaiah. "The Bent Twig: A Note on Nationalism." *Foreign Affairs* 51, 1 (October 1972), 11–30.

———. *Two Concepts of Liberty*. London: Oxford University Press, 1958.

Bienen, Henry. *Violence and Social Change: A Review of Current Literature*. Chicago: University of Chicago Press, 1968.

Blasi, Augusto. "Bridging Moral Cognition and Moral Action: A Cultural Review of the Literature." *Psychological Bulletin* 88, 1 (July 1980), 1–45.

Braudel, Fernand. *The Perspective of the World*. Translated by Sian Reynolds. Vol. 3 of *Civilization and Capitalism: 15th–18th Century*. New York: Harper & Row, 1984.

Brinton, Crane. *The Anatomy of Revolution*. Englewood Cliffs, N.J.: Prentice-Hall, 1952.

Bronfenbrenner, Urie. *Two Worlds of Childhood*. New York: Russell Sage Foundation, 1970.

Brownlie, Ian, ed. *Basic Documents on Human Rights*. 2d ed. Oxford: Clarendon Press, 1981.

Candee, Dan. "Ego Developmental Aspects of New Left Ideology." *Journal of Personality and Social Psychology* 30, 5 (1974), 620–30.

———. "Structure and Choice in Moral Reasoning." *Journal of Personality and Social Psychology* 34 (1974), 1293–1301.

Caplan, Arthur L., and Bruce Jennings, eds. *Darwin, Marx, and Freud: Their Influence on Moral Theory*. New York: Plenum Press, 1984.

Cardoso, Fernando Henrique, and Enzo Faletto. *Dependency and Development in Latin America*. Translated by Marjorie Mattingly Urquidi. Berkeley: University of California Press, 1979.

Carens, Joseph H. *Equality, Moral Incentives, and the Market: An Essay on Utopian Politico-Economic Theory*. Chicago: University of Chicago Press, 1981.

Carroll, Terrance G. "Secularization and States of Modernity." *World Politics* 36, 3 (April 1984), 362–82.

Chilton, Stephen. *Defining Political Development*. Monograph Series in World Affairs, Graduate School of International Studies, University of Denver. Boulder: L. Rienner, 1988.

Cipolla, Carlo M. *Before the Industrial Revolution: European Society and Economy, 1000–1700*. New York: W. W. Norton, 1976.

Clark, Rodney. *The Japanese Company*. New Haven: Yale University Press, 1979.

Coble, Parks M., Jr. *The Shanghai Capitalists and the Nationalist Government, 1927–1937*. Harvard East Asian Monographs no. 94. Cambridge: Council on East Asian Studies, Harvard University, 1980.

Cochran, Sherman. *Big Business in China: Sino-Foreign Rivalry in the Cigarette Industry*. Cambridge: Harvard University Press, 1980.

Cohen, Mitchell, and Dennis Hale, eds. *The New Student Left*. Boston: Beacon Press, 1966.

Cohn, Norman. *The Pursuit of the Millennium*. 2d ed. New York: Harper and Brothers, 1961.

Colburn, Forrest D. "Current Studies of Peasants and Rural Development: Applications of the Political Economy Approach." *World Politics* 34, 3 (April 1982), 437–49.

Conklin, John E. *"Illegal But Not Criminal": Business Crime in America*. Englewood Cliffs, N.J.: Prentice-Hall, 1977.

Craig, Stephen C. "The Mobilization of Political Discontent." *Political Behavior* 2, 2 (1980), 189–209.

Cranston, Maurice. "Are There Any Human Rights?" *Daedalus* 112, 4 (Fall 1983), 1–17.

Crozier, Michael, Samuel P. Huntington, and Joji Watanuki. *The Crisis of Democracy*. New York: New York University Press, 1975.

Dahl, Robert. "Democracy in the Workplace: Is It a Right or a Privilege?" *Dissent* 31 (Winter 1984), 54–60.

———. *Dilemmas of Pluralist Democracy: Autonomy vs. Control*. New Haven: Yale University Press, 1982.

———. *Polyarchy: Participation and Opposition*. New Haven: Yale University Press, 1971.

Dahrendorf, Ralf. *Class and Class Conflict in Industrial Society*. Stanford: Stanford University Press, 1959.

DasGupta, Jyotirindra. "Development and Poverty Reduction in South Asia—A Review Article." *Journal of Asian Studies* 42, 1 (November 1982), 105–17.

Davies, James C. *Human Nature in Politics: The Dynamics of Political Behavior*. New York: John Wiley & Sons, 1963.

———. "The Proper Biological Study of Politics." *Political Psychology* 4, 4 (December 1983), 731–43.

Deutsch, Karl W. "On Political Theory and Political Action." *The American Political Science Review* 45, 1 (March 1971), 11–27.

De Vries, Jan. "The Rise and Decline of Nations in Historical Perspective." *International Studies Quarterly* 27, 1 (March 1983), 11–16.

Dittmer, Lowell. "Political Culture and Political Symbolism: Toward a Theoretical Synthesis." *World Politics* 29, 4 (July 1977), 552–83.

Djilas, Milovan. *Memoir of a Revolutionary*. Translated by Drenka Willen. New York: Harcourt Brace Jovanovich, 1973.

———. *The New Class: An Analysis of the Communist System*. New York: Frederick A. Praeger, 1957.

Donaldson, T., and P. H. Werhane. *Ethical Issues in Business*. Englewood Cliffs, N.J.: Prentice-Hall, 1983.

Downs, Anthony. *An Economic Theory of Democracy*. New York: Harper & Row, 1957.

Easton, David. *A Systems Analysis of Political Life*. New York: John Wiley & Sons, 1965.

Eckstein, Harry. "Authority Patterns: A Structural Basis for Political Inquiry." *The American Political Science Review* 47, 4 (December 1973), 1142–61.

———. "On the Etiology of Internal Wars." *History and Theory* 4, 2 (1965), 133–63.

———. "The Idea of Political Development: From Dignity to Efficiency."

World Politics 34, 4 (July 1982), 451–86.

———, ed. *Internal War: Problems and Approaches*. New York: The Free Press of Glencoe, 1964.

Edwards, John D., and Thomas M. Ostrom, "Value-Bonded Attitudes: Changes in Attitude Structure as a Function of Value Bonding and Type of Communication Discrepancy." *Proceedings of the 77th Annual Convention of the American Psychological Association*, part 1, vol. 4, 1969, 413–14.

Eisenstadt, S. N. *Revolution and the Transformation of Societies: A Comparative Study of Civilizations*. New York: The Free Press, 1978.

Eisenstadt, S. N., and Louis Roniger. "Patron-Client Relations as a Model of Structuring Social Exchange." *Comparative Studies in Society and History* 22, 1 (January 1980), 42–77.

Elder, Glen H., Jr., ed. *Linking Social Structure and Personality*. Beverly Hills: Sage Publications, 1973.

Elvin, Mark. *The Pattern of the Chinese Past: A Social and Economic Interpretation*. Stanford: Stanford University Press, 1973.

Emler, Nicholas, Stanley Renwick, and Bernadette Malone. "The Relationship Between Moral Reasoning and Political Orientation." *Journal of Personality and Social Psychology* 45, 5 (1983), 1073–86.

Erikson, Erik H. *Childhood and Society*. New York: W. W. Norton, 1950.

———. *Young Man Luther: A Study in Psychoanalysis and History*. New York: W. W. Norton, 1958.

Ermann, M. David, and Richard J. Lundman, eds. *Corporate and Governmental Deviance: Problems of Organizational Behavior in Contemporary Society*. New York: Oxford University Press, 1978.

Feldman, Shel, ed., *Cognitive Consistency: Motivational Antecedents and Behavioral Consequents*. New York: Academic Press, 1966.

Fine, Reuben. "The Protestant Ethic and the Analytic Ideal." *Political Psychology* 4, 2 (June 1983), 245–64.

Fishkin, James S. *Beyond Subjective Morality: Ethical Reasoning and Political Philosophy*. New Haven: Yale University Press, 1984.

———. "Moral Principles and Public Policy." *Daedalus* 108, 4 (Fall 1979), 55–67.

Fishkin, James, Kenneth Keniston, and Catherine MacKinnon. "Moral Reasoning and Political Ideology." *Journal of Personality and Social Psychology* 27, 1 (July 1973), 109–19.

Fitzgerald, Ross. "Human Needs and Politics: The Ideas of Christian Bay and Herbert Marcuse." *Political Psychology* 6, 1 (1985), 87–108.

Foucault, Michel. *Discipline and Punish: The Birth of the Prison*. Translated by Alan Sheridan. New York: Pantheon Books, 1977.

Fried, Charles. *Right and Wrong*. Cambridge: Harvard University Press, 1978.

Frohlich, Norman, Joe A. Oppenheimer, and Oran R. Young. *Political Leadership and Collective Goods*. Princeton: Princeton University Press, 1971.

Fromm, Erich. *Escape From Freedom*. New York: Holt, Rinehart and Winston, 1941.

Garson, G. David, and Michael P. Smith, eds. *Organizational Democracy: Participation and Self-Management*. Beverly Hills: Sage Publications, 1976.

Geertz, Clifford. *The Interpretation of Cultures: Selected Essays*,. New York: Basic Books, 1973.

Gerth, H. H., and C. Wright Mills, eds. *From Max Weber: Essays in Sociology*. New York: Oxford University Press, 1946.

Gibbs, John C. "Kohlberg's Stages of Moral Judgment: A Constructive Cri-

tique." *Harvard Educational Review* 47, 1 (February 1977), 43–61.
Gilbert, G. M. *Nuremberg Diary*. New York: Signet Books. New American Library, 1947.
Gilligan, Carol. *In a Different Voice: Psychological Theory and Women's Development*. Cambridge: Harvard University Press, 1982.
Glaser, Kurt, and Stefan T. Possony. *Victims of Politics: The State of Human Rights*. New York: Columbia University Press, 1979.
Goldstein, Joseph, Burke Marshall, and Jack Schwartz, eds. *The My Lai Massacre and Its Cover-up: Beyond the Reach of Law?* New York: The Free Press, 1976.
Goldstone, Jack A. "Theories of Revolution: The Third Generation." *World Politics* 32, 3 (April 1980), 425–53.
Golubovic, Zagorka. "Marx's Concept of Man vs. a Stalinist Ideology of the 'New Man.'" Paper presented at the sixth annual meeting of the International Society of Political Psychology, Oxford, England, July 1983.
Goslin, David A., ed. *Handbook of Socialization Theory and Research*. Chicago: Rand McNally, 1969.
Greenblatt, Sidney L., Richard W. Wilson, and Amy A. Wilson, eds. *Organizational Behavior in Chinese Society*. New York: Praeger, 1981.
Greenstein, Fred I. *Children and Politics*. New Haven: Yale University Press, 1965.
Greenstein, Fred. I., and Nelson W. Polsby, eds. *Handbook of Political Science, II, Micropolitical Theory*. Reading: Addison-Wesley, 1975.
Griffin, Keith, and Jeffrey James. *The Transition to Egalitarian Development: Economic Policies for Structural Change in the Third World*. New York: St. Martin's Press, 1981.
Gurr, Ted. "Psychological Factors in Civil Violence." *World Politics* 20, 2 (January 1968), 245–78.
———. *Why Men Rebel*. Princeton: Princeton University Press, 1970.
Haan, Norma, M. Brewster Smith, and Jeanne Block, "The Moral Reasoning of Young Adults: Political-Social Behavior, Family Background and Personality Correlates." *Journal of Personality and Social Psychology* 10 (1968), 183–201.
Hagan, Everett E. *On the Theory of Social Change: How Economic Growth Begins*. Homewood, Ill.: Dorsey Press, 1962.
Hammer, Richard. *Court Martial of Lieutenant Calley*. New York: Coward, McGann and Gehegan, 1971.
Harding, Harry. *Organizing China: The Problem of Bureaucracy 1949–1976*. Stanford: Stanford University Press, 1981.
Hay, James. "A Study of Principled Moral Reasoning Within a Sample of Conscientious Objectors." *Moral Education Forum* 7, 3 (Fall 1982), 1–8.
Hess, Robert D., and Judith V. Torney. *The Development of Political Attitudes in Children*. Chicago: Aldine, 1967.
Hill, Christopher. *Puritanism and Revolution: Studies in Interpretation of the English Revolution of the 17th Century*. London: Secker and Warburg, 1958.
Hirschman, Albert O. *Exit, Voice, and Loyalty: Responses to Decline in Firms, Organizations, and States*. Cambridge: Harvard Unversity Press, 1970.
Hoffer, Eric. *The True Believer: Thoughts on the Nature of Mass Movements*. New York: Harper & Brothers, 1951.
Hoffman, Louise E. "Psychoanalytic Interpretations of Political Movements, 1900–1950." *The Psychohistory Review* 13, 1 (Fall 1984), 16–29.
Hogan, Robert. "Moral Conduct and Moral Character: A Psychological Per-

spective." *Psychological Bulletin* 79, 4 (April 1973), 217–32.

Horowitz, Irving Louis. *Genocide: State Power and Mass Murder*. New Brunswick: Transaction Books, 1976.

Hsu, Cho-yun. *Ancient China in Transition: An Analysis of Social Mobility, 722–222 B.C.*. Stanford: Stanford University Press, 1965.

Hummel, Ralph P. *The Bureaucratic Experience*. New York: St. Martin's Press, 1977.

Huntington, Samuel P. *Political Order in Changing Societies*. New Haven: Yale University Press, 1968.

———. "Transnational Organizations in World Politics." *World Politics* 25, 3 (April 1973), 333–68.

Huntington, Samuel P., and Joan M. Nelson. *No Easy Choice: Political Participation in Developing Countries*. Cambridge: Harvard University Press, 1976.

Hutchison, Henry. "An Eighteenth-Century Insight into Religious and Moral Education." *British Journal of Educational Studies* 24, 3 (October 1976), 233–41.

Inkeles, Alex, and Daniel J. Levinson. "The Personal System and the Sociocultural System in Large-Scale Organizations." *Sociometry* 26 (1963), 217–29.

Jackman, Robert W. "Dependence on Foreign Investment and Economic Growth in the Third World." *World Politics* 34, 2 (January 1982), 175–96.

———. *Politics and Social Equality: A Comparative Analysis*. New York: John Wiley & Sons, 1975.

Jackson, Helene Ann Cooper. "The Impact of Combat Stress on Adolescent Moral Development in Vietnam Veterans." Ph.D. dissertation, Smith College School for Social Work, 1982.

Jahoda, Gustav. "Children's Concepts of Nationality: A Critical Study of Piaget's Stages." *Child Development* 35, 4 (December 1964), 1081–92.

Jacoby, Henry. *The Bureaucratization of the World*. Translated by Eveline L. Kanes. Berkeley: University of California Press, 1973.

Jenkins, Iredell. *Social Order and the Limits of Law: A Theoretical Essay*. Princeton: Princeton University Press, 1980.

Johnson, Chalmers. *Revolutionary Change*. 2d ed. Stanford: Stanford University Press, 1982.

Johnson, James Turner. *A Society Ordained by God: English Puritan Marriage Doctrine in the First Half of the Seventeenth Century*. Nashville: Abingdon Press, 1970.

Kaplan, Barbara H. *Social Change in the Capitalist World Economy*. Beverly Hills: Sage, 1978.

Katope, Christopher, and Paul Zolbrod, eds. *The Rhetoric of Revolution*. Toronto: Macmillan, 1970.

Katz, Daniel, and Robert L. Kahn. *The Social Psychology of Organizations*. New York: John Wiley & Sons, 1966.

Katz, Daniel, Robert L. Kahn, and J. Stacy Adams, eds. *The Study of Organizations*. San Francisco: Jossey-Bass Publishers, 1980.

Kaufman, Herbert. *The Limits of Organizational Change*. University: University of Alabama Press, 1971.

Kautsky, John H. *The Politics of Aristocratic Empires*. Chapel Hill: University of North Carolina Press, 1982.

Kegan, Robert. *The Evolving Self: Problem and Process in Human Development*. Cambridge: Harvard University Press, 1982.

Kelman, Herbert C. "Compliance, Identification, and Internalization: Three

Processes of Attitude Change." *The Journal of Conflict Revolution* 2, 1 (March 1958), 51-60.

———. "Processes of Opinion Change." *Public Opinion Quarterly* 25 (1961), 57-78.

Kenniston, Kenneth. *Young Radicals*. New York: Harcourt, Brace and World, 1968.

Kindleberger, Charles. "On the Rise and Decline of Nations." *International Studies Quarterly* 27, 1 (March 1983), 5-10.

Kirkland, Edward C. ed. *The Gospel of Wealth and Other Timely Essays*. Cambridge: Harvard University Press, 1962.

Koch, Sigmund, ed. *Psychology: A Study of a Science*. Study II. Empirical Substructures and Relations with Other Sciences. Volume 6. Investigations of Man as Socius: Their Place in Psychology and the Social Sciences. New York: McGraw-Hill, 1963.

Kohlberg, Lawrence. *The Philosophy of Moral Development: Moral Stages and the Idea of Justice*. Volume 1 of *Essays on Moral Development*. San Francisco: Harper & Row, 1981.

Korzec, Michel, and Martin King Whyte. "Reading Notes: The Chinese Wage System." *The China Quarterly* 86 (June 1981), 248-73.

Kramnick, Isaac. "Reflections on Revolution: Definition and Explanation in Recent Scholarship." *History and Theory* 11, 1 (1972), 26-63.

LaBier, Douglas. "Bureaucracy and Psychopathology." *Political Psychology* 4, 2 (June 1983), 223-43.

Lane, Robert E. "Motives for Liberty, Equality, Fraternity: The Effects of Market and State." *Political Psychology* 1, 2 (Autumn 1979), 3-20.

Lasswell, Harold. *Who Gets What, When, How*. Cleveland: Meridian Books, 1958.

Lebra, Takie Sugiyama. *Japanese Patterns of Behavior*. Honolulu: University Press of Hawaii, 1976.

Leonard, H. Jeffrey. "Multinational Cororations and Politics in Developing Countries." *World Politics* 32, 3 (April 1980), 454-83.

Levy, Marion J., Jr. *Modernization and the Structure of Societies: A Setting for International Affairs*. Princeton: Princeton University Press, 1966.

Lichter, S. Robert, and Stanley Rothman. "The Radical Personality: Social Psychological Correlates of New Left Ideology." *Political Behavior* 4, 3 (1982), 207-35.

Lickona, Thomas, ed., *Moral Development and Behavior: Theory, Research, and Social Issues*. New York: Holt, Rinehart & Winston, 1976.

Lindblom, Charles E. *Politics and Markets: The World's Political-Economic Systems*. New York: Basic Books, 1977.

Lindzey, Gardner, and Elliot Aronson, eds. *The Handbook of Social Psychology*. 2d ed. Reading, Mass.: Addison-Wesley, 1969.

Lipset, Seymour Martin, and William Schneider. *The Confidence Gap: Business, Labor and Government in the Public Mind*. New York: The Free Press, 1983.

Little, David. *Religion, Order, and Law: A Study in Pre-Revolutionary England*. New York: Harper & Row, 1969.

Long, Samuel L., ed.*The Handbook of Political Behavior*. New York: Plenum Press, 1981.

Lowi, Theodore J. "American Business, Public Policy, Case Studies, and Political Theory." *World Politics* 16 (July 1964), 677-715.

Lukacs, Georg. *History and Class Consciousness: Studies in Marxist Dialec-*

tics. Translated by Rodney Livingstone. Cambridge: M.I.T. Press, 1968.

McClintock, Cynthia. "Why Peasants Rebel: The Case of Peru's Sendero Luminoso." *World Politics* 37, 1 (October 1984), 48–84.

McClosky, Herbert, and Alida Brill, *Dimensions of Tolerance: What Americans Believe About Civil Liberties*. New York: Russell Sage Foundation, 1983.

MacCrimmon, Kenneth R., and David M. Messick. "A Framework for Social Motives." *Behavioral Science* 21, 2 (March 1976), 86–100.

McNeill, William H. *The Pursuit of Power: Technology, Armed Force, and Society since A.D. 1000*. Chicago: University of Chicago Press, 1982.

McWilliams, Wilson Carey. *The Idea of Fraternity in America*. Berkeley: University of California Press, 1973.

Magruder, Jeb Stuart. *An American Life: One Man's Road to Watergate*. New York: Atheneum, 1974.

———. *From Power to Peace*. Waco: World Books, 1978.

[Mao Zedong.] *Selected Works of Mao Tse-Tung*. Vol. 3. Peking: Foreign Language Press, 1965.

Margolis, Howard. *Selfishness, Altruism, and Rationality: A Theory of Social Choice*. Cambridge: Cambridge University Press, 1982.

Marquette, Jesse F. "A Logistic Diffusion Model of Political Mobilization." *Political Behavior* 3, 1 (1981), 7-30.

Masters, Roger D. "The Biological Nature of the State." *World Politics* 35, 2 (January 1983), 161–93.

Mazlish, Bruce. *The Revolutionary Ascetic: Evolution of a Political Type*. New York: McGraw-Hill, 1976.

Mead, Margaret. *Soviet Attitudes Toward Authority*. New York: McGraw-Hill, 1951.

Merelman, Richard M. "The Development of Political Ideology: A Framework for the Analysis of Political Socialization." *The American Political Science Review* 43, 3 (September 1969), 750–67.

Metzger, Thomas A. *The Internal Organization of Ch'ing Bureaucracy: Legal, Normative, and Communication Aspects*. Cambridge: Harvard University Press, 1973.

———. "Max Weber's Analysis of the Confucian Tradition: A Critique." *National Taiwan Teacher's College History Journal* 11, 379–416.

Michels, Robert. *Political Parties*. New York: The Free Press, 1962.

Migdal, Joel S. *Peasants, Politics, and Revolution: Pressures Toward Political and Social Change in the Third World*. Princeton: Princeton University Press, 1974.

Miller, James G. "The Nature of Living Systems." *Behavioral Science* 21, 5 (September 1976), 295–319.

Millgram, Stanley. *Obedience to Authority*. New York: Harper & Row, 1974.

Mischel, Theodore, ed., *Cognitive Development and Epistemology*. New York: Academic Press, 1971.

Moody, Harry R. "Moral Development Over the Lifespan." *Moral Education Forum* 9, 3 (Fall 1984), 2–13.

Moore, Barrington, Jr., *Injustice: The Social Bases of Obedience and Revolt*. White Plains, N.Y.: M. E. Sharpe, 1978.

———. *Social Origins of Dictatorship and Democracy: Lord and Peasant in the Making of the Modern World*. Boston: Beacon Press, 1966.

Morgan, Edmund S. *The Puritan Family: Religion and Domestic Relations in Seventeenth-Century New England*. New York: Harper & Row, 1966.

Nader, Ralph, and Mark J. Green, eds. *Corporate Power in America.* New York: Grossman Publishers, 1973.

Nef, John U. *War and Human Progress: An Essay on the Rise of Industrial Civilization.* New York: Russell and Russell, 1968.

O'Connor, James. *The Fiscal Crisis of the State.* New York: St. Martin's Press, 1973.

Offe, Claus. *Industry and Inequality: The Achievement Principle in Work and Social Status.* Translated by James Wickham. London: Edward Arnold, 1976.

Olson, Mancur, Jr., *The Logic of Collective Action.* Rev. ed. New York: Schocken, 1971.

———. *The Rise and Decline of Nations: Economic Growth, Stagflation, and Social Rigidities.* New Haven: Yale University Press, 1982.

Olson, Richard Stuart. "Economic Coercion in World Politics: With a Focus on North-South Relations." *World Politics* 31, 4 (July 1979), 471–94.

Oppenheimer, Joe A. "Small Steps Forward for Political Economy." *World Politics* 33, 1 (October 1980), 121–51.

Ostrom, Thomas M., and Timothy C. Brock. "Cognitive Bonding to Central Values and Resistance to a Communication Advocating Change in Policy Orientation." *Journal of Experimental Research in Personality* 4, 1 (July 1969), 42–50.

Paige, Glenn D. *Political Leadership: Readings for an Emerging Field.* New York: Praeger, 1972.

Paige, Jeffrey M. *Agrarian Revolution: Social Movements and Export Agriculture in the Underdeveloped World.* New York: The Free Press, 1975.

Parsons, Talcott. *Societies: Evolutionary and Comparative Perspectives.* Englewood Cliffs, N.J.: Prentice-Hall, 1966.

Parsons, Talcott, and Edward A. Shils, eds. *Toward A General Theory of Action.* Cambridge: Harvard University Press, 1951.

Pateman, Carole. *Participation and Democratic Theory.* London: Cambridge University Press, 1970.

Pervin, Lawrence A. *Current Controversies and Issues in Personality.* New York: John Wiley & Sons, 1978.

Peters, Richard. "The Place of Kohlberg's Theory in Moral Education." *Journal of Moral Education* 7, 3 (May 1978), 147–57.

Peters, R. S. "Moral Development and Moral Learning." *The Monist* 58, 4 (October 1974), 541–67.

Peters, Thomas J., and Robert H. Waterman, Jr. *In Search of Excellence: Lessons from America's Best-Run Companies.* New York: Harper & Row, 1982.

Petras, James F., with Morris H. Morley, Peter DeWitt, and A. Eugene Havens. *Class, State, and Power in the Third World.* Montclair, N.J.: Allanheld, Osmun, 1981.

Piaget, Jean, assisted by Anne-Marie Weil. "The Development in Children of the Idea of the Homeland and of Relations With Other Countries." *International Social Science Bulletin* 3, 3 (Autumn 1951), 561–78.

Piaget, Jean. *The Moral Judgment of the Child.* New York: Collier Books, 1962.

Pittel, Stephen M., and Gerald A. Mendelsohn. "Measurement of Moral Values: A Review and Critique." *Psychological Bulletin* 66, 1 (July 1966), 22–35.

Polanyi, Karl. *The Great Transformation.* Boston: Beacon Press, 1944.

Polanyi, Karl, Conrad M. Arensberg, and Harry W. Pearson, eds. *Trade and Market in the Early Empires: Economies in History and Theory.*

Glencoe, Ill.: The Free Press, 1957.

Popkin, Samuel L. *The Rational Peasant: The Political Economy of Rural Society in Vietnam.* Berkeley: University of California Press, 1979.

Poulantzas, Nicos. *Political Power and Social Classes.* London: NLB and Sheed and Ward, 1973.

Presthus, Robert. *The Organizational Society.* Rev. ed. New York: St. Martin's Press, 1978.

Pye, Lucian. *The Dynamics of Chinese Politics.* Cambridge, Mass.: Oelgeschlager, Gunn and Hain, 1981.

Rawls, John. *A Theory of Justice.* Cambridge: Harvard University Press, 1971.

Rejai, Mostafa, and Kay Phillips. *World Revolutionary Leaders.* New Brunswick: Rutgers University Press, 1983.

Reich, Charles A. *The Greening of America.* New York: Random House, 1970.

Renshon, Stanley A., ed. *Handbook of Political Socialization.* New York: The Free Press, 1977.

Rokeach, Milton. *Beliefs, Attitudes, and Values: A Theory of Organization and Change.* London: Jossey-Bass Publishers, 1968.

———. *The Nature of Human Values.* New York: The Free Press, 1973.

Rosenblum, Nancy L. "Moral Membership in a Postliberal State." *World Politics* 36, 4 (July 1984), 581–96.

Rubenstein, Richard L. *The Cunning of History: Mass Death and the American Future.* New York: Harper & Row, 1975.

Salert, Barbara. *Revolutions and Revolutionaries: Four Theories.* New York: Elsevier, 1976.

Schmidt, Matthias. *Albert Speer: The End of a Myth.* Translated by Joachim Neugroschel. New York: St. Martin's Press, 1984.

Schneider, Peter R., and Anne L. Schneider, "Social Mobilization, Political Institutions, and Political Violence: A Cross-National Analysis." *Comparative Political Studies* 4, 1 (April 1971), 69–90.

Schochet, Gordon J. *Patriarchalism in Political Thought.* Oxford: Blackwell, 1975.

Schumpeter, Joseph A. *Capitalism, Socialism, and Democracy.* 3d ed. New York: Harper & Brothers, 1950.

Schwartz, David C. *Political Alienation and Political Behavior.* Chicago: Aldine, 1973.

Scott, James C. *The Moral Economy of the Peasant: Rebellion and Subsistence in Southeast Asia.* New Haven: Yale University Press, 1976.

Scott, William A. *Values and Organizations: A Study of Fraternities and Sororities.* Chicago: Rand McNally, 1965.

Searing, Donald D., Joel J. Schwartz, and Alden E. Lind. "The Structuring Principle: Political Socialization and Belief Systems." *The American Political Science Review* 47, 2 (June 1973), 415–32.

Sennett, Richard. *Authority.* New York: Alfred A. Knopf, 1980.

Sennett, Richard, and Jonathan Cobb, *The Hidden Injuries of Class.* New York: Alfred A. Knopf, 1972.

Sereny, *Into that Darkness: From Mercy Killing to Mass Murder.* New York: McGraw-Hill., 1974.

Sigel, Roberta S., ed. *Learning About Politics: A Reader in Political Socialization.* New York: Random House, 1970.

Simmel, Georg. *Conflict.* Translated by Kurt H. Wolff. *The Web of Group Affiliations.* Translated by Richard Bendix. New York: The Free Press of Glencoe, 1955.

Singer, J. David. "Man and World Politics: The Psycho-Cultural Interface." *The Journal of Social Issues* 24, 3 (July 1968), 127–56.
Sizer, N. F., and T. R. Sizer, eds. *Moral Education: Five Essays*. Cambridge: Harvard University Press, 1970.
Skinner, B. F. *Beyond Freedom and Dignity*. New York: Alfred A. Knopf, 1971.
Skocpol, Theda. *States and Social Revolutions: A Comparative Analysis of France, Russia, and China*. Cambridge: Cambridge University Press, 1979.
Smelser, Neil J. *Theory of Collective Behavior*. New York: The Free Press, 1962.
Smigel, Erwin O., and H. Laurence Ross, eds. *Crimes Against Bureaucracy*. New York: Van Nostrand-Reinhold, 1970.
Smith, M. Brewster. *Social Psychology and Human Values*. Chicago: Aldine, 1969.
Smith, Tony. "The Underdevelopment of Development Literature: The Case of Dependency Theory." *World Politics* 31, 2 (January 1979), 247–88.
Sorokin, Pitirim A. *The Crisis of Our Age: The Social and Cultural Outlook*. New York: Dutton, 1941.
Sprinthall, Richard C., and Norman A. Sprinthall, eds. *Educational Psychology*. New York: Van Nostrand-Reinhold, 1969.
Stokols, Daniel. "Toward a Psychological Theory of Alienation." *Psychological Review* 82, 1 (January 1975), 26–44.
Stone, Gregory P., and Harvey A. Farberman, eds. *Social Psychology Through Symbolic Interaction*. Waltham, Mass.: Xerox College Publishing, 1970.
Stone, Lawrence. "Theories of Revolution." *World Politics* 18, 2 (January 1966), 159–76.
Sullivan, John L., James Pierson, and George E. Marcus. *Political Tolerance and American Democracy*. Chicago: University of Chicago Press, 1982.
Sutton, Francis X., Seymour E. Harris, Carl Kaysen, and James Tobin. *The American Business Creed*. Cambridge: Harvard University Press, 1956.
Sweezy, Paul M. *Modern Capitalism and Other Essays*. New York: Monthly Review, 1972.
Talmon, J. L. *The Origins of Totalitarian Democracy*. London: Secker and Warburg, 1955.
Tapp, June L., and Lawrence Kohlberg. "Developing Senses of Law and Legal Justice." *The Journal of Social Issues* 27, 2 (1971), 65–91.
Tawney, R. H. *Religion and the Rise of Capitalism*. New York: Harcourt, Brace, Mentor Books, 1926.
Theophanous, Andrew C. "In Defense of Self-Determination: A Critique of B.F. Skinner." *Behaviorism* 3, 1 (Spring 1975), 97–115.
Tilly, Charles, Louise Tilly, and Richard Tilly. *The Rebellious Century: 1830–1930*. Cambridge: Harvard University Press, 1975.
De Tocqueville, Alex. *Democracy in America*. Vol. 2. New York: Alfred A. Knopf, 1956.
Toffler, Alvin. *The Third Wave*. Toronto: Bantam Books, 1981.
Trainer, F. E. "A Critical Analysis of Kohlberg's Contributions to the Study of Moral Thought." *Journal for the Study of Social Behavior* 7, 1 (April 1977), 41–63.
Trimberger, Kay Ellen. *Revolution from Above: Military Bureaucrats and Development in Japan, Turkey, Egypt, and Peru*. New Brunswick: Transaction Books, 1978.
Tucker, Robert C. *The Marxian Revolutionary Idea*. New York: W. W. Norton, 1969.

Tufte, Edward R. *Political Control of the Economy*. Princeton: Princeton University Press, 1978.

Veblen, Thorstein. *The Theory of the Leisure Class*. New York: Penguin Books, 1979.

Vivas, Eliseo. *The Moral Life and the Ethical Life*. Chicago: University of Chicago Press, 1950.

Wallerstein, Immanuel. *The Modern World-System: Capitalist Agriculture and the Origins of the European World-Economy in the Sixteenth Century*. New York: Academic Press, 1974.

Walzer, Michael. *Obligations: Essays on Disobedience, War, and Citizenship*. New York: Simon and Schuster, 1970.

———. *The Revolution of the Saints: A Study in the Origins of Radical Politics*. London: Weidenfeld and Nicolson, 1965.

———. *Spheres of Justice: A Defense of Pluralism and Equality*. New York: Basic Books, 1983.

Waterman, Harvey. "Insecure 'Ins' and Opportune 'Outs': Sources of Collective Political Activity." *Journal of Political and Military Sociology* 8, 1 (Spring 1980), 107–12.

Weinreich-Haste, Helen, and Don Locke, eds. *Morality in the Making: Thought, Action, and the Social Context*. Chichester: John Wiley & Sons, 1983.

Whitaker, C. S., Jr. "A Dysrhythmic Process of Political Change." *World Politics* 19, 2 (January 1967), 190–217.

Wilson, Edward O. *On Human Nature*. Cambridge: Harvard University Press, 1978.

———. *Sociobiology: The New Synthesis*. Cambridge: Harvard University Press, 1975.

Wilson, Richard W. *Learning to Be Chinese: The Political Socialization of Children in Taiwan*. Cambridge: M.I.T. Press, 1970.

———. "Moral Development and Political Change." *World Politics* 36, 1 (October 1983), 53–75.

———. "Political Socialization and Moral Development." *World Politics* 33, 2 (January 1981), 153–77.

———. "Some Comments on Stage Theories of Moral Development." *Journal of Moral Education* 5, 3 (June 1976), 241–48.

Wilson, Richard W., and Gordon J. Schochet, eds. *Moral Development and Politics*. New York: Praeger, 1980.

Wolf, Eric R. *Peasant Wars of the Twentieth Century*. New York, Evanston, and London: Harper & Row, 1969.

Wolfe, Alan. *The Limits of Legitimacy: Contradictions of Contemporary Capitalism*. New York: The Free Press, 1980.

Wolfenstein, Victor. *The Revolutionary Personality: Lenin, Trotsky, Gandhi*. Princeton: Princeton University Press, 1967.

Woodruff, William. *The Struggle for World Power 1500–1980*. New York: St. Martin's Press, 1981.

Wright, J. Patrick. *On A Clear Day You Can See General Motors: John Z. De Lorean's Look Inside the Automotive Giant*. Grosse Pointe, Mich.: Wright Enterprises, 1979.

Index